Skills to Make a Librarian

CHANDOS

INFORMATION PROFESSIONAL SERIES

Series Editor: Ruth Rikowski
(email: Rikowskigr@aol.com)

Chandos' new series of books is aimed at the busy information professional. They have been specially commissioned to provide the reader with an authoritative view of current thinking. They are designed to provide easy-to-read and (most importantly) practical coverage of topics that are of interest to librarians and other information professionals. If you would like a full listing of current and forthcoming titles, please visit www.chandospublishing.com.

New authors: we are always pleased to receive ideas for new titles; if you would like to write a book for Chandos, please contact Dr Glyn Jones on g.jones.2@elsevier.com or telephone +44 (0) 1865 843000.

Skills to Make a Librarian

Transferable Skills Inside and Outside the Library

Edited by

Dawn Lowe-Wincentsen

AMSTERDAM • BOSTON • CAMBRIDGE • HEIDELBERG
LONDON • NEW YORK • OXFORD • PARIS • SAN DIEGO
SAN FRANCISCO • SINGAPORE • SYDNEY • TOKYO
Chandos Publishing is an imprint of Elsevier

Chandos Publishing is an imprint of Elsevier
225 Wyman Street, Waltham, MA 02451, USA
Langford Lane, Kidlington, OX5 1GB, UK

Notice
Knowledge and best practice in this field are constantly changing. As new research and experience broaden our understanding, changes in research methods, professional practices, or medical treatment may become necessary.

Practitioners and researchers must always rely on their own experience and knowledge in evaluating and using any information, methods, compounds, or experiments described herein. In using such information or methods they should be mindful of their own safety and the safety of others, including parties for whom they have a professional responsibility.

To the fullest extent of the law, neither the Publisher nor the authors, contributors, or editors, assume any liability for any injury and/or damage to persons or property as a matter of products liability, negligence or otherwise, or from any use or operation of any methods, products, instructions, or ideas contained in the material herein.

British Library Cataloguing in Publication Data
A catalogue record for this book is available from the British Library.

Library of Congress Control Number: 2014955044

ISBN 978-0-08100-063-2 (print)
ISBN 978-0-08100-065-6 (online)

For information on all Chandos Publishing publications
visit our website at http://store.elsevier.com/

Typeset by SPi Global
www.spi-global.com

Printed in the UK and USA

Dedication

To M, for whom I do everything.

Contents

List of figures

List of tables

Preface

More than a measure of skills

In a survey of 92 librarians conducted in 2010, I asked how many previous careers they had. The median was 2, and the average was 1.197. Thinking about this, the average librarian probably has had some work experience before becoming a librarian. Assuming that there is some educational requirement to be a librarian, even those who do not have prior careers or work experience, will have some life experience. (In the United States it is a Masters Degree, this varies by country and educational system though.) All of this comes into play in the day-to-day workings of being a librarian or information professional.

For the survey, I was focusing on those who identified in a specific generation, Generation X. Even within those slim results there was a diversity of the experience they were bringing to the information profession. These ranged from: education, business, arts, engineering, and to retail. All of this professional experience and diversity amount for something, and add to us as a whole, and as individuals. It is my intent that this text explores how these outside experiences contribute to the information professions, and make us better librarians.

In my own experience, I worked in food service (haven't we all) and for a political party, prior to college. During college I worked in the university library; while I earned a degree in Creative Writing. I went straight from university to university—where I earned a graduate degree in Library and Information Science. As a friend has told me: "You never left school". After graduate school, I went to work at a university, in a library. It was here where one of my outside passions: food—began to mix with librarianship, and the cross-disciplinary skills started to shine.

Food service aside, I have a passion for cooking and entertaining with food. My home and my waistline are usually flush with new concoctions, and recipes that I am trying or developing. I have delved into food blogging, but never with enough discipline to endure. I have had the opportunity to share this love of food in both large and small settings; learning a few more skills that have proven useful in the library along the way.

Time management and "to do" lists

When was the last time you read a recipe? Not the text or story behind a recipe, but the list of ingredients and how to put them together? Not recently? Go ahead, grab one now, I will wait . . . .

Back? Now look at the recipe. Specifically look at the list of ingredients and how they are arranged. For baking these are usually separated out into dry and wet, or by process. I have a cheesecake recipe that has three parts: the crust, the cheesecake, and the topping. At a minimum, most recipes are organized by the order in which each ingredient is added to the recipe. Once you look at the list of ingredients, notice what order they are mentioned in the instructions—it should be the same order.

The list of ingredients is like a "to do" list. In most cases, a long ingredient list means a longer prep time. The three ingredients: 15-minutes model; or the five ingredients: in less than 30 minutes—is a great selling gimmick to attract the new, or short-on-time cook.

In my own "to do" lists I have learned to group items by process (dry ingredients = resource management tasks; wet ingredients = public services, etc.). I have also learned to manage my time according to the number of items on my list. For example, my current list is a few pages long, and therefore, I am blocking-out time for each task, and meticulously scheduling my life to get everything accomplished.

As I complete things, or other tasks change in priority; I adapt my schedule and my list accordingly. The same is true in my kitchen. As I use the last head of broccoli, I substitute in shredded brussels sprouts to the winter slaw, or use another ingredient available at the time; instead of running out to the shops to find exactly what was called for in the recipe.

Evaluation

Many of the chapters in this text talk about "evaluation". It would seem that this is something we all learn in some capacity or another. It is also something we all try to teach the various groups of users we work with. For me, right here, I am talking about evaluating texts for collection development. Don't judge a book by its cover. Do, however, judge a head of lettuce by its outer leaves.

Books, journals, and library materials are very different from food produce. Beyond checking to see if the pages or leaves are moldy, the outward evaluation techniques would seem very different as well. The mold and dust questions of materials usually only come into account when the material is a gift item that may have lived in storage for a bit. For new items (and new-to-you items) I look for:

- *Is it fresh?*
- *Will my users eat it?*
- *Is it easily available elsewhere?*

Is it fresh? Is the material new information? A new take, on something? A new edition? While I don't only focus on date, I do look at timeliness. I work in engineering and the sciences: new research in these areas comes out every day. For the scientists that I work with; to keep up, I need to focus on getting them the freshest, crispest, content in their areas that I can.

Will my users eat it? While I hope that most university populations have moved beyond book-chewing, I do want them to use the library collection, and to be interested in the materials being purchased. Just as I find out the food preferences, allergies, and needs of those I cook for; I find out the interests, research areas, and information needs of the populations I work with. As I would not cook beef for a vegetarian, I would not buy Shakespeare for a future paramedic.

Is it easily available elsewhere? When entertaining, I try to make dishes that are not my guests' everyday cuisine. For one friend, this is Indian food. She does not have the spices usually used in this cuisine, and does not go out to eat very often. She has asked for this cuisine before so I know it meets the previous criteria. In collection development I look up to see where a title may also be available, and how easy it is for my population to access, before I purchase. We are part of a regional consortium, and can easily obtain items from 37 different universities' libraries within a few days. If more than a handful of these have the item I am contemplating acquiring for the collection, I pass, on that item. Even if it is not available immediately, it is available within a few days.

Learning to experiment

Let's face it: I am no Julia Child. I cook for fun. I cook because I love food. I am not a professional chef. (Definitely a back-up career as a personal chef though.) I like to experiment in the kitchen. I like to try new recipes and new ideas, see what works. And yes, see what doesn't work. Last week, there was a chickpea Provençal that failed horribly—*far* too much garlic. It did succeed in keeping the pests away from the compost. The chickpeas that survived the experience found a new purpose in a salad. The family and I went out for take-out in the face of this garlicky disaster, and have a new memory to taunt myself with, when something goes awry in the kitchen.

Outside of the kitchen, I have found great use for this experimental attitude: developed when working on new dishes. I have an idea, I try it out, then evaluate its effectiveness. Whether it works or not, I try to learn from it, move from chickpea Provençal to chickpea parmesan—where the mozzarella softens the flavor of the garlic, and also maybe a bit less garlic to begin with.

In my current position I supervise all functions of a small campus library. Think of this as my kitchen. While I do have supervision both at a local operational level, and from the other campus, I also have a fair amount of room to experiment without having to get something approved. Since we are moderately small, I also have close connection to the students, and the faculty. This gives me the chance to see what is going on and where a need might be. After a year of offering a "Review work for citation use" service, and talks with various professors, I came up with the idea to offer workshops on copyright and fair use of information in the students' papers. These workshops are offered mainly during the day, and advertised through a variety of media to the local general student population. One method of advertising has been direct contact with the professors. Some of these professors have then required or recommended that their students attend the workshops: that guarantees some attendance; while others have either mentioned that the workshops were being held, or not. We are on a quarter system. The first workshop was offered during the Fall Quarter. This workshop gave an overview of copyright and plagiarism with some suggestions on how to not plagiarize. The attendance was modest, and mostly comprised of students required to attend. I asked the students to complete a five-question evaluation after the session. This was an anonymous assessment that has so far only been seen by me. I also spoke with a few of the students afterwards: asking what more they would like to know. These two forms of feedback, plus my observations in the classes, gave me enough information to change the controls for the next quarter. In the winter quarter I offered a "Part II" workshop. This workshop built on the information conveyed in the first workshop (cut back on garlic) and built on that information (add mozzarella) while still giving enough basis that someone could attend "Part II" without the prerequisite of having attended "Part I". Where the first workshop had been primarily lecture-based; the second was much more hands-on with students working together to evaluate previous works; and where they may have accidentally plagiarized. A similar evaluation was conducted on this second workshop, and led to the development of a third workshop offered during the spring quarter. This final workshop of the series focusses on one section that seems to breed much more confusion: the copyright and fair use of images. Evaluation of the workshop is yet to come, but current responses indicate that it, and the second workshop should be repeated again next academic year.

The experimentation from my kitchen has given me a structure, and an ability to experiment outside the kitchen. In the case above, it is a two-thirds success. Next academic year, I will build on "Part II", and offer the three workshops again. Measuring the success of these against the first lecture, I will condense the first, and give it as a preamble to the second, in a single session, both experimenting, and learning from a past experiment to fulfill a need. What isn't better with cheese on top?

Perhaps next, an information professional cookbook should be in the works?

This book explores how the skills from business, to nonprofit, to retail, instructional design, biology, and indeed motherhood: connect and enrich the library, and the information professional. Read these as a whole, or as snippets, into the workings of professionals. We have all experimented, and worked in different industries, or learned skills outside the information professions that make us stronger librarians. I hope that you too can see how your prior careers, and life experiences enrich, and add to your experience as an information professional. And also, how your experiences as an information professional may add to future careers, and life experiences.

Dawn Lowe–Wincentsen

About the editor

Dawn Lowe–Wincentsen is the Wilsonville Campus librarian for the Oregon Institute of Technology. She graduated with an MLIS from Louisiana State University in 2003, though she has been involved in libraries since 1996. Dawn has been editor for the *Learning Exchange*—a newsletter of the Learning Round Table of the ALA since 2008. She has co-authored *A Leadership Primer for New Librarians: Tools for Helping Today's Early Career Librarians to Become Tomorrow's Library Leaders* (Chandos Publishing, 2009) and co-edited, *Mid-Career Library and Information Professionals: a leadership primer* (Woodhead Publishing, 2011) as well as having written various chapters, and articles about librarianship.

About the contributors

Cara Ball is a records analyst for Records Management, at the University of Washington (UW). She spends her days empowering and advocating for the UW community to effectively manage their records. Connecting people with information is her passion. Cara holds a Masters in Library and Information Science from the University of Washington's *i*School, and a BA in Accounting from Seattle University.

Carrie E. Byrd is a reference and instruction librarian living in Kentucky. She spends much of her time at work trying to convince students not to use Wikipedia as a scholarly source. In her downtime she enjoys container gardening and reading voraciously.

Beth R. Canzoneri received her Master's degree in Library and Information Studies (MLIS) from the University of Alabama in 2012. She incorporates skills from her previous career in marketing and communications in her position as a reference and instruction librarian at the University of Idaho Library.

Robin L. Ewing is a reference librarian and assessment coordinator at St Cloud State University in St Cloud, MN. She earned her MLIS at the University of Oklahoma in 2001. Her research interests include information literacy assessment, leadership, and reference models.

Anne V. Hiller Clark spent almost eight years as an environmental project manager for a State agency, and then 12 years as an academic librarian. She has published articles in historical and geological journals and field guides, as well as coordinated production of ten annual issues of the *Journal of the Shaw Historical Library*. She is currently a consulting librarian and archivist as well as a registered geologist in the State of Oregon.

Megan Hodge is a teaching and learning librarian at Virginia Commonwealth University in Richmond, Virginia. She earned her Master of Science in Library Science from the University of North Texas in 2010, and is the 2014–15 President of the American Library Association (ALA) New Members Round Table. In 2011, she was an ALA Emerging Leader, and co-founded the Virginia New Members Round Table. Her professional interests are instructional design, services for young/emerging adults, and library human resources.

Kevin Michael Klipfel is an information literacy coordinator at California State University, Chico. He received a Masters in Philosophy from Virginia Tech in 2007, and was subsequently a university lecturer in philosophy for several years: teaching moral, political, and existential philosophy. His Master's paper, an application of the existentialist ethic of authenticity to student motivation and information literacy learning, won the "Dean's Achievement Award" for the Best Master's Paper in the School of Information and Library Science at the University of North Carolina at Chapel Hill, in May 2013. His scholarly work has appeared, and is forthcoming in *College & Research Libraries*, *Reference Services Review*, and *Communications in Information Literacy*. Kevin is also a monthly contributor to the "Intellectual Spaces" forum of *Ethos: A Digital Review of Arts, Humanities, and Public Ethics*, a journal sponsored by the Institute for the Arts & Humanities at The University of North Carolina at Chapel Hill, and Kevin is a co-founder of *Rule Number One: A Library Blog* (*www.rulenumberoneblog.com* [Accessed 17.8.14]) devoted to discussing issues in educational theory, information literacy instruction, and the library profession.

Leo Lo is assistant professor and research & development librarian at Kansas State University. He holds a MS in Information Studies from Florida State University, and a MFA in Screenwriting from Hollins University. His thesis screenplay was an Official Finalist in the 2009 Mexico International Film Festival.

Meredith Lowe Prather is currently head librarian at The Museum of Flight in Seattle, Washington. She landed there after various stints as a catering kitchen manager, flight attendant, and academic librarian. When not lost in a book or planning new travels, she enjoys knitting, baking, rooting for her Sounders, and playing with her family. She lives in the Puget Sound with her husband, and two spoiled cats.

Michael Saar is an assistant professor at Lamar University's Mary & John Gray Library whose primary responsibilities include reference services and instruction. In addition to a Masters in Library Science from the University of Arizona, Michael has a second Masters in Theatre Historiography from the University of Minnesota. Michael remains active in the theatre community both as a theatre director, and as an actor.

Samantha Schmehl Hines received her MS in Library and Information Science from the University of Illinois Urbana-Champaign in 2003. In 2004 she was hired as social science librarian by the Mansfield Library at The University of Montana-Missoula, and is currently head librarian for the Missoula College campus library of The University of Montana. She writes and presents widely on the issues of: online library services, information literacy instruction, and library middle management; and is the author of *Productivity for Librarians* (Chandos Publishing, 2010) and *Revolutionizing the Development of Library and Information Science Professionals* (IGI-Global, 2014).

Judith Schwartz is an assistant professor and librarian at Medgar Evers College, City University of New York. She received her MSLIS from the Palmer School of Library and Information Science, Long Island University Post. She is a reference and interlibrary loan librarian, and also designs marketing pieces for the library. With over 15 years of prior experience working as an art director in publishing; Judith has expertise in all forms of visual-design communication.

Mary J. Snyder Broussard is an associate professor and librarian at Lycoming College. She received her MLS from Indiana University, and has designed numerous games and tutorials for her library. She has published a number of articles and chapters on game-based learning, and formative assessment in academic libraries.

Susan Beth Wainscott is a science, technology, engineering, and mathematics librarian at the University of Nevada, Las Vegas. She transitioned to librarianship; after receiving a MLIS from San Jose State University in 2012. Her previous career as a conservation biologist included work for an international environmental non-profit organization, and a county government agency's Endangered Species Act Compliance Division. She also has a Masters degree in Biology from Illinois State University.

Kimberly Fu-Jia Yang is research, education and outreach librarian, and the School of Pharmacy librarian at the University of Maryland, Baltimore (UMB) Health Sciences and Human Services Library. She authored "Centralizing distributed resources and making them searchable", in recently *Best Practices for Government Libraries: Managing Evolving Resources: Strategies, Capabilities, and Alternatives* (LexisNexis, 2013). In her prior career as a corporate attorney, Kim represented hospitals, physicians, and healthcare providers in the health law practice of a large law firm. She has extensive grant proposal writing, and grant reporting experience, and worked as a nonprofit administrator prior to earning her MLS from the University of Maryland, College Park. She holds a JD from UCLA School of Law, and a BA in Human Biology from Stanford University.

The benefits of earning a Master of Fine Arts to library leadership

1

Leo Lo

Introduction

There are countless articles and research on leadership qualities. Daniel Goleman, who first brought the term "emotional intelligence" into the discussion, observes, "Everyone 'knows a story about a highly intelligent, highly-skilled executive who was promoted into a leadership position only to fail at the job. And they also know a story about someone with solid—but not extraordinary—intellectual abilities and technical skills who was promoted into a similar position and then soared'" (2004). The same could be said of library leadership, which suggests that the attributes or qualities of a successful leader are different, than what we normally perceive to be the indicators of future success. We tend to associate qualities such as intelligence, toughness, determination, and vision: to be the prerequisites of a successful leader. However, after conducting research at over 200 large, global companies, Goleman discovered that, although those qualities are important, they are insufficient. "Truly effective leaders are also distinguished by a high degree of emotional intelligences, which includes self-awareness, self-regulation, motivation, empathy, and social skills" (2004).

When we look at the graduate education in a Master of Business Administration (MBA) degree that prepares future business leaders, or the Master of Library and Information Studies (MLIS), that nurtures the next generation of library leaders; they tend to focus on the technical skills, but do not seem to offer nearly as much training in developing the so-called soft skills of a successful leader, such as those that comprise emotional intelligence.

As the economy and our library profession face unprecedented changes, Daniel Pink offers another view of the necessary qualities to solve our problems. He suggests in his book, *A Whole New Mind* the solutions to the complex problems in today's new economy demand a new way of thinking—a creative, "right-brain" way of thinking that more and more corporations increasingly value (2006). He proposes that in this "conceptual age", we need to complement our left-brain directed reasoning, by mastering some right-brain directed aptitudes. He lists storytelling as one of those aptitudes. "When our lives are brimming with information and data, it's not enough to marshal an effective argument [....] The essence of persuasion, communication, and self-understanding has become the ability also to fashion a compelling narrative" (2006). He also suggests empathy as an important aptitude. "The capacity of logical thought is one of the things that makes us human. But in a world of ubiquitous information, and advanced analytic tools, logic alone won't do. What distinguish those who

Skills to Make a Librarian. http://dx.doi.org/10.1016/B978-0-08-100063-2.00001-6

thrive will be their ability to understand what makes their fellow woman and man tick, to forge relationships, and to care for others" (2006).

However, since our primary education (MBA for businesses, and MLIS for libraries) do not emphasize developing those aptitudes, how do we nurture the next generation of leaders? Katherine Bell takes Pink's idea one step further, and suggests in her Harvard Business Review blog post that the Master of Fine Arts (MFA) is the new Master of Business Administration (MBA) because students hone a lot of the so-called "soft" leadership skills in the program naturally (Bell, 2008). She also suggests that creative writing can teach students persuasion and empathy, two of the aptitudes that Pink values so much:

> If you can create a world, a completely imaginary world that a reader believes in, you can manage to do pretty much any persuasion that you have to do in the business world. A PowerPoint presentation is nothing after that. Also, the most important thing that a fiction writer does is put him or herself in the shoes of his characters. And that's really empathy, which is something that is absolutely crucial in business as well. You're constantly needing to think about things from the perspective of your direct reports, of your boss, of your colleagues, and, importantly, also of your customers (Bell, Ideacast, 2008).
>
> (Bell, Ideacast, 2008)

In fact, Goleman's analysis revealed that such "soft-skills" played, "an increasingly important role at the highest levels of the company, where differences in technical skills are of negligible importance" (2004). In other words, the higher up the leadership ladder, the more important these soft skills become.

In this chapter, I will use my own personal experience in earning a MFA in Screenwriting to expand upon Bell's ideas on why a MFA program is a valuable management and leadership training course for librarian leaders, and how I apply those skills in my professional life.

My path to librarianship

When I enrolled in the graduate film program at Hollins University, I was planning to go on to earn a PhD in film studies and become a film scholar. Nothing was more appealing to me at the time than to just watch movies all day, think about them all day, and write about them. It seemed like a perfect lifestyle, especially for a shy and introverted person, which I certainly was. At that stage of my life, I seemed to have accepted that I would never enjoy dealing with "people". I lacked self-confidence, and the social skills to feel comfortable speaking my mind in front of people. Immersing myself in the movie world was actually my way of escaping the real world.

I was drawn to the Hollins MFA in Film and Screenwriting program: First, because it was a summer-only program that allowed me to do other things during the academic year. Second, because it was a summer-only program, it was able to attract very high caliber professors from top screenwriting, and films studies programs at universities such as the University of California, Los Angeles (UCLA), New York University

(NYU) and the University of Southern California, to teach in Roanoke, Virginia for the summer. However, as it says in the name of the program, it is a film AND screenwriting program. The unique part of this degree is that students study both film studies, and screenwriting, which meant that I would have to take at least one screenwriting class. The thought of sharing my writing with everyone in class terrified me so much I actually considered not enrolling in the program!

I took that screenwriting class the first summer I enrolled. The idea was to get it out of the way as soon as possible. As in most things in life, the anxiety of something is usually worse than the actual event. It turns out I actually really enjoyed the class once I allowed myself to enjoy it. If you think about it, creative writing is a very fun thing to do. You get to day-dream and make-up stories. It is almost like you are a kid again. The anxiety inducing part, was the sharing of the story in public, and being critiqued in public. However, the interesting was, I discovered that every time I stepped outside of my comfort zone: the comfort zone got a little bit bigger. In other words, I grew as a person during that period of stress-meets-anxiety-meets-creativity. I gained confidence from that experience, and realized that I actually really loved writing. Later, I even switched my degree from the MA in Film Studies and Screenwriting to a MFA in Screenwriting: in which I concentrated on just screenwriting. In fact, my thesis screenplay got placed, and won awards in various screenplay competitions, which was something that I never thought could happen in my life before I took that first screenwriting workshop class. Even though I did not really have any desire to move to Hollywood, and become a professional screenwriter, I felt that this training in screenwriting introduced me to a whole new world of thinking, and behaving. It was transforming me into a different person, dare I say an improved version of me. However, it was much later, when I entered the librarianship profession, that I was able to realize what exactly, had I really learned, from the training.

The summer before I graduated, a visiting professor from UCLA's Film Archives and Preservation program taught at Hollins. I asked him about the program and expressed interest in it, which led to a discussion on other preservation programs, such as the highly regarded one at University of Texas at Austin's Library School. Before this discussion, I had absolutely no awareness of the existence of librarianship. When I began to do some research on it, I discovered a whole new, fascinating, and now rapidly changing profession. It has so many different facets that it almost seems like there is a library job for every personality type. As I was searching for a future career direction, it was the perfect timing. I applied to Florida State University's School of Information Studies, and received a graduate assistantship to work in the University's Main Library. A few months later, I packed my car and moved to Tallahassee, Florida to begin the Master's in Library and Information Studies program. After graduation, I secured a position at Kansas State University Libraries as their Multicultural Studies Librarian, and officially began my librarian career. I stayed in that position for about a year, until my library had a major reorganization, and I took on the new role of research & development librarian with the responsibilities to conduct assessment, and drive innovation.

As I gained progressively more responsibilities in my library, and in professional organization, I realized how much my MFA training has helped me developed a set of skills, and aptitudes, to stand apart from others in my profession. While I believe some people are able to develop these skills naturally when they were young, most people require some training. I also believe that by understanding why a MFA training is useful, one can adapt that philosophy into other achievable plans to develop those skills.

The MFA workshop format

The Master of Fine Arts in Screenwriting (or Creative Writing) is the definitive degree in the field (although there are now a growing number of PhDs in Creative Writing programs). Depending on the program, there are usually some required film theory, and/or film history courses, but the bulk of the program has always consisted of writing workshops. Unlike a lecture-style class, in which the instructor gives an oral presentation of the subject matter, and there is little to no student participation; or a graduate seminar class, in which the instructor leads a small group of students on discussions on a specific topic; a writing workshop requires students to share their written work for peer critique in class. This format demands much more student participation than the lecture style class, or even a seminar class, as every student will have to have their work critiqued, and to critique others' work.

The student shares a draft version of the script with the rest of the class and the professor ahead of class time. During class time, the class discusses the work in front of the student. It could be an intimidating environment. "When you're dealing with creative work it's very, very close to you. You're about at your most vulnerable when you're putting forth something that is from that deep inside you and that you've created. And that you know isn't finished. You know that there are flaws with it" (Bell, Ideacast, 2008). However, it is this unique way of teaching and learning that nurtures in a MFA graduate some of the highly important skills that library leadership requires.

How to take and give criticism

> *"It was confusing", one classmate said. "The flash backs and flash forwards are too much!"*
>
> *"I liked the premise of the story, and the concept", another commented. "But I don't think the execution is there yet".*
>
> *"I think it's meant to be confusing", yet another classmate chimed in. "The protagonist doesn't know where, or when he is supposed to be. And we are deliberately being led to feel the same confusion".*

My classmates were critiquing a draft of my screenplay in class. I remained silent, because I had to. It was not that I did not want to respond, or to explain myself, or simply agree, or disagree with the feedback. In the workshop format, it is customary for each writer to remain silent while the draft of their writing is being read out, and discussed by their classmates, and instructor. "This allows the writer to actually hear what other has to say, and train him or herself to listen openly to all criticism" (Bell, Ideacast, 2008).

Giving and receiving criticism are two of the most delicate professional skills. Naturally people do not like to be criticized because it implies that they are wrong, or not good enough. Many people are sensitive about criticism and take it very personally, and this could negatively affect workplace harmony. Therefore, the ability to give constructive criticism "in a way that people could perceive it and actually hear it" (Bell, Ideacast, 2008) is very valuable in our profession. The writing workshop environment provides a very natural setting to hone this difficult skill. Giving and receiving criticism is part of life in a MFA program. In fact, it is the only way to improve your work. Every time you revise your draft, you have to take those criticisms into consideration, and then pick and choose, the ones that would make your work better. I apply the same attitude to my library work. As one of my main job responsibilities is to create new services, and products for my library, I regularly propose new ideas for consideration. Inevitably, there is feedback on the feasibility of the proposals. However, I actually look forward to the feedback, whether it is positive or negative; because I now know that by having collective critiques from different perspectives— that I alone would not able to come up with—could only help improve my work. While not everyone at the workplace is able to deliver criticism in a thoughtful, constructive, or diplomatic manner, I have been trained to receive criticism positively, and not take criticism personally.

A leader who knows how to give, and receive criticism could also establish a culture of giving constructive criticism in such a way that it empowers the receiver to improve. In a workshop, the readers respond to the work and say:

> *this is how I'm reacting to this. This is where I'm confused. This is where I am having this kind of reaction. This is where I have no idea what's happening, or I don't understand the character. And then let the writer, who is the creative owner of the work, come up with a solution for that. I think that's really useful as a manager in terms of giving advice to employees, that you let them come up with the response. You provide the feedback, they provide the solution*
>
> *(Bell, Ideacast, 2008).*

What motivates people

> *"By creating realistic fictional characters and their interactions, the writer must think about people's mix of motives and learn what drives a person. The more the writer immerses him/herself in this mindset, the better he/she can empathize with real life people"*
> *(Bell, HBR Blog, 2008).*

Empathy is the ability to see from other people's perspectives; to feel the way they feel; to understand where their actions, or thoughts come from. For example, a former smoker is more likely to have empathy with someone who is trying to quit, because he/she has experienced it firsthand how difficult the process was, and is now able to understand what the person is going through. Pink (2006) suggests that: "it is something we do pretty much spontaneously, an act of instinct rather than a product of deliberation". However, can it be learned or developed?

When we write a screenplay, we very often create a character profile for each main character. It gives us a backstory of the character, which may or may not, appear in the story proper. However, that informs us of how the character would act, speak, and react in our story. By creating this profile, we are forced to think, and see from this character's perspective. In other words, we try to understand our characters, and by extension, people. For a story to work, these characters must have goals to motivate them to do the things they do.

> *Writers always talk about how there's a point when you're writing, a novel especially, where your characters really take on a life of their own and they become real people. [...] Once a character comes to life, [...] you're not the god in control of that character. That character will refuse to do things and will want to do things that you maybe are surprised by or don't expect. And then sometimes it can be very inconvenient. But you really have to think about why they're doing what they're doing in order to know what they're going to do next*
>
> *(Bell, Ideacast, 2008).*

So, when we craft a story, and try to make these characters behave the way we want them to, we are very much "managing" and "leading" them by understanding their motivations. The same philosophy could be applied to the real world. In order to effectively persuade my colleagues, or our library users, I must understand their motivations, what drives them to do what they do.

Before we write a screenplay, a common practice is to write a log line for the film, which is basically a brief summary of the entire story in one sentence, to provide a "hook" to stimulate interest. Here are some loglines for well-known movies, and see if you recognize what they are:

- "A lawyer who loses his ability to lie for 24-hours, clashes with his ex-wife for the affection of his son and the healing of his family."
- "A naïve young man battles heartless authorities to protect the life of his girlfriend when it's revealed that she is not human—she's a mermaid."
- "A Parisian rat teams up with a man with no talent to battle convention and the critics that anyone can cook and open their own restaurant" (Williams, 2014).

They are, of course, *Liar Liar, Splash,* and *Ratatouille*. Notice that in each logline, there is a protagonist (a lawyer, a naïve young man, a Parisian rat), with a goal (win the affection of his son and healing of his family; to protect the life of his girlfriend; to prove that anyone can cook and open their own restaurant), and an obstacle (his inability to lie for 24 hours; heartless authorities; convention, and critics). It is that goal (or motivation) that *drives* the protagonist to act. Without it, there would not be a movie. So, another valuable lesson I learned in my MFA program was the importance of *setting a goal*. Whether it is for the story, for a character, for a project, or for myself. We must have a vision to lead others. Without a destination, we would be wandering aimlessly, without a sense of purpose. A vision of where we want to go allows us to draw up a roadmap of how to get there. Another common practice of screenwriting is "know your ending". It is a very effectively a way to *focus* the story if you want: how you want to end it, that is. We very often come up with a final image, a final scene. Then everything before is designed to lead to that destination. An organization needs a vision first, before we can craft a narrative to get there.

When to let go of good ideas

"An idea may be great on its own, but if it doesn't serve your larger venture, you have to be ruthless and cut it. Brilliant but misplaced ideas can derail a project or keep you from seeing bigger, better solutions. It can be almost impossible to recognize your own darlings"

—(*Bell, HBR Blog, 2008*).

Writing is about rewriting. When we revise a script, we very often have to give up good ideas in order to make changes to make the story work. And it is a very difficult process for a writer, as these ideas are the writer's "babies", and in many way they are priceless. Just as ideas for an organization, for a library service or product are difficult to let go. It comes back to knowing the vision. If the idea does not fit in with the bigger picture, it does not matter how brilliant an idea it is, it would get in the way of achieving the overall goal. And it must go!

For example, when I was writing a comedy, I would come up with a funny joke, or a scene that I really liked, and I naturally wanted it to be in the script because I knew it would get a big laugh. However, if it slows down, or deviates from the main story just to have this laugh, then it actually weakens the script. Bell offers this solution:

So the key thing there is to not think about deleting it permanently, but to rather cut and paste it. So if it's a product, there might be an aspect to it that just doesn't work this time. But maybe will work in another iteration, or maybe will work for a different product, or maybe it will completely change itself and become a different idea in the future. But never completely delete your ideas. Just save them in a separate place and go back to them later (2008).

The power of storytelling

Persuasion is the centerpiece of business activity. Customers must be convinced to buy your company's products or services, employees and colleagues to go along with a new strategic plan or reorganization, investors to buy (or not to sell) your stock, and partners to sign the next deal. But despite the critical importance of persuasion, most executives struggle to communicate, let alone inspire. Too often, they get lost in the accoutrements of companyspeak: PowerPoint slides, dry memos, and hyperbolic missives from the corporate communications department. Even the most carefully researched and considered efforts are routinely greeted with cynicism, lassitude, or outright dismissal

(Fryer, 2003).

The most important training I got from the MFA in Screenwriting program was, of course, storytelling. It was when I stepped outside of the screenwriting environment; and into a professional setting that I realized what a powerful tool I had acquired. It might sound strange that storytelling is a necessary skill to persuade people in a professional setting where hard facts, numbers, charts are the typical tools most people tend to use to convey their messages. However, I argue that the storytelling is what separates great leaders, from the average ones.

Robert McKee, a screenwriting guru, also coaches many CEOs of well-known corporations on how to tell stories. He explains that there are two ways to persuade people.

> *The first is by using conventional rhetoric, which is what most executives are trained in. It's an intellectual process, and in the business world it usually consists of a PowerPoint slide presentation in which you say, 'Here is our company's biggest challenge, and here is what we need to do to prosper'. And you build your case by giving statistics, facts, and quotes from authorities. But there are two problems with rhetoric. First, the people you're talking to have their own set of authorities, statistics, and experiences—while you're trying to persuade them, they are arguing with you in their heads. Second, if you do succeed in persuading them, you've done so only on an intellectual basis. That's not good enough, because people are not inspired to act by reason alone*
>
> *(Fryer, 2003).*

If you have been to any library conferences, you would probably agree that these are the most common types of presentations you see. The presentations tend to be dry, and uninspiring, and instead of helping the audience "get" the message they try to deliver, the presenters actually create an obstacle (i.e. the presentation) for the audience to get to the message. However, there is a better way to persuade people. McKee further explains:

> *The other way to persuade people—and ultimately a much more powerful way—is by uniting an idea with an emotion. The best way to do that is by telling a compelling story. In a story, you not only weave a lot of information into the telling but you also arouse your listener's emotions and energy. Persuading with a story is hard. Any intelligent person can sit down and make lists. It takes rationality but little creativity to design an argument using conventional rhetoric. But it demands vivid insight and storytelling skill to present an idea that packs enough emotional power to be memorable. If you can harness imagination and the principles of a well-told story, then you get people rising to their feet amid thunderous applause instead of yawning and ignoring you*
>
> *(Fryer, 2003).*

Due to my MFA training, whenever I communicate with my colleagues, I instinctive apply the storytelling principles to make my message more engaging.

Daniel Pink explains what story is in another way: "Story exists where high concept and high touch intersect. Story is high concept because it sharpens our understanding of one thing by showing it in the context of something else" (2006).

Libraries are in a critical period of transitioning. The concept and the identity of libraries are being transformed. It is, therefore, necessary for library leaders to articulate what we are, and what we are becoming. To deliver a message about the future, about change, about unpredictability, we need good storytellers to rouse our emotions, and our stakeholders' emotions.

The most important thing for a library leader is to accept that storytelling is a necessary leadership skill. Steve Denning, an expert in organizational storytelling, came up with a list of reasons why leadership storytelling is important, and here are some of them:

- Storytelling is a key leadership technique because it's quick, powerful, free, natural, refreshing, energizing, collaborative, persuasive, holistic, entertaining, moving, memorable and authentic. Stories help us make sense of organizations.
- Storytelling translates dry and abstract numbers into compelling pictures of a leader's goals.
- Narrative helps us make sense of a world that is rapidly mutating, as compared to conventional management, which is more suited to activities that are stable, linear, and predictable.
- Narrative is a key tool for leadership, because it helps us deal with organizations as living organisms that need to be tended, nurtured, and encouraged to grow. It thrives on inspiration rather than administration, fostering change rather than stasis.
- Narrative is a tool for the instigators of change, who aim at continuing transformation and the creation of a fruitful tomorrow.
- When we hear a story that touches us profoundly, our lives are suffused with meaning. As listeners, we have had transmitted to us, that which matters. Once we make this connection, once a sense of wonder has come upon us, it does not last long, and we inevitably fall back into our daze of everyday living, but with the difference that a radical shift in understanding may have taken place.
- A story is something that comes from outside. But the meaning is something that emerges from within. When a story reaches our hearts with deep meaning, it takes hold of us. Once it does so, we can let it go, and yet it remains with us. We do not weary of this experience (Denning, 2011).

Conclusion

Whether it was teaching information literacy classes, persuading colleagues to try new ideas, or simply delivering any message in any forum; I have applied so many of the tools I acquired in my MFA program to my librarianship career. While I don't believe it is feasible for every leader to take time out to earn a MFA, I believe that we should recognize the benefits of such training, and try to develop ways to provide similar training for future library leaders. There could be an elective class in a MLIS curriculum that follows the writing workshop format that allows MLIS students to practice those skills. Or, libraries could provide professional development incentives for staff to take a creative writing class. Professional associations could develop leadership courses that focus on storytelling. The possibilities are endless.

References

Bell, K. (2008). *The MFA is the new MBA.* HBR Ideacast. [podcast: 3 May 2008a]. Available from, http://blogs.hbr.org/2008/05/harvard-business-ideacast-92-t/, Accessed 14.04.14.

Bell, K. (2008). *The MFA is the new MBA.* Harvard Business Review. [blog: 14 April 2008b]. Available from, http://blogs.hbr.org/2008/04/the-mfa-is-the-new-mba/, Accessed 14.04.14.

Denning, S. (2011). *Why leadership storytelling is important*. Forbes. [blog: 8 June 2011].
    Available from, http://www.forbes.com/sites/stevedenning/2011/06/08/why-leadership-
    storytelling-is-important/, Accessed 16.04.14.
Fryer, B. (2003). Storytelling that moves people: A conversation with screenwriting coach
    robert McKee. *Harvard Business Review*.
Goleman, D. (2004). *What makes a leader?* Available from, http://hbr.org/2004/01/what-
    makes-a-leader/ar/1, Accessed 14.04.14.
Pink, D. H. (2006). *A whole new mind*. New York: Riverhead Books.
Williams, S. D. (2014). *Writing good log lines*. Available from, http://www.movieoutline.com/
    articles/writing-good-log-lines.html, Accessed 16.04.14.

Transferable skills: from rocks to books

2

Anne V. Hiller Clark

Introduction

At first glance, it may seem that there is little relationship between working as a geologic project manager, supervising hazardous waste site cleanup for a State agency, and working as an academic librarian. However, in my experience I have found that many skills transfer and are valuable aids in managing time and tasks, providing effective instruction and reference services, as well as serving on library management teams. First, this chapter explores the more immediately obvious transferrable skill of project management—the need for which has been discussed in library literature for quite a while, with a closer look at how in-depth those skills need to be effective: in a library setting. Second, the perhaps less obvious, but often related, skills of facilities care and maintenance, and disaster preparedness are considered. The author argues that these skills and knowledge from a previous career can be very effective tools in many librarians' toolbox. Many second career librarians bring important transferable skills with them; this chapter will hopefully provoke readers into examining in more detail how some of their own more esoteric skills may be useful in the library setting.

Transferable skills for librarians and geologists

When I began thinking about transferrable skills from geologists to librarians beyond my own personal experience, I did what most librarians would do: research. I started with the *US Bureau of Labor Statistics' Occupational Outlook Handbook* that lists "important qualities" for each job category. These are "characteristics and personality traits that are likely needed for workers to be successful in given occupations" (Bureau of Labor Statistics, 2014b). Table 2.1 is the author's compilation of these qualities for librarians and geologists. The two categories share three sets of "important qualities": communication skills, interpersonal skills, and problem-solving skills (Bureau of Labor Statistics, 2014c; Bureau of Labor Statistics, 2014a). Communication and interpersonal skills are important to most jobs these days so it is logical that they occur on both lists. Problem-solving skills are also on both lists. In their everyday work both librarians and geologists are presented with many problems to solve. They may be small or quick problems, such as a student's request for help with a citation at the reference desk—or much larger—such as a geologist's need to determine the extent of groundwater contamination at a hazardous waste spill site. In either event, both the librarian and the geologist need to use various types of problem-solving skills to meet

Skills to Make a Librarian. http://dx.doi.org/10.1016/B978-0-08-100063-2.00002-8

Table 2.1 Author's compilation of qualities for librarians and geologists

Geologist important qualities	Librarian important qualities
Communication skills	Communication skills
Critical-thinking skills	Computer skills
Interpersonal skills	Initiative
Outdoor skills	Interpersonal skills
Physical stamina	Problem-solving skills
Problem-solving skills	Reading skills

Source: US Bureau of Labor Statistics' Occupational Outlook Handbook, Bureau of Labor Statistics, 2014a,b,c).

the requestor's need. The *Occupational Outlook Handbook* includes three other skills for geoscientists: critical-thinking skills, outdoor skills, and physical stamina (Bureau of Labor Statistics, 2014a). I would argue that librarians also need critical-thinking skills, and in some cases physical stamina.

Looking for a resource that delved deeper into occupational skills and abilities; I turned to O*NET OnLine, *www.onetonline.org*. O*NET OnLine is an interactive database developed by the National Center for O*NET Development for the US Department of Labor to bring together vast amounts of occupational data that can be used by employers, job seekers and human resources professionals (National Center for O*NET Development, (n.d.)). Table 2.2 is the author's compilation of the skills and abilities from O*NET OnLine's summary reports for geologist and librarian occupations (National Center for O*NET Development, (2013a), National Center for O*NET Development, (2013b)). Of the skills required 50 per cent, and 80 per cent of the abilities listed, for the two occupations are the same. The same skills listed for the two occupations are: active listening, critical-thinking, reading comprehension, speaking and writing. Most librarians would agree with that list. These skills are important in many professions. Additional librarian skills are coordination, instructing, monitoring, service orientation, and social perceptiveness; while the additional geologist skills are active learning, complex problem-solving, judgment, and decision-making, mathematics, and science. Individual librarians may say that some of those other skills also apply to them.

The list of the two occupations' *shared abilities* is as follows: category flexibility, inductive reasoning, information ordering, oral comprehension, oral expression, speech clarity, written comprehension, and written expression. The additional librarian abilities are near vision, and speech recognition, while the additional geologist abilities are deductive reasoning, and problem sensitivity.

When I reviewed these two tables of important qualities, skills and abilities, one reason why librarianship had appealed to me as a second career became obvious: so much of the skill sets are similar. Even though on the surface my two careers seem very different, the similarities in qualities, skills and abilities helped make my transition easier. In addition to those skills and abilities, I have found that I have other

Table 2.2 Author's compilation of the skills and abilities for librarian and geologist occupations

Geologist skills	Librarian skills
Critical thinking	Reading comprehension
Reading comprehension	Active listening
Science	Speaking
Speaking	Writing
Active listening	Monitoring
Complex problem solving	Critical thinking
Judgment and decision making	Coordination
writing	Instructing
Active learning	Service orientation
Mathematics	Social perceptiveness
Geologist abilities	**Librarian abilities**
Inductive reasoning	Oral comprehension
Category flexibility	Written comprehension
Deductive reasoning	Oral expression
Oral comprehension	Written expression
Oral expression	Information ordering
Problem sensitivity	Near vision
Written comprehension	Speech clarity
Written expression	Speech recognition
Speech clarity	Category flexibility
Information ordering	Inductive reasoning

Source: O*NET OnLine's summary reports for geologist and librarian occupations, National Center for O*NET Development, (2013a,b).

skills that proved to be valuable in my librarianship career that are discussed in the later sections.

Project management

One skill set that transferred well into my work as a librarian was project management. Actively managing projects calls on many of the skills and abilities discussed in the previous section such as inductive reasoning, active listening, information ordering, critical-thinking, category flexibility, oral and written comprehension, and expression. It was a skill set I could bring to my library that added value to the overall sets of skills the staff possessed. Carpenter (2011) partially attributes the lower rate of use of project management techniques in service organizations (libraries being one) to either unawareness of the approach's usefulness at various levels of management, or poor implementation of the project manager's role that leads to unsatisfactory outcomes. However, that does not mean that these techniques cannot be valuable in many different library settings.

In my previous career I worked as a project manager on environmental cleanup projects that ranged from short-term, tens of thousands of dollar projects to—multi-year, multi-million dollar projects. These projects progressed through many phases with associated tasks, teams, assessment, and decision processes. Using project management techniques was a key to successful progress in the heavily regulated clean-up process.

A variety of project management standards, tools and techniques have been developed in different countries. In the United States the Project Management Institute, Inc. publishes *A Guide to the Project Management Body of Knowledge* (PMBOK), offers project management (PM) courses, and certification to project manager professionals. The *PMBOK® Guide* (currently in its fifth edition) presents the basic concepts every project manager needs to know, and is revised periodically to reflect changing practices (Project Management Institute, 2014a). Carpenter (2011) describes using the PRINCE2 method that is often used in Great Britain and European projects. Horwath's (2012) study of library project management practices in Ontario, Canada indicates that a variety of approaches were used by her study set. Some library management classes briefly address the topic of project management, but based on recent literature and personal experience, it appears that it is often a skill set learned on the job (Allen, 2004; Carpenter, 2011; Condit Fagan & Keach, 2009; Horwath, 2012; Smallwood, Kuhl & Fraser, 2013). For good overviews of recent literature on project management in libraries, see Horwath's (2012) literature review and Kinkus (2007).

Project management in libraries

Before delving into project management specifically in libraries, it is helpful to define what a project is, and what it is not. In a general sense most projects have a common set of characteristics: specific desired objectives or results, a limited timeframe, and a predetermined set of resources (Carpenter, 2011). Projects are different from operational workflows, especially in the limited timeframe and sometimes in the resources available; although parts of workflows can sometimes be treated as projects, especially when piloting changes in them.

The Project Management Institute (2014b) presents the following general steps in the project management process: initiating, planning, executing, monitoring and controlling, and finally, closing. In order to successfully complete these steps, certain knowledge areas are needed including: integration, human resources, costing, stakeholder management, scoping, time management, quality control, procurement, communications, and risk management (Project Management Institute, 2014b). A number of the common skills and abilities described in Table 2.2 relate to the knowledge areas above.

Many activities in the library workplace can be thought of as projects, and successfully addressed using project management techniques. Even tasks that we think of as part of our operational workflows can sometimes be broken down into projects, and addressed or improved, through use of project management techniques. Projects may be one time or recurring activities. Using project management techniques is valuable for recurring projects because by documenting the process and the outputs, valuable time and effort can be saved when it is time for that particular activity again.

The decision of whether or not to use project management techniques is partly a matter of perspective on whether that approach can add value to the activity, or does the project "just need to be done now" as so often happens in the very busy world of libraries. Another factor in deciding whether or not to use project management techniques is training and experience. If a manager isn't familiar with the process or has had a bad experience when project management was not implemented well, then it is unlikely that her/his unit will use the process, even when it may be very beneficial.

Horwath (2012) surveyed Ontario-based, Canadian librarians about project management practices, and found that the most common categories where project management is used are: technology, collection development, "marketing and communications/community outreach", and facilities. Projects that fall into each of these categories often have many steps or involve lots of details that must be managed. One example is building digital collections. Project management techniques are particularly helpful in keeping grant-funded projects on track, as well as when preparing complex grant applications to large non-profit funders or government agencies. Facilities and building projects will be addressed later.

There are many tools a project manager may use ranging from simple paper lists to sophisticated software suites. The decision as to what tools and techniques are appropriate often depends on the scale of the project. If it is a campus campaign to increase awareness of new electronic resources at the library: a shared spreadsheet workbook, and a shared calendar may be the most effective and simplest tools. If the project is on the scale of designing and building a new library, an experienced project manager using the Project Management Institute, or PRINCE2 tools, associated with sophisticated software; is probably the most appropriate approach.

Important questions for any librarian starting to manage a project are:

- What is the desired goal or end result of this project?
- What is the time frame for this project?
- What resources (people, equipment, funding, etc.) are available for this project?
- Are these resources adequate? A librarian project manager may have to be creative to find the resources needed to complete the project in this time of limited budgets, and staffing restraints.
- To whom is the project manager accountable, or what is the communications path?
- What is the preferred communication method the project manager should use to communicate with those she/he is accountable to about progress and/or problems?
- What style of leadership is most appropriate for the project team? What are the limits of the project manager's authority to require activities to be accomplished, especially if the team is an ad hoc one composed of staff members who usually work for different supervisors? A situation where failure is more likely; is when the project manager has all of the responsibility for the project's success—but little authority over team members, or has few relationships with other entities involved in the project, such as the business side of the organization.
- Are there other aspects of the overall project that will be handled by other offices? For example, is the project manager responsible for the accounting/financial aspects of the project or is this handled by another office?
- Are there risks associated with this project that will need to be addressed or mitigated?
- What type of project management tool(s) is most appropriate for monitoring and controlling this project?

Lessons learned from managing library projects

In addition to the ideas discussed above, here are some lessons I have learned from projects I have managed for both libraries, and government agencies. Knowing your own strengths, and weaknesses, is important because you will want to have team members with skills that fill in those gaps for you if possible. Know your personality and style of leadership. For example, as a less than five-foot tall, young-looking woman, I had to find an effective way to get cleanup work done according to State regulations beyond commissioning contractors, and expecting them to jump to it. So, I would find the largest four-wheel drive truck with the State seal available, drive up to the site, and then jump out, and personally say hello to everyone. The contrast between the truck and myself was usually good for a chuckle, and got things started-off well.

How in-depth do librarians need their project management skills to be? In my opinion, it depends on the types of projects managed. A good rule-of-thumb is that the more complex the project, the more experienced the project manager should be with both managing projects, and the various techniques and tools available to support the project. One important thing that all librarian project managers should take to heart is the idea of completing all of the project steps identified by the Project Management Institute, Inc. Sometimes we are so eager to get the project going that we don't do enough in the initiation phase, and we may end up without enough support to finish the project. On the other hand, we may be so tired of the project by the end; that we don't complete and file all of the documentation; so that when that type of project occurs again, we find ourselves recreating items unnecessarily.

Soft skills are important too: for example, building relationships with team members as well as staffers in offices that can have an impact on the project can make the difference between getting an issue resolved quickly or not. Adaptability and flexibility are key characteristics to cultivate in yourself. I always told my library student workers and volunteers that we had a Plan B for each project that gave us all confidence when progress may have looked a little rocky.

One final lesson I learned, is the universal one of keeping things as simple as possible. Use the simplest project management tools and techniques that are appropriate. Keep communication lines open. Complexities easily arise, and can complicate or stymie an ill-defined project. Some people find that the project-tracking activities, and associated management software: can sometimes seem to involve more effort than the actual project activities, but both activities are necessary for success.

Facilities care and maintenance

Another valuable transferrable skill when I became a librarian was my experience working with contractors and facilities management. Librarians at many levels often have some type of responsibility for all or a part of a facility. This may range perhaps from just your desk area—to one or more buildings. Even if it is just your desk area, it is a good idea to understand where the buildings systems—such as heating, air-conditioning, plumbing electricity, and network cabling are located. I once worked in a space that was subject to leaks through cracks in the concrete walls if the wind blew rain or snow in certain directions. To protect my computer and other materials it was important for me to understand how the building and its systems functioned. Ultimately my solution was to install seven permanent buckets around my desk to catch drips and plastic sheets to cover my desk each evening while I waited for the building to be remodeled.

Understanding your facility

In terms of facilities, however, most of us think on the larger scale of a building. Knowing where the building's systems are located, and generally how they operate are just one part of understanding a facility. Library facility management involves many aspects: security, information technology requirements, and capacity, energy management, space utilization, pest management, and even cleanliness. A wide array of literature exists on these topics and is well worth exploring if needed. However, my experience has been that while the literature is useful in helping to learn the right questions to ask of the staff who maintain the building and its systems; creating direct relations with these staff members is equally important. For example, I always made it a point to introduce myself to each new custodial staff member who cleaned the special collections area I managed. I would give them a quick tour, and we would talk about the cleaning schedule, and the special cleaning supplies needed to protect the materials; since that information sometimes was not always communicated by the supervisor. Afterward the new custodial staff member felt more a part of the team that cared for that area, not just the cleaner, and I had reassurance that the materials I was charged to protect would be taken care of when unsupervised staff were in the space.

Understanding bidding and procurement processes

Organizations use various processes to purchase items or procure services. It is important to understand not only the processes, but also the details about when and how each process is used. For example, governmental organizations may have very detailed bidding processes, and if a small step is not followed, it could invalidate the process or open it up to challenges from the losing bidders. In certain cases, the amount of money to be spent determines the procurement process to be used. Usually, the larger the sum, the more involved the process will be. Building relationships with staff who handle contracting, accounting, procurement, and other similar activities can help prevent costly mistakes.

Working with contractors and subcontractors

Working with contractors and subcontractors is a place where the soft skills mentioned above come into play. It is important to remember that their work is often bid on a time and materials basis, so be respectful of their time when interacting with them. Like most people they take pride in their work and can be sources of improvement ideas that can turn a project: into something special.

I was involved with the replacement of the climate control system in a special collections unit—within one that covered a greater area—and required expanded duct work. As the project's contractors and I were meeting about the plans; the heating, ventilation and air conditioning (HVAC) engineer on the project brought up his concerns about the placement of vents and returns. After talking about the budgetary constraints of the project he suggested using a system of doors to connect the rooms that were to be added to the system's coverage as one way to address the issue. Privately, one of the top items on my wish list for the space was for just such connections. Since, he and I had an established relationship, he felt comfortable bringing up the non-traditional idea. I jumped at the chance, and the end result was a facility that not only had expanded climate-controlled storage areas, but a space that was much more efficient to use, and could serve more patrons and workers.

Disaster preparedness

Disaster preparedness has been a popular topic in library literature and conferences, especially since Hurricane Katrina in New Orleans, USA. In one sense disaster preparedness is taking the understanding of a library facility and considering threats outside the four walls—as well as within them. Organizations such as the Western States and Territories Preservation Assistance Services (WESTPAS) in the US, provide preparedness training, and consultation during a disaster. (For more information see *westpas.org* [Accessed 16 August 2014].)

Preparation of a disaster preparedness plan is based partly on knowledge of the facility, and its surroundings. Each area is vulnerable to various types of natural disasters; and every building has its known and hidden problems—so it is important to understand each individual situation. When writing the plan it is also important to connect with those who maintain the building as well as the risk management staff of the organization. Existing insurance policies may have an effect on some of the activities that should, or should not, be included in the plan.

One way in which my first responder training, namely, preparation of site health and safety plans, and experience teaching Industrial Safety and Health to undergraduate engineers—transferred to my librarian activities was to help me identify potential problems, assess preparedness needs and write a disaster preparedness plan for the special collections area for which I was responsible. However, when I attended disaster preparedness workshops put on by WESTPAS, or by Connecting to Collections; one of the things I saw my colleagues struggle with a bit was the Federal Emergency Management Agency (FEMA) incident command system (ICS) used in a major disaster, and where they and their collections, would fit into the system. As librarians we sometimes feel personally responsible for the materials we care for, and provide to our users, and it can be a bit hard to learn that ICS responders have higher priorities such as people's health and safety than collections preservation during a disaster, and we will probably not have immediate access to the damaged area to try to use the preservation skills we learn in the workshops. While we all will agree that preservation of life and minimizing the effects of the disaster must be top priorities, and a centralized system for managing activities is the most efficient way to deal with the disaster situation, we may still feel that our valuable collections are being ignored. Hopefully, most of us will never have to experience a disaster of this scale. For more information about the ICS system visit the FEMA website at *http://www.fema.gov* [Accessed 10 August 2014].

There are many aspects of disaster preparedness which are extensively covered in the literature, and in various training options which cannot be covered in this chapter. One useful reference is *Disaster management in archives, libraries and museums* by G. Matthews, Y. Smith, and G. Knowles (2009).

Conclusion

Second career librarians can bring some surprising skills to the libraries where they work. I have always appreciated the opportunities to use skills I had learned in my earlier career in my library career, partly because it made that knowledge still seem worthwhile, but also because of the opportunity to bring something to an effort that could make it richer.

References

Allen, B. (2004). *Project management: tools and techniques for today's professional*. London, UK: Facet Publishing.

Bureau of Labor Statistics, US Department of Labor. (2014a). *Geoscientists occupational outlook handbook, 2014–15 edition*. Available from, http://www.bls.gov/ooh/life-physical-and-social-science/geoscientists.htm, Accessed 04.03.14.

Bureau of Labor Statistics, US Department of Labor. (2014b). *Glossary. Occupational outlook handbook, 2014–15 edition*. Available from, http://www.bls.gov/ooh/about/glossary.htm, Accessed 13.03.14.

Bureau of Labor Statistics. US Department of Labor. (2014). *Librarians. Occupational outlook handbook, 2014–15 edition*. Available from, http://www.bls.gov/ooh/education-training-and-library/librarians.htm, Accessed 04.03.14.

Carpenter, J. (2011). *Project management in libraries, archives and museums: working with government and other external partners*. Oxford, UK: Chandos Publishing.

Condit Fagan, J., & Keach, J. A. (2009). *Web project management for academic libraries*. Oxford, UK: Chandos Publishing.

Horwath, J. A. (2012). How do we manage? Project management in libraries: an investigation. *Partnership: The Canadian Journal of Library and Information Practice and Research*, 7(1), 1–34, Available from: Wilson, H.W. (24 February 2014).

Kinkus, J. (2007). Project management skills: a literature review and content analysis of librarian position announcements. *College and Research Libraries*, 68(4), 352–363, Available from: Wilson, H.W. (24 February 2014).

Matthews, G., Smith, Y., & Knowles, G. (2009). *Disaster management in archives, libraries and museums*. Farnham, Surrey, UK: Ashgate Publishing Ltd.

National Center for O*NET Development. (2013a). *Summary Report for: 19-2042.00– Geoscientists, Except Hydrologists and Geographers. O*NET OnLine*. Available from, Accessed 04.03.14, http://www.onetonline.org/link/summary/19-2042.00.

National Center for O*NET Development. (2013b). *Summary Report for: 25-4021.00–Librarians.* *O*NET OnLine.* Available from, http://www.onetonline.org/link/summary/25-4021.00, Accessed 19.03.14.

National Center for O*NET Development. (n.d.), O*Net OnLine Help: OnLine Overview. *O*NET OnLine.* Available from: *http://www.onetonline.org/help/online/* [Accessed 19 March 2014].

Project Management Institute, Inc. (2014a). *Library of PMI Global Standards.* Available from, http://www.pmi.org/en/PMBOK-Guide-and-Standards/Standards-Library-of-PMI-Global-Standards.aspx, Accessed 23.03.14.

Project Management Institute, Inc (2014b). *What is Project Management?* Available from, http://www.pmi.org/About-Us/About-Us-What-is-Project-Management.aspx, Accessed 19 March 2014.

Smallwood, C., Kuhl, J., & Fraser, L. (Eds.), (2013). *Time and project management strategies for librarians.* Toronto, Canada: The Scarecrow Press, Inc.

More than just story time: how librarianship prepares you for parenting, and vice versa

3

Samantha Schmehl Hines

Introduction

The truism that "becoming a parent changes everything" of course applies to us in libraries as well as anyone else. This fundamental human experience alters an individual's perspective in a number of ways, and requires parents to learn new skills in order to cope with the demands of raising a new human being. A WorldCat search on 11 February 2014 turned up over 5000 items dealing with "parenting skills" as a keyword search. Skills addressed in these works include the practical and physical: feeding, clothing, cleaning, and so on. However, the skills adopted in parenting also include more nebulous concepts such as communication, reasoning, teaching, emotional intelligence, and the like. It makes sense that these skills can go beyond the parenting experience, and provide parents with career advantages.

However, the transfer between parenting skills and career skills has been less examined. A keyword search on WorldCat for both "parenting skills" and "career skills" brings up slightly more than 200 titles, and a number of those focus on "mommy wars" issues of working mothers, or how to raise children to possess good employable skills. Similar keyword searches on Google Scholar, LISTA and the University of Montana Mansfield Library's Summon iteration, on February 11, 2014 yielded few results.

Despite the lack of hard research, it stands to reason that parenting skills would be transferable—that is, that the particular things you learn to do as a parent to manage that role, would be useful in other circumstances. It also makes sense that the skills we learn as librarians can be applied to our lives as parents, in order to better facilitate that role. In my own experience, becoming a parent has developed my skills in interpersonal relations, including becoming more patient and understanding as is required when dealing with a small and impatient human, and helped me hone my time management, and organizational skills; which is key when you take on managing the life of a child—and all the requisite appointments, meetings, events, and materials. My career has helped me in parenting through the ability to research issues from sleep to nutrition, to health, to behavior, and given me the critical-thinking, and analysis skills to determine what is relevant and credible in a sea of information. Both roles have shaped my skills in budgeting from various perspectives, and in presenting information in a wealth of environments. This chapter will examine both parenting and librarianship's place in transferable skills building and use, through a look at existing research, and via an analysis of qualitative data gathered in an informal survey.

Skills to Make a Librarian. http://dx.doi.org/10.1016/B978-0-08-100063-2.00003-X

Literature review

General discussion of transferable skills

As mentioned above, there has been little formal analysis of transferable skills between parenting and career. Some writers have discussed the issue on blogs and other social media, where there seems to be a tacit understanding that such transferable skills exist. One of the most succinct and eloquent discussions came from a post on a blog devoted to the intersection of parenting and religious practice, where the author writes:

> *[The parent] who has spent time at home with kids may well have, in that time, developed much better clinical skills in areas of communication, organization, self-control, stamina and empathy than her colleague. I mean this in all seriousness—I'm not being cute or flippant. Trying to get inside the head of a two-year-old, for twelve hours, so you can successfully negotiate the day with everyone's sanity and property intact— and then do it again tomorrow—gives these skills a serious workout. The vast majority of my time spent mothering isn't niche stuff that won't be useful elsewhere. Motherhood stretches my transferable skills*
>
> *(Rowden, 2013).*

The blog post goes on to discuss the gendered nature of discussion on parenting, and that mothers are often the parents whose careers are impacted by parenting. It is worthwhile to note that librarianship is considered a 'gendered' career, like teaching, nursing and social work, and that these occupations as a whole face barriers in obtaining professional status (England & Folbre, 2005). Those in these occupations already garner low pay, lack benefits, and receive little social recognition, and respect (Ackerman, 2006), and the question arises as to what impact parenting status may have on those in the library profession. The larger question also arises that perhaps the transfer of parenting skills to career skills may not be studied due to institutionalized sexism in fields of research dealing with career preparedness and efficacy, as parenting is still primarily seen as a female objective.

Academia

One area in which family status and professional status has been studied increasingly in recent years is in higher education. When addressing the issue of impact of family status on tenure, Mason and Goulden (2004) learned that women with children under six years of age were least likely to obtain a tenure-track position but, conversely, that men with young children were the most likely to obtain such a post. The same article stated that women with children were the most likely to report stress from family status as affecting travel, research, publishing and other career-related tasks.

Todd, Madill, Shaw, and Bown (2008) showed that both women and men felt that having children would negatively impact an academic career. However, they felt that perhaps men overcompensated for children in a way that led them to greater success than women in the same position. The authors state:

Prior research suggests that women with children are disadvantaged in the academy (Mason & Goulden, 2004), and so this perhaps shows a realistic assessment of the situation. However, some of the same research suggests that actually men with children are more productive than men without, which is contrary to the expectations of our male participants. Perhaps men with children are more productive because, feeling that it will negatively influence their career, they work very hard to overcome that (p.773).

Librarianship in academia

Graves, Xiong, and Park (2008) studied attitudes a group of library faculties held toward parenting. They found that only a small segment of their sample, 27 per cent, actually had children during the years in which they were attempting to achieve tenure (p.205). This was surprising compared to other disciplines, in which more than half of women were parents (p.208). They found that female faculty seeking promotion and tenure generally considered children a "hindrance (p.206)" to advancement. The study raised several questions. Were librarians in the academic process truly less likely to have small children than other faculty? Were they entering their career path after having children, perhaps?

Zemon and Bahr (2005) surveyed 347 library deans or directors to see if parenting status impacted their careers, and discovered that the answer was, generally speaking, no. The majority of directors and deans had children (p.398) and were fairly happy with their careers, and family lives (p.400). Graves, Xiong and Park (2008) felt that librarians could be a bellwether to an improved situation in academia overall, concluding: "As a female-dominated discipline, librarians can open the doors to this discussion for their campus communities (p.209)."

Generational differences

Graves et al. (2008) also suggested that librarianship consider how parenting status is supported within the profession, as a signal to young professionals about how adaptable our profession is (p.208). The best point of analysis with regard to young professionals might be to look at the research describing the attitudes and desires of millennials, as the upcoming generation of workers. This generation is defined as those born between 1982 and 2001 (Emanuel, 2012: p.4).

The desires of millennials as newly matriculating library workers was examined by Emanuel's 2012 dissertation. She noted several traits of millennials, chiefly:

- ubiquity of technology (p.34);
- acceptance of multi-tasking (p.35);
- adoption of mobile devices (p.37);
- skeptical consumer behavior (p.43);
- flexibility between work and personal life (p.46);
- work in a team environment (p.46); and
- a sense of relevance for and engagement in their work (p.47).

Emanuel noted in her research that several of these traits overlapped with developing trends in librarianship, primarily the use of technology, and adoption of mobile devices (p.165) and the desire to change the work patterns of librarianship to reflect a team environment, and build in more flexibility and engagement (p.167–70). Emanuel's research also confirmed that librarianship is highly gendered, with a range of 80–90 per cent of various study respondents being female (p.175).

When examining the traits of millennials and library work, what might be noteworthy for studying transferable career and parenting skills? Deal, Altman, and Rogelberg (2010) point out that generally millennials have been avoiding positions of responsibility in the workforce, perhaps due to concerns over balance and flexibility. They point out that employees today are already expected to work more hours than ever before, and that management roles expect even more hours of face time (p.195). The authors go on to say that this objection may be less of a generational disagreement, than a life-stage one, citing in particular parents of young children desiring a more flexible schedule regardless of parental generational status (p.196).

An area of relevance, however, might be the changing family structure for millennials. Millennials have firmly left behind the traditional nuclear family in favor of many other arrangements (Ray, 2013). Managers and library administrations ought especially to never presume to know what family structure exists for their employees.

In-depth analysis: therapists as parents

One of the best pieces of scholarly research I found on parenting skills as transferable career skills and vice versa is a dissertation focusing on the effect of motherhood on psychotherapists. Robinson (2012) found overall that motherhood gave therapists increased empathy, clearer, and firmer boundaries, and a fuller understanding of developmental issues as compared to non-parents. She also found that mothers were better at compartmentalizing professional life than non-parents, and were more understanding of their patients with children (p.17).

In her study, Robinson interviewed nine women from across the US about their experiences as psychotherapists and mothers (p.21). After her semi-structured interview with each participant, she identified fourteen general themes; and four master themes on how parenting affected a therapist's career; or how being a therapist affected parenting styles and skills. The general themes that reflect transfer between parenting and career skills are as follows:

- *Theme 1:* Becoming a mother changed how participants understood themselves and the world, and this had an effect on their roles as therapists (p.38).

This theme states that lived experiences of parenthood help therapists relate better to their clientele. This could be easily applied to library work, especially in those positions that work with the public.

- *Theme 2:* Motherhood changed participants' career plans (p.40).

Universally, this theme reflected a slowing-down and reassessing of participants' career plans, from goals, to hours worked, to training, to professional association involvement. However, participants stressed universally that their careers were still important to them.

- *Theme 3:* Being a mother affects the way participants practice psychotherapy (p.45).

Due to their careers dealing directly with family structure in many cases, the new insights into parenting that the participants gained directly changed how they practiced their profession. This was mostly described as an improved ability to empathize or relate to their clients, and setting boundaries. This could translate well to library work, especially with regard to front-line work with the public.

• *Theme 4:* Being a mother changed the logistics of being a therapist (p.50).

This meant that participants gained time management skills, and adopted different boundaries and methods of managing the time impact of parenting on their professions. This is a theme that I expect is universal for parents in any profession.

• *Theme 6:* Participants' mothering was influenced by their profession (p.57).

As therapists, all participants had training and education in child development issues. This influenced how they parent, as they had knowledge and skills that the layperson would not. This may be true of library workers as well—I would expect to see a lot of our knowledge about literacy, and critical evaluation of information, to be reflected in our parenting practices.

• *Theme 9:* Motherhood creates change (p.66).

While on the surface this theme is a platitude, the discussion of the theme demonstrates that participants feel that mothering connects them with human society, and the human experience on a fundamental level like no other experience. This connection helps minimize some of the day-to-day drama that these professionals experienced prior to having children. Perhaps library workers who are also parents feel this deep connection in a way that affects their career skills.

• *Theme 11:* Participants have a worldview that reflects psychoanalytic values (p.70).

As a helping profession, the psychotherapists participating in the study viewed parenting as the opportunity to raise productive and functional members of society—the psychoanalytic values mentioned. Would librarianship, as a similar helping profession, have the same view of parenting?

• *Theme 13:* Mothers and therapists have substantial commonalities (p.76).

The coaching and attunement required by psychotherapists has a good deal in common with mothering. This may not be as true with librarianship, but as a gender-coded profession and a helping profession, there may be some commonalities between librarianship and parenting.

The four master themes identified by Robinson (2012) are considered the largest, overarching concepts from the study data. They are listed below:

• *Master Theme 1:* Motherhood changes everything (p.82).

This was mostly listed as a master theme because all participants agreed with this statement, and felt it was fundamental to the understanding of their experience as parents and psychotherapists. The "everything" refers to their thought processes, their practice, their worldview, and their relation to and connection with clients.

- *Master Theme II:* Insight changes everything (p.84).

Insight in this sense is the practice of psychotherapy. This theme drills directly into the mindset and skills that therapists bring to parenting. All the participants felt that their career choice had a huge impact on how they parent.

- *Master Theme III:* Therapists' experiences of motherhood are complex (p.87).

Parenting affected all the participants in personal world-changing ways that cannot be easily explained or condensed.

- *Master Theme IV:* Therapists have a worldview that encompasses both their parenting, and their professional lives (p.88).

Due to their training, skills and experiences, therapists' worldview was applicable to both their parenting life and career life. Their professional outlook is expansive enough to conceptualize beyond their work to larger issues in society, which obviously impinge on how they parent.

Faced with the literature I discovered and especially the dissertation by Robinson, I was keen to discover whether my experiences with parenting skills aiding my career, and vice versa were applicable to a larger population of librarians.

Methodology

In order to discover how library workers' skill set affects parenting skills and vice versa, I constructed a survey on Google Drive. The survey text can be found at the end of this chapter. This survey consisted mostly of open-ended questions soliciting anecdotes and perceptions of how librarianship influences parenting skills, and how parenting affected the respondent's practice of librarianship. I then sent a link to the Google Drive survey to my Facebook audience (n=312) and Twitter audience (n=349), as well as the ACRL Balancing Baby and Books Discussion Group listserv (123 subscribers). I received 33 responses during the last week of January 2014. Google Drive provided a painless and simple way to set up and collect responses online for the survey, and I highly recommend it for small surveys.

Results

Of the potential audience of 784 individuals, I received 33 responses. Of those 33: 21 respondents were from academic libraries; 8 were from public libraries; 1 was from a special library; and 1 was from a school library. Based on my Twitter and Facebook audience, as an academic librarian, and that the Association of College and Research Libraries provided the listserv I used; the lack of balance among library types is understandable. Of the respondents: 11 identified themselves as managers, and 8 said they worked with children in some aspect of their jobs.

There were three survey respondents who were in positions that did not require an MLIS or equivalent. Four survey respondents had been in librarianship for less than

5 years, while 12 had been in librarianship for 5–9 years. Seven respondents had been library workers for 10–14 years, while 5 had been working in libraries for 15–19 years. The remaining 3 had been in librarianship for 20 or more years.

Of my 33 survey respondents, all but 3 felt that being a parent has affected their librarianship skills. (A single respondent was undecided, and 2 felt that it had not.) Analyzing the content of responses I received, I identified the following library worker skills that were positively influenced by parenting, followed by the number of respondents listing the skill.

• Compassion or understanding (n=11)

From helping with topic development for obstetric nursing classes, to offering to carry books for those with their hands full, this was the top skill developed by parenting for our library workers. "I know first-hand how hard it can be to get things done when you have a little one in tow", stated a respondent. This connects with Robinson's *Theme 1*, on parents' understanding of themselves and the world.

• Championing issues of work/life balance (n=6)

Work/life balance challenges many working parents, and several of my respondents said that their experiences as a parent led them to become champions in their workplace for better balance for their coworkers and their clientele. One respondent realized that, in order to draw in patrons aged in their twenties and thirties to programs: it would be helpful to provide corresponding children's programming. Several respondents mentioned adopting or pushing for flexible scheduling in their workplaces. This relates to Robinson's *Theme 3*, on parenting changing career practices, and *Theme 4*, on parenting changing career logistics.

• Patience (n=5)

Tied in with compassion or understanding, but deserving of its own listing, the development of patience is a primary parenting skill that has relevance in any workplace setting. The ability to deal with the public, or coworkers, is improved, and respondents mentioned that patience with the day-to-day struggles of work life improved as well. One respondent said, "I've learned to just slow down because being a parent of a young child is such a beautiful part of life that passes unbelievably fast". (This also connects with Robinson's *Theme 1*.)

• Efficiency (n=3)

Several respondents mentioned a new found ability to get things done in limited amounts of time as a positive skill for both their work and home lives. "I have learned to work quickly and efficiently to stay ahead of the game, so when/if I get called out for not being present, I can show that going to my daughter's winter program isn't ruining the library world!" exclaimed one respondent. (This also connects with Robinson's *Theme 4*.)

• Story time and work with children (n=3)

Of course, several respondents mentioned that their story time skills at work improved now that they had a test audience at home. Even after their own children outgrew story time, respondents noted that they could relate to children better at differing ages when performing their job duties. (This relates well with Robinson's *Theme 3*.)

• Decreasing perfectionism (n=2)

Two respondents noted that they had become far less concerned about perfection in their lives overall and that this transferred over into their work. (Again, this connects with Robinson's *Theme 1*.)

Individual respondents also mentioned other relevant skills developed by parenting, including listening skills, acknowledging feelings, organization, conflict resolution, and setting limits. A respondent said: "I think [parenting] has broadened my skills, especially the type they don't teach you in library school. I am more competent at resolving conflicts, setting limits with patrons, and juggling multiple priorities because I am a parent".

Some respondents mentioned negative impacts of parenting on library skills. Lack of focus was mentioned by four respondents, time constraints by three, and guilt by two. According to one respondent, "I feel like it should make me better at juggling, but in reality I think I'm even more disorganized and 'just staying afloat'".

On the other hand, of my 33 respondents, all but 6 felt that being a library worker has affected their parenting skills. Four respondents were undecided, and two felt that it had not. Analyzing the content of responses I received, I identified the following parenting skills that were positively influenced by working in a library, followed by the number of respondents listing the skill. All these connect with Robinson's *Theme 6*, on how parenting is influenced by profession.

• Love of books/reading/literacy (n=13)

This was by far the most mentioned skill in the entire survey. Respondents felt strongly they were instilling a love of books, reading, and literacy in their children by virtue of their professional training and skills. "Reading and spending time with our books is a BIG part of our together time", said one respondent.

• Assisting with schoolwork (n=6)

Several respondents discussed how their careers in librarianship made it far easier for them to assist their children with schoolwork and research for assignments, and in preparing reports and presentations.

• Understanding the benefits of technology (n=4)

Our jobs in libraries lead us to understand how technology works, and how it helps with learning and reading. Several respondents cited this as a positive skill brought to their parenting. In the words of one respondent, "I am prepared to acknowledge the benefits technology can bring to my child's education, so while time on the iPad is limited, I definitely let her use it". Another respondent stated, "I definitely plan to use screen time as a way to learn, explore and be interactive more than mindless entertainment. Sort of like giving them an apple for a snack, which they love anyway, instead of a sweet".

• Awareness of media influence (n=2)

An interesting skill that two respondents said librarianship lent them was an increased or clearer awareness of how media influences children. One respondent put it succinctly: "Good—keenly aware of media and its influence on cognition and attention. Bad—Perhaps too aware of media's influence? I worry she won't be a normal kid".

Some other important themes, were mentioned by a single respondent each. Patience, was one skill that a respondent felt had been developed by her practice of librarianship, and useful in parenting, and this was a skill we saw on the other side of the equation. Story time skills popped up again, as did organizational skills taught, and used in the field of librarianship.

One particularly interesting skill that a library worker parent felt her career had given her that impacted her parenting was the concept of community. "I'm excited to instill in my son the value of sharing a library with a community versus individual consumerism", she stated.

Some negative impacts of library skills on parenting also arose. The generic concern of the working parent, that there was too much work to enjoy parenting, arose. "I don't feel that I have time and energy to focus on my children. My job consumes my day," wrote one respondent. She concluded, "I feel sad because I don't have a lot of downtime to interact with the children".

One respondent felt that she should promote reading more to her child, as a library worker. She said, "Because I work in a library, I feel like I should be reading to my son ALL THE TIME! So when I am not, I feel guilty, like somehow I am letting him down".

Discussion

Based even on my brief and nonscientific poll, it is clear that career skills, and parenting skills are transferable. Respondents could best articulate how parenting skills transferred to librarianship, but also had well-drawn library worker skills that transferred to their parenting. It is interesting to note that many of the skills of parenting could also be said to be life values—patience, understanding, compassion—but multiple people defined them as skills and described them as such. Likewise, some of the skills of librarianship could be described more broadly as life values, particularly the understanding of community good.

An expected, but still unfortunate, outcome of the survey was a confirmation of the pervasive sense of guilt, and the sense of being overwhelmed that many working parents espouse. This manifested in the obvious ways, when respondents spoke of time constraints, lack of focus, and worries about not spending enough time on both parenting, and work, in turn. The unexpected concern about how one respondent felt she should be reading to her child all the time was at first amusing, but at its root is another worry about not spending enough time on what is important, because it is all important in this context both for our careers but also for our families.

I had expected to see some connection between management skills and parenting, due to popular views that management and parenting roles share similar traits. An exemplar of this is *Forbes'* 2007 article entitled 'Do Parents Make Better Managers?'—that tracked a study conducted by the Center for Creative Leadership. That study concluded that active and involved parents do indeed develop skills useful for management, for example, multi-tasking, dealing with stress, and negotiating (Clark, 2007). However, none of my respondents addressed the relationship between parenting, and managing in a meaningful way.

Another expectation I had was for respondents to be more representative of gender, but all my respondents seemed to be female. This is understandable based on the gendering of our profession, and the gendering of discussions on parenting, but it would be useful to broaden any study of transferable skill to include males.

Future directions of research

More research on the intersection between career skills generally and parenting skills is needed. Librarianship, as a gendered career, could be an interesting starting point for this research. A more scientifically conducted survey, with a random, unbiased, inclusive sample from across the profession, could lead to further exploration of how the transferable skills of parenting, and librarianship, develop and interact. This type of research could aid parents in the workforce in demonstrating their worth despite the additional outside demands on their time.

Research of this sort could also contribute to the normalization of working parents. Nearly 88 per cent of US families have one working parent, according to the 2012 Bureau of Labor Statistics *Employment Characteristics of Families Report*, and 59 per cent of traditional nuclear families had both parents employed outside the home (US Department of Labor, 2013). Studying the impact of parenting status on career skills and vice versa would allow for a more holistic view of workers, and perhaps improve work/life balance issues. Simply conducting this research could legitimize working parents, and the skills they develop both on the job and in caring for their children, and help banish the institutionalized sexism that stymie such conversations.

Also useful in addressing institutionalized sexism would be to further examine the differences in perception and practice between mothers and fathers with relation to the impact children have on their careers. Do fathers develop better skills in reconciling parenting with work demands, as indicated in some of the research described above? Or do mothers endure most of the work of parenting, or discrimination due to family status?

Conclusion

The intersection between parenting and career skills is ripe for research and exploration, and is critically relevant for recruitment to the library profession in many ways. Family and work/life issues are of importance to our profession from a humanist perspective, in order to provide the best possible work experience. In addition, with the upcoming millennial generation's concerns and desires, understanding and celebrating the transferrable skills between parenting and librarianship will only make our profession more attractive. Parents in the workforce accept the truism that parenting "changes everything". The field could be a groundbreaker in demonstrating how this is true with the intersection of parenting skills and librarianship skills.

Appendix 1   Intersection between parenting and librarianship survey text

Thank you so much for completing my informal survey! The purpose of this survey is to gather "anecdata" about parenting and librarianship for a forthcoming book chapter. Does being a parent influence how library workers practice librarianship? Does working in a library influence how you parent your child? Please share your thoughts below or feel welcome to email me directly at samantha.hines@umontana.edu. You don't have to be currently working in a library to participate. The book focuses on transferable skills, so try to think about your responses in that framework.

Responses WILL be kept confidential and WILL be anonymized unless you give permission to use your information. The textual responses (anecdotes) are not required, but are very much appreciated to broaden understanding and extend the dialog on the topic. If you are interested in participating in a short interview beyond these questions, please give me your email address at the end of the survey. Thanks!

Samantha Hines

Head, Missoula College Library

samantha.hines@umontana.edu

* Required

Do you feel that being a parent has affected your skills as a library worker?*

Perhaps you understand your users (or your boss) better now that you have children, or maybe you have been forced to address your work/life balance. If you feel parenting has affected your career skills for good, or for bad, please choose yes and explain why.

Yes

No

Not Sure

If yes, please explain how. Anecdotes/stories/rants are appreciated!

Do you feel that being a library worker has affected your skills as a parent?*

Maybe you really rock at bedtime stories. Perhaps you make your child log-in for computer time. If you feel that working in a library has affected your parenting skills, for good or for ill, please select yes below and explain why.

Yes

No

Not Sure

If yes, please explain how. Anecdotes/stories/rants are appreciated!

Demographics and permissions

These questions are purely optional, but can help me to see if there are any trends in the people responding to the survey. Demographic data will NOT be linked to individual responses.

Please also indicate on this page if you want your responses to be credited to you or anonymous, and if you might be interested in a follow-up interview.

Which type of library is/was your primary library type?

Academic/Public/School/Special/Other

Do/Did you work in library management?

Yes

No

Not Sure

Do/Did you work directly with children in your library work?

Yes

No

Not Sure

How long have/had you worked in libraries?

0–4 years/5–9 years/10–14 years/15–20 years/more than 20 years

Does your current position, or did your last position, require an MLIS or equivalent?

Yes

No

Not Sure

If your long-form responses are used in my writing, would you prefer your anecdotes to be anonymous or credited?*

Anonymous

Credited

If you would be willing to be contacted with follow up questions, please enter your email address below. Thanks!

Bibliography

Ackerman, D. (2006). The costs of being a child care teacher: Revisiting the problem of low wages. *Educational Policy*, *20*(1), 85–112.

Clark, H. (27 February 2007). *'Do parents make better managers?'* Forbes. Available from: http://www.forbes.com/2007/02/27/parents-bosses-managers-leadership-careers_cx_hc_0227parents.html, Accessed: 12 March 2014.

Deal, J. J., Altman, D. G., & Rogelberg, S. G. (2010). Millennials at work: What we know and what we need to do (if anything). *Journal of Business and Psychology*, *25*(2), 191–199.

Emanuel, J. (2012). *The Millennials: Assessing the next generation of academic librarians.* Columbia: University of Missouri.

England, P., & Folbre, N. (2005). Gender and economic sociology. In N. J. Smelser & R. Swedberg (Eds.), *The handbook of economic sociology* (pp. 627–649). New York: Russell Sage Foundation.

Graves, S. J., Xiong, J. A., & Park, J. (2008). Parenthood, Professorship, and Librarianship: Are They Mutually Exclusive? *The Journal of Academic Librarianship*, *34*, 202–210.

Mason, M. A., & Goulden, M. (2004). Marriage and baby blues: Redefining gender equity in the academy. *The Annals of the American Academy of Political and Social Science*, *596*, 86–103.

Ray, J. A. (2013). Today's young families: Successful strategies for engaging millennial parents. *Childhood Education*, *89*(5), 332.

Robinson, L. C. (2012). *Therapist as mother, and mother as therapist: The reciprocity of parenting and profession for female psychoanalytic psychotherapists*. Rutgers The State University of New Jersey: Graduate School of Applied & Professional Psychology.

Rowden, T. (2013). *Parenting as Professional Development*. Available from, http://sacraparental.com/2013/12/08/parenting-as-professional-development/, Accessed 13 March 2014.

Todd, Z., Madill, A., Shaw, N., & Bown, N. (2008). Faculty Members' Perceptions of How Academic Work is Evaluated: Similarities and Differences by Gender. *Sex Roles*, *59*, 765–775.

United States Department of Labor. (26 April 2013). *Employment Characteristics of Families Summary*. Available from: http://www.bls.gov/news.release/famee.nr0.htm, Accessed 10 March 2014.

Zemon, M., & Bahr, A. H. (2005). Career and/or Children: Do Female Academic Librarians Pay a Price for Motherhood? *College and Research Libraries*, *66*, 394–406, September.

From nonprofits to libraries: information-gathering, communication, and relationship-building—skills that transcend fields

4

Kimberly Fu-Jia Yang

Grant writing and fundraising defined

The nonprofit professional who works in grant writing, fundraising, or administration acquires a plethora of information-gathering, communication, and relationship-building skills transferable to librarianship. Although all grant writers can be described as fundraisers, not all fundraisers are grant writers. Fundraising is a broader term encompassing a multitude of activities with the ultimate goal of cultivating donors and contributions. Although there are similarities between a grant writer and a fundraiser (indeed, a grant writer is as a type of fundraiser) the differences between the roles, and responsibilities of a grant writer versus a fundraiser, create different skill sets that are assets to a career in librarianship in distinct ways. A discussion of these various roles and their corresponding skills will illustrate how the skills translate into librarianship.

In the nonprofit world, the term "development" is often used to describe both grant writing and fundraising staff. Hence, larger nonprofits might have a chief development officer or director of development who oversees a development department comprised of staff who write grant proposals ("grant writers") and/or staff who fundraise in other ways. These other ways might include soliciting individual donors, soliciting major donors or corporations, holding special event fundraisers, galas, online fundraising emails, and written, or oral requests to an individual for funding.

A very large nonprofit might even have staff dedicated to "prospect research", a version of intelligence gathering on potential donors ("prospects"), their capacity, and ability to give money, and their likelihood of giving. In a small nonprofit, there might be only one staff member dedicated to the entire constellation of grant writing, and fundraising activities described above.

Skills to Make a Librarian. http://dx.doi.org/10.1016/B978-0-08-100063-2.00004-1

Information-gathering

Information-seeking

While librarians are presented with reference questions that require information-seeking skills, development professionals are presented with questions about funding opportunities, and donor prospects that require information seeking skills. Grant writing, as used in this chapter, means writing and preparing written proposals requesting funding for a stated purpose. A grant writer must constantly be alert to new, and recurring funding opportunities and their submission deadlines. The grant writer both actively seeks new funding opportunities by searching for them online, and passively stays tuned to new, and recurring funding opportunities by subscribing to relevant listservs, newsletters, and alerts. Similarly, a librarian actively seeks information when responding to specific-user inquiries, and stays tuned to trends in librarianship by subscribing to listservs, newsletters, RSS feeds, and monitoring blogs.

Grant writing subject matter specialization and expertise

In the course of identifying potential funders, and crafting persuasive funding proposals, grant writers become knowledgeable about the subject matter of their organization's programs, and the focus area in which their nonprofit or institution operates. For example, a grant writer for a children's charity would become familiar the subject matter/focus area of the charity (such as children aged 0–5, early education, child abuse prevention). Such things include data, statistics, and research about the charity's geographic service area, demographics of its population served, and the benefits of its programs and projects. In essence, a needs assessment, or problem statement supported by data and research, is necessary to demonstrate the need for the service or program provided by the nonprofit. Developing expertise in the subject matter is necessary for a grant writer to craft compelling grant proposals.

Librarian subject matter specialization and expertise

In a similar vein, an academic librarian, especially a liaison to a university department or professional school, might acquire information-seeking expertise relevant to a specific discipline, such as chemistry, law, social or health sciences, to support their liaison activities. Academic librarians would become familiar with subject-specific information (information about library resources, databases, and any tools relevant to that particular discipline) in order to understand the information needs of users within that academic discipline. A librarian serving the chemistry department would obviously need to be familiar with different resources, than the librarian serving the history department.

Knowing the audience/user

Grant writers/fundraisers know their audience

A grant writer understands who the audience is for their proposals. Although the audience generally is the funder, funders come in a variety of forms: corporations, foundations, government agencies, individuals, groups of individuals, or other funding entities. One thing that all funders have in common is that the grant writer's proposal must persuade them that what they are to fund is both viable, and relevant. The proposal must align with the mission, interest, and agenda of the funder. At the same time, different types of funders have different expectations, and preferences for what they want to see in a funding proposal. A corporation might prefer proposals that specify how they impact communities where the corporation has locations, whereas a government agency might require an evaluation plan, or data management plan. A successful grant writer acquires knowledge of the particular interests, and submission requirements for each type of funder. Similarly, a fundraiser understands the interests of their individual donor prospects. Before making a pitch to a potential donor, the fundraiser gathers information on that individual's degree of interest in the nonprofit's mission, the person's financial capacity to give, and whether the nonprofit has a contact with that potential donor (either a direct relationship with the donor, or a connection with another person who has a relationship with and can broker an introduction to that donor).

Librarians know their users

While grant writers' target audience are potential funders, and fundraisers' audience are prospective donors, academic librarians' audience are their users, which might be faculty, staff, and students. Understanding which particular audience they are addressing, librarians will adapt their presentation of information, or instruction to the target audience. For example, knowing that faculty are interested: in promotion, tenure, and maximizing their research impact, librarians might market services related to those topics (bibliometrics, strategic publishing workshops, etc.) specifically for the benefit of faculty. Librarians would acquire discipline-specific information about their user population (faculty research interests, curriculum, and student course assignments, etc.) to inform how to provide relevant library services, and instruction to those users. Librarians might also tailor instructional opportunities, and services to be discipline-specific. For example, providing patient communications workshops at the medical school, or offering instruction on discipline-specific databases, for example, the Cumulative Index to Nursing and Allied Health (CINAHL) for nursing students, or SciFinder for chemistry researchers.

Online research skills

Grant writers online search skills

A grant writer must constantly be alert to both new, and recurring funding opportunities; to opportunities to renew existing grants; and all corresponding submission deadlines. The grant writer both actively seeks new funding opportunities by searching for them online, and passively stays tuned to funding opportunities by sub-scribing to relevant listservs, newsletters, and funding alerts. To search actively for funding opportunities, the grant writer might become proficient at searching databases such as Foundation Directory Online from the Foundation Center, and grants.gov. Seeking funding opportunities requires excellent research skills, and excellent research skills are an asset for any librarian.

Librarians online research skills

While grant writers research funding-related resources online, a librarian actively seeks information in databases, or resources that they determine are most likely to help them respond to user-inquiries. Academic librarians attempt to become expert searchers of these databases, and topical online resources. Whereas grant writers might subscribe to listservs, newsletters, and funding alerts so funding opportunities are "pushed" to them, librarians subscribe to listservs, newsletters, and alerts (e.g. RSS feed, or other mechanisms), that contain updates about the online resources they use, developments in their subject area of expertise, or topics in librarianship relevant to their work. Staying abreast of topics in librarianship might include information literacy, instructional tech-nology, scholarly communication, open access, and a wide variety of topics.

Professional development

Staying current on funding trends

Staying abreast of funding trends is critically important to grant writers, so they can monitor the continued viability of existing funding opportunities as well as new ones. This includes researching, and monitoring the funding practices and preferences of current, past, and potential new funders. From time-to-time, funders change their focus areas of funding, develop new strategic initiatives, discontinue past initiatives, or institute guidelines limiting previously-funded organizations from re-applying for funding. After including an *evaluation component* became a more commonplace funding requirement, nonprofits have had to adjust their programs to include evalu-ation in order to even submit a proposal or grant application.

Staying current on trends in librarianship

Staying abreast of subject-specific resources is relevant to librarians; in the same way as staying informed of current funding trends is to grant writers. Academic librarians monitor trends in instructional techniques, developments in their subject disciplines, issues relevant to scholars, and researchers (e.g. open access, research impact metrics, the flipped classroom model, massively open online courses (MOOCs), copyright, etc.). While grant writers adapt their proposals, and funding applications to the sub-mission requirements of funders in accordance with funding trends, academic librarians adapt to the demands/interests of their constituencies (faculty, students, staff) according to educational, and research trends. For example, some libraries provide instruction, and guidance to support faculty compliance with the NIH Public Access Policy (Stimson, 2009). With increased faculty interest in demonstrating the value, and impact of research, academic librarians have also provided instruction, and support to faculty on research impact (Drummond & Wartho, 2009; Sarli, Dubinsky & Holmes, 2010). The adaptive abilities of grant writers seeking funding are transferable to librarianship; in that librarians must be similarly adaptive in serving their academic community.

Evaluating information

Grant writers and fundraisers evaluate funding opportunities

When grant writers are presented with a potential funding opportunity, they evaluate that opportunity, and its submission guidelines, to determine whether to invest the time, and resources to prepare, and submit a proposal. Nonprofit fundraisers who work with individual donors undergo a similar process by evaluating whether a prospective donor might have sufficient interest in the nonprofit's activities, whether that prospect has the capacity/ability to donate at certain monetary levels, and whether the nonprofit has access to the prospective donor, i.e. whether the nonprofit has a relationship with the prospective donor, or has a relationship with an intermediary who will introduce the prospective donor to the nonprofit.

Librarians evaluate information sources

A nonprofit grant writer can transfer analytical skills used to evaluate the viability of funding opportunities or donor prospects to the library profession. Librarians use similar analytical skills when evaluating sources of information to answer research or informational queries (see Table 4.1, below).

Information-gathering

Program or project?

Although the terms "program" and "project" are sometimes used interchangeably, or synonymously by some nonprofits, others will treat the two as distinct concepts with regard to funding: "Program" will be used to describe a service, or cluster of services, provided on an ongoing basis by the organization. "Project" will be used to describe a service, or cluster of services, to be provided for a finite period of time, with project start dates and end dates. Even if it does not yet have a fixed end date initially, a project is typically not considered a perpetual, ongoing part of an organization's services, and is not planned to exist for an indefinite period of time. Occasionally, successful projects will be made regular, ongoing parts of an organization's services, or will be converted into ongoing programs because of their success.

Table 4.1 Comparison of analytical questions used to evaluate sources of funding by nonprofit grant writers, and sources of information by librarians

Sample questions used by grant writers to evaluate funding source	Sample questions used by librarians to evaluate information source
• **Eligibility**: Does the grant writer's organization meet the eligibility requirements for grant applicants to this particular funder? • **Compatibility**: Does the nonprofit's activities, programs, or area of focus match the funder's interest and guidelines? If the nonprofit is considering establishing a new project/program/activity to meet the funding guidelines, is the new project/program/activity consistent with the nonprofit's mission? • **Feasibility**: Is it feasible to prepare a grant proposal by the deadline? Is it feasible to carry out the proposed activities? Can they be implemented within the prescribed grant period? • **Likelihood of award**: Is there a reasonable likelihood that the grant writer's organization will be funded?	• **Relevance:** Does this source (database, journal, etc.) contain information appertaining to my topic or question? Am I likely to retrieve results for my research? • **Reliability**: Is the source of information reliable? Is the source of the information potentially biased? Is the research methodologically sound?

The distinction between a program versus a project is relevant in grant-seeking, because some funders will only fund discrete projects, new projects, or pilot projects, as opposed to services that are part of the ongoing, or regular operations of the nonprofit. Other funders are willing to fund services only if they feel confident that the nonprofit, or its services, are capable of securing sufficient funds from other funders to continue to exist. In those cases, an ongoing program has the advantage of being able to demonstrate a track record of having been funded in the past, and the likelihood of sustained funding, or continued existence.

The distinction between the terms "program" and "project" also have a role in libraries. Academic libraries will also have time-defined projects, such as launching outreach projects, evaluation projects, holding conferences or symposia, or conducting internal projects. Rather than using the term "program", the straight-forward term "service" is used to describe a function that academic libraries provide on a regular, ongoing basis to their users.

Information-gathering for programs versus projects

Grant writers who have gathered information to prepare funding proposals for both programs, and projects will note some differences in approach to the two tasks. Due to the ongoing nature of a program, there is more likely to be existing, documented information, even past proposals, program budgets, evaluation plans, or other prior grant proposal elements that can be reused in a new grant proposal or funding application. The ability to recycle parts of past written proposals is an immense timesaver. However, projects often involve a new or non-recurring service, assembling information on a project is often more time-consuming. Brainstorming sessions, and meetings of stakeholders, might be held by the grant writer to obtain the planning details related to the startup of a new project. These details and information gathered are key elements that a grant writer will need to include in a written proposal.

Project information-gathering

A nonprofit grant writer's information-gathering skills for new projects are transferable to the academic library setting. When a library plans a project, the process of involving stakeholders, holding meetings, and assembling a plan to implement the project are all steps with which a grant writer is likely to be familiar. Identifying existing sources of information (individuals, documents, or materials) that are helpful to the current project are also tasks with which a grant writer will already be acquainted. Just as funders for nonprofits have become more insistent on funding proposals including an evaluation plan, or component, the library world has become more interested in demonstrating the value of library services. Hence, libraries have increasingly focused on including an evaluative component to their services, or have even launched projects focusing entirely on evaluation. Nonprofit grant writers who have included evaluation in their funding proposals, and evaluation results in their grant reports can point to these experiences to bolster their credentials in the area of evaluation planning in the library world.

Information-gathering from colleagues at a nonprofit

In order to prepare a grant proposal, a grant writer gathers information from various colleagues. At larger nonprofits, this can involve engaging staff from multiple departments, such as the development office, finance, human resources, information technology, and planning/evaluation, and even executive leadership. If the nonprofit operates in multiple locations, or provides services off-site, information might be gathered from staff who work at various sites. Since program or project staff have roles or responsibilities delivering services to the nonprofit's client population, or implementing a program or project, information is gathered from those staff to verify that what is written in the proposal is both accurate, and feasible.

Information gathered from colleagues for library services

A nonprofit grant writer who used information-gathering skills to prepare funding proposals can apply these information-gathering skills in the library profession. A librarian takes comparable steps when gathering information to plan a library project, service, or activity (see Table 4.2, below). Since libraries also apply for grant funding, in those instances, a professional grant writer has the advantage of being able

Table 4.2 Comparison of information-gathering activities of grant writers and librarians

Common information gathered by grant writers to prepare funding proposal (NB not all categories of information are required by every funder)	Common information gathered by librarians to plan project, service or activity
• **Project description/timeline:** Information from program or project staff who have operational responsibilities might be gathered to confirm proposed activities, and deliverables that will be described in the proposal. • **Project description/timeline:** Information from program or project staff might be gathered about the appropriate time frames, and timeline, to assign to proposal activities, or deliverables. • **Staffing/bios:** Biographical sketches, resumes, or CVs might be gathered for staff who conduct activities described by the proposal, and staff whose positions will be funded by the grant. • **Budget:** Financial information about personnel, equipment, technology, direct and indirect expenses, and other sources of funding for the proposed project or program might be obtained from the nonprofit's finance department, or staff. • **Evaluation:** Information about an evaluation plan for the proposed project or program might be gathered from staff.	• **Existing resources:** Information from colleagues about existing and available resources (materials, documentation, in order to avoid re-inventing the wheel). • **Evaluation:** Information about past evaluation plans or evaluation tools (e.g. SurveyMonkey) that can be used for the proposed project, or service. • **Grant proposal elements:** Information commonly gathered for nonprofit grant proposals would similarly be gathered for library grant proposals.

to directly apply his or her grant writing experience towards preparing grant applications on behalf of their library.

Information-gathering for grant reports

At some nonprofits, grant writers might also be charged with grant reporting responsibilities. Those grant writers would track deadlines for the preparation of grant reports as well as information (content) required for those reports. Just as gathering information for the grant proposal requires contacting staff from various departments, gathering information for grant reports requires requesting information from various departments (e.g. financial reports of grant expenditures; numbers of clients served, outcomes, etc.).

Information curation

A "curator" is defined as "one who has the care and superintendence of something" (Merriam-Webster n.d.). Thus, "curating information" means caring for and superintending information. Nonprofit fundraisers, and administrators, as well as fundraisers, and administrators in academic institutions: care for information related to their grant applications. They also guard their funder/donor/member/alumni information that make them curators of information—comparable to librarians who care for, and superintend digital repositories.

Information curation for fundraisers

Nonprofit fundraisers, and fundraisers at academic institutions, use databases to track donors and their contributions. At larger nonprofits or in the academic setting, there may be a separate administrator who is responsible for maintaining the donor, membership, or alumni database. While fundraisers track donor names, gift amounts, and gift dates in their donor databases, grant writers track information related to their grant proposals, such as date submitted, amount requested, proposed grant period, proposal topic, award outcome (awarded/declined). These fields or data elements function like metadata that describe the proposal, grant application, or funder/donor. Regardless of whether such information (metadata) is maintained in a donor database, or a spreadsheet: they serve a vital function in helping fundraisers maintain consistent information about past, pending, current, or future (planned) funding requests, their outcomes, and facilitate retrieval of such data.

Information curation for librarians

Skills with databases are useful in the library setting where databases are used to track patron, and service interactions. Librarians also become curators of information when they function as catalogers, indexing content that appears on information databases, or when they are charged with starting, or maintaining an institutional repository. Both tasks might require familiarity with setting-up, assigning, or applying metadata.

While fundraisers might confront the challenge of retrieving the information they need from a donor database where data entry was inconsistent, librarians might confront the challenge of retrieving information from databases that are inconsistently indexed. Both fundraisers and librarians have a vested interest in having their information databases set up, and maintained in a way that facilitates retrieval of data or information they need; to fulfill their job responsibilities. Thus, lessons learned by fundraisers who manage donor databases can be instructive in the field of librarianship.

Communication

Nonprofit fundraisers tailor communications

As mentioned above, successful grant writers acquire knowledge of the particular interests, and submission requirements of various types of funders. Accordingly, their proposals are tailored to the special interests, expectations, and requirements of each type of funder. The style, tone, and content of their funding proposals, or grant reports will vary according to the funder type. For example, a family foundation's grant-making operations might be run by individual family members. These individual decision-makers might find proposals, or grant reports with human impact stories, or testimonials more compelling than a government agency. Government agencies, and large foundations might require formal grant application components, such as a needs assessment, an evaluation plan, and program/project timeline.

In addition to being able to identify potential funders, nonprofit grant writers should be able to write convincing proposals explaining why their nonprofit is exceptionally suited to implement program/project/activities worthy of the funder's commitment of funds. The nonprofit fundraiser who asks individuals for monetary donations must be able to communicate well both in writing and orally, sometimes making the "ask" face-to-face with prospective donors.

Librarians tailor communications

Whereas grant writers tailor their funding requests to the funder, librarians similarly tailor their communications according to their target audience, and according to the media in which they communicate. Librarian communications through the library's social media channels (such as Facebook or Twitter) will differ dramatically from their communications in other sources, such as library webpages, blog posts, or conference posters. The content, tone, and style of their communications will further change if the communication involves publishing an article in an academic journal. A grant writer who is accomplished at tailoring communications according to various types of grant applications to foundations, corporations, government agencies, or other funding entities; can apply diverse communication styles skills in librarianship as well. Moreover, since grant writers are accustomed to writing compelling arguments to persuade funders to support their causes, those persuasive writing skills are transferable to marketing, and evoking compelling reasons for library-users to avail themselves of library services.

Grant writers and fundraisers accustomed to tailoring their communications according to whether the prospective funder is an individual, group, foundation, corporation, or government agency can apply those skills in librarianship. Academic librarians adjust their oral presentations according to their audience. The following examples illustrate the diversity of audiences that an academic librarian might communicate with:

- An introductory class of freshman undergraduates in a basic library orientation, and information literacy class/workshop.

- A faculty department meeting presentation on a research database.
- A library conference presentation, or poster session.
- A one-on-one research consultation with a student, faculty member, or research staff.

The clarity with which a nonprofit fundraiser must communicate can be applied in the context of librarianship. Librarians who have instructional responsibilities may need to teach, and communicate clearly on topics ranging from: information literacy (explaining to a user how to distinguish reliable, from unreliable information—especially in the context of online information—even more so, in the area of health information on the internet); copyright; to online research skills for specific research databases or resources. Communication skills are also used by librarians to communicate internally with library management and staff to develop, and evaluate new, or existing library services.

Relationship-building

Relationship-building skills are critical for nonprofit development professionals, because relationship success with colleagues within their organization, and with funders outside their organization are the basis of career success. Relationship-building skills are crucial to nonprofit fundraisers as they cultivate relationships with individual, and corporate donors to engage their support, and financial contributions. These same skills foster academic librarians' outreach efforts to forge relationships with faculty, researchers, and students to support research efforts, build collaborative relationships, and publicize library services.

Grant writer relationships with colleagues

Grant writers must build strong relationships with a variety of staff, often from different departments, in order to gather information necessary for assembling a grant proposal. Since proposal budgets can require itemized staff salaries, otherwise confidential personnel information is disclosed to them for the purposes of preparing a proposal budget. Grant writers must inspire the trust and confidence of finance, and human resources staff that they can keep information such as staff salaries confidential.

Grant writers rely on the timely provision of information from colleagues in order to complete a proposal in time for its submission deadline. Sometimes, notice of a funding opportunity arrives so late that the grant writer has barely enough time to assemble a proposal. At larger nonprofits, assembling a proposal might involve engaging staff from multiple departments, such as the development office, finance, human resources, information technology, planning/evaluation, and even executive leadership who might be required to, or wish to review, and sign-off on the proposal. If the nonprofit operates in multiple locations, or provides services off-site, information might be gathered from staff who work at various sites. Since program or project staff have roles, or responsibilities delivering services to the nonprofit's client population, and implementing a program or project, meetings must be scheduled, and information gathered from various staff to verify that what is written in the proposal is desirable, accurate, and feasible.

Nonprofit fundraisers who raise money in special events must also maintain good relationships with colleagues. They might need to ask colleagues to assist in staffing fundraising events (e.g. golf tournaments, galas, silent auctions, dinners, etc.) that take place in the evenings, or on weekends.

Grant writer relationships with funders

Cultivating good relationships with funders, either prospective or existing funders, is vital to fundraisers, and their nonprofits' success. For a grant writer, cordial relationships with prospective funders is the basis upon which the grant writer can make inquiries related to preparing, and following up with a proposal, and grant application. Once the grant writer's organization is funded, maintaining a good relationship, and open channels of communication with the funder is important if the nonprofit intends to ask for renewed funding. For example, cultivating good relationships with program officers from the National Institutes of Health (NIH) or foundation funders are beneficial strategies for funding recipients. Good relationships help when grantees have issues, or questions arise, with their funded projects. When bad things happen to good projects, when a project falls short of enrolling the proposed number of clients/patients/research subjects, a good grantee-funder relationship paves the way for the funder to work with the grantee (whether at a nonprofit, or academic institution) to mitigate funder dissatisfaction with the outcome of their funded project or program. This also preserves the possibility of applying for, and receiving future funding.

Fundraisers who cultivate donations from individuals work in an area sometimes called "individual giving" or "major gifts". The term, major gifts, is used for contributions from donors at a significantly higher monetary level than their usual contributions. Fundraisers who solicit gifts in face-to-face requests to individuals must be skilled in building relationships, and rapport with these prospective donors in order to reach a point at the relationship where the donor is likely to respond affirmatively to an "ask" for a specific donation amount.

Librarian relationships with colleagues

Applying good relationship-building skills forges success in librarianship also. Academic librarians build, and cultivate relationships with colleagues, and with library users. Whereas grant writers rely on their colleagues to supply information needed for their grant requests or reports; academic librarians rely on fellow librarians to assist with teaching responsibilities. Especially with information literacy classes or library orientations offered to each year's new class of students, the number of classes/orientations might be so numerous at the beginning of the school year that each librarian relies on their fellow librarians to help teach the requested classes within the necessary time period. Academic librarians have committees, and projects on which they serve. It behooves a librarian to develop good relationships with their library colleagues to smooth working collaborations on both committees, and projects.

Another important avenue for relationship-building is participating in professional organizations for librarians/information professionals. Professional organization involvement is viewed as a service to the library profession, and is a critical part of an academic librarian's portfolio when reviewed for promotion (or tenure, a possibility at institutions that have tenure-track faculty librarian positions). Professional organizations, and the advancement opportunities that they hold for both fundraising professionals, and librarians are discussed further, below.

Librarian relationships with users

The relationship-building skills that fundraisers use to cultivate positive relationships with funders are equally applicable in the library profession. Academic librarians cultivate positive relationships with users of library services to improve their ability to serve those users. Librarians' outreach efforts to faculty, researchers, and students aim to support their research efforts, build collaborative relationships, and publicize library services. When librarians succeed in building trust, and confidence among users of the librarians' skills, and ability; these users are more likely to refer their peers, staff, or students to consult with the librarian.

By engendering confidence in users, especially faculty, librarians might become partners in research projects by conducting literature searches, and developing online search strategies. The librarian might write the methods portion of research papers, and potentially receive co-authorship credit. An example of a collaborative relationship emerging between librarians, and faculty members is the involvement of a librarian in a systematic review. The Institute of Medicine Standards for Systematic Reviews, Standard 3.1 states: "Work with a librarian or other information specialist trained in performing systematic reviews to plan the search strategy" (Institute of Medicine, 2011).

Nonprofit professional organizations for development professionals

Grant writers and fundraisers have professional organizations, and various certifications similar to the professional organizations, and certifications within the library profession. Grant writers and fundraisers can become involved with the American Fundraising Professionals (AFP) or the American Grant Writers' Association (AGWA) or the Grant Professionals Association (GPA). The Certified Fund Raising Executive (CFRE) designation is a professional designation, and credential requiring, "a written application, a written examination, and agreement to uphold a code of ethics and Accountability Standards" plus a recertification requirement every three years (CFRE International, n.d.). Professional certification, and engagement offer the potential for career advancement through networking, building leadership skills, and demonstrating professional service.

Professional organizations for librarians

A nonprofit professional who has actively participated in, or led professional organizations, can engage in similar roles in professional organizations for librarians. Several professional organizations exist for librarians, and each has committees, or special interest groups within the organization tailored to areas of interest. The American Library Association (ALA), Special Libraries Association (SLA) and the Medical Library Association (MLA) are a few professional organizations for librarians. In the field of health sciences librarianship, the Academy of Health Information Professionals (AHIP) designation is the "MLA's peer-reviewed professional development and career recognition program" (Medical Library Association n.d.). AHIP designation, involvement in professional organizations, and assuming leadership roles in professional organizations: are avenues to build a network of relationships advancing the librarian/information professional's career.

Conclusion

Information-gathering, communication, and relationship-building skills gained from working as a nonprofit fundraiser or administrator are valuable assets: transferable to librarianship. Information-gathering expertise includes skill in both information-seeking, and curating. In both academic, and community settings, seeking funding opportunities requires excellent research skills, as well as an ability to curate, and track information on funding proposals submitted, awarded or declined.

References

Certified Fund Raising Executive (CFRE) International. *CFRE FAQs: What are the requirements for the CFRE Programme?* Available from: *http://www.cfre.org/about/faqs/* Accessed 21 April 2014.

Drummond, R., & Wartho, R. (2009). RIMS: The Research Impact Measurement Service at the University of New South Wales. *Australian Academic & Research Libraries, 40*(2), 76–87.

Institute of Medicine (2011). *Finding What Works in Health Care: Standards for Systematic Reviews (National Academies Press).* Available from: http://www.iom.edu/Reports/2011/Finding-What-Works-in-Health-Care-Standards-for-Systematic-Reviews/Standards.aspx, Accessed 21 April 2014.

Medical Library Association (n.d.). *Academy of Health Information Professionals (AHIP).* Available from: *https://www.mlanet.org/professional-development/academyofhealth informationprofessionals,* Accessed 21 April 2014.

Merriam-Webster (n.d.). *Curator—definition.* Available from: *http://www.merriam-webster.com/dictionary/curator,* Accessed 21 April 2014.

Sarli, C. C., Dubinsky, E. K., & Holmes, K. L. (2010). Beyond citation analysis: A model for assessment of research impact. *Journal of the Medical Library Association, 98*(1), 17–23.

Stimson, N. (2009). National Institutes of Health public access policy assistance: One library's approach. *Journal of the Medical Library Association, 97*(4), 238–240.

A head for business and a heart for libraries

Cara K. Ball

The MLIS—a new beginning

> *"I have a head for business and a bod for sin. Is there anything wrong with that?"*
> —*Tess McGill (played by Melanie Griffith) in Working Girl*

Throughout my career as a certified public accountant (CPA), a compliance officer, and an investment advisor; I constantly compared my current job to my all-time favorite position as a 16-year-old public library page. Upon self-reflection and research of the library science field, I was excited to begin my studies at the Information School to achieve my goal of becoming a reference librarian and ultimately library a director.

As an adult, I would frequently turn to the library in order to ground myself in a new community or receive respite from the corporate world. In my foreign travels, I have even entered libraries to observe what the other countries thought of free access to knowledge. During the sabbatical I took raising my daughters, the library became one of our shared escapes amidst the flurry of activity. Time away from the corporate world allowed reflection about my career, and what I would like to pursue in the next workplace. The key attributes I identified about myself are as follows:

- I enjoy working with the general public; the diversity and issues brought by people make the day exciting and challenging;
- I work best on my own with little to no supervision;
- I derive much satisfaction from learning what a person needs and assisting them in obtaining their goals;
- I enjoy problem-solving and suggesting the most expedient solution; and
- I like to lead a team giving direct, clear guidelines then setting them free to achieve the assigned goals.

My job as the compliance officer of capital markets at a large bank mandated; that I ensure that controls were in place for complicated financial structures. Derivatives, municipal, federal and agency bonds, as well as foreign exchange—are all complex, and unique financial instruments with their own risks. Formerly, I joked with co-workers: "our goal is to never testify before a Senate Committee". However, recent headlines illustrate what happens to companies that lack strong controls over complex transactions! As a compliance officer I learned to rely on Access databases to generate accurate reports for review of compliance with the laws, regulations and rules. The databases pulled information from various banks, and independent sources such as Reuters. Checks and balances were built within my daily routine to ensure that the data was accurate prior to my review and analysis.

Skills to Make a Librarian. http://dx.doi.org/10.1016/B978-0-08-100063-2.00005-3

When I moved onto selling investments, I needed current, accurate information about the product I was selling, and the marketplace. I relied upon financial periodicals, statistical databases and forecasters. Surprisingly, the real meaty information is not readily available to the financial counselor. Through trial and error, I found the information after wading through massive amounts of data. Information-mining clearly contributed to my success as a financial advisor. After determining the level of expertise of my client, I could educate them, and sell them the appropriate investment. This took a delicate touch as it was important not to overload the client with information to the point where they could not make a decision. I knew I succeeded when the client returned to my services for their next investment.

The above entry is an edited version of my entrance essay to the *i*School. Even after all these years, it still rings true—I really do enjoy helping people find information that will assist them in their needs and showing them how to succeed at a task. To this day, my greatest work pleasure is determining a need, analyzing the resources at hand, and making a recommendation. I just don't do this in a library setting.

Head for business

"It's like the people who believe they'll be happy if they go and live somewhere else, but who learn it doesn't work that way. Wherever you go, you take yourself with you. If you see what I mean."
—*Neil Gaiman, The Graveyard Book*

And take myself with me, I did. Among the jobs that I have worked, I have picked up many skills—skills I thought I would never use outside of a particular workplace. At the time I made that assumption, I was young. Naïve. And completely unable to think outside of my particular circumstances. Looking back, older and, hopefully, wiser, I can see that all of my experiences learned along the way contribute to my collection of "tools" that I can pull out and use as it suits my current needs.

When I studied accounting in college, I really enjoyed the topic. Except for tax, the logical natural flow of accounting theory made sense. Learning to read a financial statement has, by far, been one of the most beneficial skills that I have used over and over again, both in my personal and professional life.

Lesson learned: some skills used in your professional life can be used in your personal life and visa versa.

As I exited my academic career (never to return! I proclaimed loudly and often to anyone within hearing distance—this will be a common theme, me proclaiming I would never do "xyz" only to find myself in that exact situation 5, 10 or 20 years later. I can't wait to see what I'm doing in 30 years!). I was so excited to begin my first "real" job as an auditor. I wore a suit! I had a briefcase! I was all grown-up! I remember, vividly, by day 3 I had this sinking feeling in my stomach that I had just made the worst decision of my life. I was bored, bored, bored. Phoning my best friend, sobbing, I explained how this job was not going to work for me since the people were awful (really, they were), the tasks were tedious, and the outcomes appeared meaningless. Accounting, in the "real" world was just not that fun.

Lesson learned: I need an environment that is interesting, challenging, and I am constantly learning something.

My exposure to investments was purely by accident. The auditing group needed an entry level auditor to work on the capital markets team, and I was a living, breathing body who could "tick and tie" (meaning, perform the menial task of proving out transactions and demonstrating it by "ticking' them off with a check mark, preferably in red pencil, and "tying" them to the ending balance, again in red.) Perfect match!

The first time I walked onto the trading floor, I was taken aback. The place was swarming with people, all on telephones, speaking loudly, and pecking at computer keyboards. For the first time, I witnessed a group of people who thrived in their jobs. They clearly enjoyed themselves, and each other.

Lesson learned: find your people, and find an environment that matches your personality.

Even the air was thrumming with energy. Get it done! Now! Busy, busy like a bee, the room buzzed with energy and noise. I loved it, and for the first time since graduating from college, I became excited about my work.

Suddenly, "ticking and tying" became much more interesting as I was genuinely interested in the hows and whys of a transaction I was auditing. I began to build stories behind the numbers, a skill that I still use to this day. I also began my first initiation into regulations (something that even at the University of Washington *i*School, taking one of my favorite courses, Government Documents, I loved doing) and applying them to people, and transactions.

Lesson learned: regulations are complex, difficult to decipher and challenging to apply to 'real life'. People do not like performing this task since it is so complicated but if you enjoy it, like I do, then you become a valued member of the team.

Over the next couple of years, I was able to move from auditing into a compliance position in capital markets. Though this was not my ideal job—it is challenging to be in a position where you are constantly telling people "no" because of a particular regulation—I learned tons about myself, and how to effectively communicate with others.

Lesson learned: just like the Eskimos having 15 words for the term "snow", compliance officers must come up with variations for the term 'no'. This takes an ability to debate, negotiate, facilitate resolution, and a have strong backbone (i.e. stubbornness) in order to retain compliance in the constantly changing environment of investments.

". . . talent means nothing, while experience, acquired in humility and with hard work, means everything"

—Patrick Süskind, Perfume: The Story of a Murderer

The hard work paid-off as I moved from compliance to selling investment products. For the previous six years, I worked in a project-based environment. With sales, it was transaction-based. I was no longer in control of the pace. If the phone rang, it was answered. If a sale occurred because of picking up that phone, then all the better. I quickly fell in love with my job. I loved watching the market, applying the market movement to my sales talk, finding the right investment for the client, and maintaining that relationship with the client as they grew their portfolio.

Lesson learned: short, transaction-based processes are easier to manage than larger, analytical processes. I still spend time reminding myself of this difference, and am constantly challenging myself to balance the two types of work in my current environment.

The sales environment was extremely gratifying for me. After spending years in the "back room" in planning meetings, compliance, and audit meetings and system conversion meetings, I finally got to experience the other side of what all those meetings were all about—the customer. Furthermore, *because* I understood all the back room measures taken to support the front room: I was able to better serve the client. For example, I knew how to structure a transaction so it would settle quickly. Also, I could demonstrate to other sales staff how it was easier for all of us if we all remained in compliance with all the various rules and regulations. I am not a "natural" sales person but it turned out that if you work really hard and know your product, you can become an excellent sales person.

Lesson learned: just because something does not come easily, does not mean it should not be pursued. Sometimes the skills that have to be worked at become the most valuable.

To this day, I still use the skills I learned long ago. In my current role as records analyst, I am able to discuss with confidence any financial-based transaction and resulting record. Even if I do not have one-for-one experience with a specific type of transaction, I know enough about the financial arena to be able facilitate and liaison at a meeting because the other party does not need to educate me about what they do.

While working at a financial institution, I learned how to analyze situations, people, and detailed transactions. People get stuck on numbers—being a product of seventies math, I can understand! I found, however, if I could take those numbers and determine the story *behind* the numbers, people will understand the situation, and we can move forward in resolving either the problem or succeed in completing a sale. One tool that I encourage everyone to become familiar with is spreadsheets. Just like a word-processing program is mandatory to know, spreadsheets are just as important. They are the tool that assists you in telling the story behind the data. If you do not know how to use this tool, even at a simplistic level, then the numbers will remain hidden and the story will be lost.

Today, I continue to use my analysis skills in determining project scope, applying rules and regulations to particular situations, and winding my analysis into a story—people still like stories, even if they are learning something from it.

Reality

Graduation from the *i*School. Aah, it was marvelous! The sun shone, the quad was teaming with black robes and exciting energy—we did it! I smiled the entire time, so much so, my face was sore the next day. Well worth it.

I immediately set out to get myself my dream job—a librarian at a local library were I could serve the community which I felt so connected. However, reality has a way of kicking you in the butt whether you are prepared for it or not. And the reality of spring/summer 2009 was bleak indeed. Washington Mutual Inc. had just given up the ghost in late 2008, spilling thousands of people into the unemployment line. This had an immediate impact on local economies, and was hitting the tax base hard. There wasn't a day that didn't go by that we, as a family, heard of yet another family impacted by a lay-off. Announcements were coming fast and furious. State Agencies were laying-off employees and furloughing others, school districts were furloughing teachers and staff, and lay-offs began to occur at the holy grail of Pacific North West's library systems—Seattle Public Library.

However, I was still in denial. I was aware of all of the lay-offs but I was still riding my high of graduating, and just knew my resume would land in the right hands. What I didn't realize—all of those highly skilled and *experienced librarians—oh my!*—were laid-off at the Seattle system, and were snapped up at the regional libraries—the ones that I had worked so hard on cultivating professional relationships with. Oh, that sinking feeling as I realized that I could not compete with ten-year veterans of a public library. And from a business standpoint, I couldn't blame them. When comparing my business resume, with a touch of librarianship, next to a resume flush full of library experience, I wouldn't have picked me either.

Many members of my cohort did what I could not do—they left the region. Most found jobs and are happily puttering away as librarians. This is one (and only, but that is another essay all together) of the disadvantages of obtaining a Master's degree later in life—my life is settled, and I did not have the flexibility to relocate to another region for an entry-level job. Some don't have a mortgage, a spouse with their own career (a career which definitely brought in the bulk of the income since I was bringing in exactly *zero* since I had stayed home with the kiddos for the past ten years), kids and all the community connections around the children which makes it incredibly hard to pick up stakes and move. As a family, we did agree that if push came to shove (my husband at the time was in the failing financial industry) that we would sell the house and relocate.

However, it wasn't as if there were incredible opportunities in other parts of the States either, we were full on immersed into the Great Recession which was as close to the Great Depression than I ever wanted to get. As I began to realize I may not land my dream job, I began to assess what salvageable skills I did (or did not) have. In my inventory taking, I found many skills-identified above—and some holes. For example, I was not bilingual.

> *Lesson learned: learn Spanish or become fluent in any other language that interests you, preferably Mandarin. I learned French and loved it but, sadly, did not keep my skills current. If this should be a cautionary tale, then know this: if you have a skill, make sure that it remains current!*

When a door closes, look for a window

With my freshly inventoried skills and new mindset, I began looking for *anything* local where I could use my newly acquired skills. I figured I would take what was offered and then when the economy calmed down, I would leap (seamlessly, mind you) from one position into another at a library. Preferably as a librarian.

After a couple of weeks of searching and applying for positions, I stumbled upon a position as a records analyst. The title meant nothing to me. However, the job description had my name written all over it. The position was written as a jack-of-all-trades. Someone who had high analytical skills, someone with the ability to use a spreadsheet to track metrics, perform the financial/payroll function, and someone who could present ideas, and teach compliance to staff members at the University. I met all of the "required skills", AND all of the "recommended skills". There was no reason to *not* apply especially since this was a temporary position with a ten-month commitment. What a nice low risk proposition. I could excel in this job and if I hated it, I could leave after ten months. If I liked it, or even loved it, I would have current job experience demonstrating my ability as a records manager. Thrillingly, I was offered the position and I gladly accepted.

Mourning period

The first few months of the job was what I l now call, *the time of mourning and transition*. There was a lot of change going on all at once that was affecting me, but also my entire family. We went from me being the stay-at-home mom to full-time-job-owner and it meant many changes. I had spent ten years at home. At home. Anyone who calls a parent who rears their children, without having a full-time job, a stay-at-home parent knows full well that you are *never at home*. We were busy! Playdates and school and *volunteer opportunities* at the schools and chores, and meals and yard work. It never ended. Even when I attended graduate school, I was still able to raise over $100,000 for a school playground, plan, and install the playground, and that was on top of all the other volunteer obligations I was involved in.

All that came to a crashing halt upon my return to the workforce. I began to delegate (good skill to have!). I hired a sitter to take care of the kids in the afternoon and a cleaner to pick up some of the dirt in my house—which means I became a manager. I needed to set clear, attainable guidelines for people so when I paid them, I knew I was receiving value for the money. My children's chore list did not so much expand, it merely became consistently applied. Laundry folding/putting away, and dishwasher emptying, now needed to be done daily after school, instead of being done if/when I got tired of doing it myself. And since these chores were overseen by the sitter, this meant they got done (see above note about outlining clear expectations to the hired staff).

I also pulled out my skill set of saying "no". With my return to paid work, my work as a volunteer had to be dramatically reduced. I did not stop immediately, however. Naively, I really did believe I could continue on with all the activities. After a few false starts—I continued with heading-up, the school's major fundraiser—the realization that sleep and sanity are more important was recognized. I began transitioning from volunteer lead—to volunteer "worker bee". Initially this was challenging. I knew how to plan an event or activity—and the school knew it. As I was approached with new leadership activities, I learned to thank them for thinking of me, pausing, and recommending another parent for the volunteer job. To this day, I am still declining offers for volunteer leadership roles but I am also to the point where I know exactly how much time I have in my schedule, and am able to provide support of the activity (cookies or oversee a booth) with no guilt.

Lesson learned: once a person becomes a leader in an organization, people tend to expect you to constantly lead a group/activity/challenge. However, in order to grow more leaders, as well as to manage time constraints, it is ok to step aside and allow others to learn the position of leader. Once a leader doesn't mean you have to always lead. A supportive group is also needed and I now enjoy putting on and taking off that leadership cap, as required.

As the weeks turned into months and the family became accustomed to the new patterns, I began switching over to the mourning of not having the job title of "librarian". Oh, I so wanted that title. Do you have any idea how hard it is to explain what a records manager does on a daily basis? *Everyone* has an impression (even if it is incorrect) of what a librarian does for a living—*no one* has a clue as to what a records manager does.

Slowly but surely, I began to realize how much of my librarian skills I use on a daily basis. Over time, I began to understand, and appreciate how diverse the skill set learned at the *i*School was. Taxonomy, user-centered design, reference and research strategies—I use these newly acquired skills constantly. I also began to realize I was in an environment where I could test these ideas in real practice. The day I realized I had the job that best represented all of my skills was when I was able to answer an auditing risk question, followed by a regulation question (which needed to be researched), followed by implementing a new taxonomy finding-aid—all within one morning. I was in the right spot.

Life as a records manager

There is rarely a dull moment working in records management. And yes, I think that previous sentence is funny as well. Granted, I work with a great set of people at the University so there is always room for a chuckle or a full on burst of laughter. However, the work itself is interesting. I use my skill set from when I was an auditor, compliance officer, sales officer and all of the skills I picked up at the *i*School on a daily basis. And then there is that irreplaceable skill set obtained as a parent.

A records manager is responsible for an entities compliance with retention rules, and in my case, regulations. A record is a record, regardless of format. For example, a Word document, database, printed report, and an invoice, are all considered a record. Retention is how long a record is maintained before an entity can, or may, dispose of it.

There are two main compliance risks in records management: (1) keeping the record for too short a timespan; and (2) keeping a record for too long.

As a records manager at a State agency, my office is required by State law to define each record created and to establish retention rules around the record. As employees at a State agency, everyone who works at the University must adhere to the retention rules and regulations. If an individual disposes of a record prior to the retention period, then penalties can arise. There is also a risk in keeping the record too long. If my office has gained approval for a particular record to be retained for six years after the end of the fiscal year (a common retention) and an employee retains that record for, say, ten years after the end of the fiscal year then that record is still obtainable for audits, public records requests (our State's version of the Freedom of Information Act 1996 (FoIA)) and litigation. Some may suggest that keeping a record longer than necessary is a conservative approach. If this was the 1980s, we could probably agree with that train of thought. However, in this day and age it is so expensive, time wise, to go through any audit, public records request, or litigation—that the fewer the records needed to sift through, the better.

There are many ways to achieve compliance with the retention rules. Mainly, a records manager can either maintain the records on behalf of the entity or teach, and support employees on how to manage their own records. With such a huge University, there is no way one office can manage all the records; therefore, we have built an information infrastructure where employees can gather as much information as they need in order to maintain their own records. We offer training, a warehouse to store the records, advice on filing systems, liaison between various departments to ensure record processes are moving smoothly, and information on how to comply with the retention rules.

My day begins with me hitting the ground running. A typical day will include performing analysis on records, troubleshooting with clients, problem-solving with my fellow team members, mentoring process improvement programs at the University, meetings with various folk regarding ongoing projects, and assisting in managing the warehouse where records are stored.

The records center

Records management is a compliance function: pure and simple. We want people to keep their records for a particular period of time. In order for them to remain compliant, we also need to provide space for them to physically store their paper records. Therefore, I work out of a big old warehouse. Old, as in the building used to be used as part of a Second World War military base. Big, as in our space holds over 40,000 boxes of records. Our office oversees bringing new records in for storage (called accessioning), pulling files/boxes for clients as needed, and disposing of the records once the retention period has been met.

In order to meet client needs, we employ student workers to do the heavy lifting. My job consists of managing the students, interacting with the clients to ensure we are correctly classifying their boxes into the appropriate records category for retention, and maintaining the database that assists us in maintaining the records center.

At first glance, a person may think no skills are needed to maintain a warehouse. However, after working in this office for almost four years, I can tell you what skills I use daily:

- *Parenting skills*—my students are wonderful, wonderful young adults. However, they still need their momma at times to ensure they are managing their work/study workload, becoming strong independent adults, and performing their work correctly. There are many "growth opportunities" as a college student, and sometimes they need to learn basic concepts such as showing up on time, or learning how to clean up their space at the end of the shift. I do not treat these students as my children—but I use all of my parenting knowledge daily. Open-ended questions: how did the box pick up go? To direct questions: did you clean-up the empty boxes after dumping them? To setting expectations: I expect in an hour, you should be able to shelve all of these boxes.

  In addition, to supporting our student workers, I use my hard-earned parenting skills with my clients as well. Sometimes, a department is so overwhelmed by their records they have no idea where to start. I spend a lot of time making house calls, phone calls and having email conversations on how an employee can start the process. I am there, for hand-holding needs, commiseration of such a huge task, and cheering them to success. People need to know they are not alone, and when they are taking on responsibility for an entities records, I enjoy supporting, and empowering them through the process.
- *Database management*—I use our wonderful database daily. It is a beautifully built piece of work with so much flexibility built into it that I am always learning a new way to use it. In order to be open to learning these new ways; however, a person does need to be comfortable around new technology. The skills I picked up at the *i*School gives me the confidence to try out new search techniques. Sometime they work, other times, I fail but I continue. Since the database is only as good as what is put into the system, a person must have a strong ability to pay attention to detail. This skill set was picked up when I was an auditor.
- *Communication skills*—I work at a very large University that employs a wide variety of people who may/may not understand how to manage their records. Explaining the rules and regulations around records management to employees with this diverse skill set can be quite challenging. Finding out the best way to communicate with a person over the telephone, or via email, is a skill I picked-up when selling investments. Asking targeted questions, and then providing answers based on their response; allows me to work well with the University employees.

Website design

One of the more difficult skills I learned while attending the *i*School was html and xml. Though I am certainly not an expert, I believe I can now hold my own in any design or concept meeting around technology. Furthermore, I learned one of my most hard-earned skills—I learned how to try something new while also feeling completely out of my comfort zone in doing so. I had an excellent instructor who calmly stated "what is the worst thing that could happen?" To which I would answer "I can lose my work". His response was always the same "true—and you won't make that same mistake again". He, by Jove, was right! Most of the time, I don't know exactly how a change to a website will render—but I know that I can always fix it. And I also know that if I don't try out an idea, I may not get the opportunity of reaching that one allusive person who is searching for a different explanation/display of facts on records that will then create that "a-ha" moment for them to be able to comply with records retention rules.

Over the past few years, I have extended this lesson to other parts of technology. If I don't know how to use a program, or with the firewalls out there, how to gain the appropriate approvals to even install a program, I simply begin. I attempt to be apply logical steps to it and, of course, fail. However, the old me would have given-up. The new me, gets back up and begins again, and again.

Lesson learned: it is ok to work with a subject where you are not 100 per cent comfortable, or even 50 per cent comfortable. The only way to get comfortable is by trying and working on it.

Taxonomy

As part of a new project, I am slowly but surely turning the retention schedules into easily findable artifacts by applying a taxonomy to it on our department website. This is a new concept for our department, and it hasn't always been easy to convince others of the benefit. We held user input meetings, brought in our process partners, and asked everyone: "How do you search for a record series on our website?" and "What do you wish was included in our website?"—type of questions. The answers were diverse and sometimes conflicting, but it gave us a great roadmap for how employees use the website. The concept of taxonomy, and finding information, is definitely a skill set learned at the *i*School. Hopefully, it will allow users to easily identify their records, and apply the appropriate retentions to them. One thing is certain: this project may be launched soon, but it will never be "done". As records are added or used differently, the taxonomy structure will need to be maintained.

Process improvement

Timing is everything. Just as I was getting settled into my new career, the University determined major changes were needed on how value was delivered to their customer. In order to continue providing services to students and researchers, they needed to *focus on the students and the research.* In order to do that, they needed to stop doing the activities that got in the way of providing this valuable service. Thus, they began training individuals in the Lean Process—a process improvement concept which allows a group of individuals to fix broken processes—but to do so within 90 days of identifying a problem.

I have to admit, I was immediately star struck by this empowering process. I had been in corporate America for a long time and knew how important it was to improve processes and had been trained in many, many techniques, in order to do so. However, all the process improvements "tricks" ended-up with good, valuable recommendations for change—but then it rarely was executed. Lean took the concept of process improvement *to the people,* so to speak. Workers are encouraged to bring forth ideas that will remove waste, make a process easier, safer, better; and all ideas are taken seriously. Not only are the ideas taken seriously, once an idea is accepted, the Lean team has 90 days to implement that change. Immediate gratification (or as immediate as you can get when working in a team environment) is a huge motivator for most people, including myself.

As more and more groups within our division began taking on a Lean Process improvement challenge, we began to notice more and more inquiries about their records. As they began examining their daily tasks, departments realized huge opportunities to change, due to technology advances, communication changes, ways people reached out to them (web forms and emails instead of input paper forms). Inquires varied from: "Can we stop using this form?" (Yes!) to: How do we manage this process now that it is mostly electronic?" (still need to monitor retention of the records, regardless of format.) These inquiries led the records management team to making ourselves available for consultations throughout their 90-day Lean Process implementation. And in some cases, beyond.

Lesson learned: sometimes a project will lead to unexpected outcomes. If you are open to new experiences and trial and error, you may be able to advance your program.

Relationships with customers and process partners

Working in a University setting has some enormous communication challenges because of the siloing that takes hold. Knowing who to call, when, and keeping yourself open to new and changing relationships is something I learned early on in my career. However, I find some people do not learn this important skill. Bottom line, if you want to move a project, process, idea, etc. forward, you need to remain focused on that goal, and not become caught-up in the steps it takes to get you there. Having the ability to look broadly at a challenge, but also be able to work through the fine details is an ever-evolving growth opportunity for everyone.

Lesson learned: this ability to look at the big picture as well as to be able to analyze fine details is not something that is learned once and done; there is always more to learn.

Empowering customers

With technologies changing, what often feels like, daily, many people throw up their hands, and just use what they know—but they don't always use what they have. I have found, however, that in order for our office to run as smoothly as possibly, people need to use the technology they have—so stop using those fax machines, people, and begin submitting a request online! Explaining how to use a new application, encouraging a change-resistant person to attempt something new, and to celebrate it when they succeed; is a skill I learned from when I sold investments. Managing the office records is a simple task, in theory. However, once a person begins analyzing how the records are filed and stored, the black and white answers quickly lead to a broad expanse of gray area. I find I enjoy the challenging of finding and using just the right words and tone with the various people I interact with, in order to push them to grapple with all the change around them.

Lesson learned: I may not appreciate the circumstances in which a person is asking a question but by asking questions and having the right attitude (even if I have answered this same question a multitude of times) assures the customer they have come to the right place to gain support.

There seems to be always something new to learn or a challenge to overcome in records management. It could be something as simple as onboarding new student workers—all the way to working on a team for implementing an enterprise wide system. Thankfully, I am rarely bored. And if I do find myself looking at my watch one too many times in an afternoon, I usually can rearrange my task list to find something more engaging to my current mood.

Lesson learned: I may not always like a particular task but I do know if I can push through it, there is always something different for the next task.

I may not have landed my dream job out of iSchool, but I do use my dream skills, every day. And for that I am thankful. As long as I continue to remain challenged, and interested in my day, I will remain in records management.

Information matters: critical-thinking skills in the library (and out)

6

Carrie E. Byrd

Introduction

The combination of journalism and librarianship has helped contribute to my world-view. Studying journalism has made me a better librarian, and becoming a librarian has given me a chance to share what I learned. The idea that research can be fun; the idea that research skills can have a positive impact on your life outside of your grades—these are things I hope I can pass on to my students. These are skills that don't have to stop at the classroom. They can and should be, something you carry with you. This is a lesson I learned, and that I want them to take away. Knowing how to do research for yourself, and to take a critical eye to what you find—it makes life so much easier. Whether you are researching a new vacuum, or deciding which politician to vote for, or learning about the prescription your doctor wrote, understanding how to find, and assess this information is invaluable.

I never expected to be a librarian. To be perfectly honest, the idea had never occurred to me. I didn't even know how you became a librarian. Although, I've had a library card for as long as I can remember, and I volunteered at my local public library during high school, and I worked in the library in college—however, the idea of being a librarian as a career never occurred to me. It wasn't until my senior year in college that the director of my college library said to me: "Have you ever considered library school?" and the seed was planted. Now, I work as a reference and instruction librarian at a small liberal arts school, and have made that same suggestion to a few of my students. Although, this is not where I ever planned, or expected to be, I think I ended-up in the right place.

I headed to college with my eye on a Communications degree, focusing on print journalism. I had a dream of being a cross between Lois Lane, and Edward R. Murrows. I wanted to be half-intrepid girl reporter, and half-trusted voice of a nation. I had worked on my high school newspaper, and done an internship at a Pulitzer Prize winning paper. I felt ready to take on the world. Unfortunately, for me the model for what the news looked like was in transition. We were moving from the *6 o'clock News* and the local paper—to a 24-hour news cycle that competed with itself on TV, radio, and internet. The local paper was beginning to disappear and the idea of being a journalist seemed both less realistic, and less like what I wanted to do. I loved writing, and I was instilled, through the hard work of my professors, with a love of research. I believed that journalism had a place for someone with those passions, and more to the point, I couldn't think of any other career that did.

Skills to Make a Librarian. http://dx.doi.org/10.1016/B978-0-08-100063-2.00006-5

I don't want to give the impression that my degree in Communications killed my interest in journalism. I was taught by committed professionals who had a real passion for the kind of old school journalism that rarely seems to be practiced now in an age of "clickbait" headlines—promising to show you one weird thing you never knew about dolphins. The skills that I learned as a journalism student made me more aware of how I consume information, and more aware of how that type of headline is designed to manipulate the reader. My life as a librarian has made me more aware of how other people consume information, and how I can teach them what skills they need to become more savvy consumers.

I wasn't sure what to expect from a Communications degree. It ended-up being an amazing educational experience where I got to learn a lot of practical skills, such as editing and graphic design for layouts; I was also able to explore a wide variety of topics and ideas. While focusing on print journalism I took classes on politics and pop culture, and most importantly—research skills. After all—how can you report on something if you don't know what you are talking about? When I watch cable news now, this seems like something they don't worry about any more, but if they won't worry about it: then the viewers need to.

Evaluating authoritative sources

Two classes in particular stand out to me. One was about politics and journalism, and in it, we followed the 1998 election season. For many of us, it was the first election we were old enough to vote in. We followed the various elections from our home states, writing mock articles, and learning to understand the political process. We learned to understand poll numbers and statistics—and to understand how those numbers could be presented, and manipulated. It was an exercise in journalism, but also in critical-thinking, and in becoming active, and aware citizens. Learning to both watch, and read the news with critical eyes; was a key part of this class—and although I didn't end up as a political reporter those skills have become a huge part of my day-to-day life; as well as part of what I try to teach my students.

Since students don't understand how to do these things, I see them struggling every day to find information that their teachers will accept. They have a hard time not only finding information on their topic, but to find "good" information on their topic. When I ask students to assess a source I see the same answer again and again—the idea that information is good simply because it exists! "This article is good because it has lots of information on my topic", but they don't understand why the information is good, or not good, as the case may be. They have a world of information at their fingertips, and yet no idea how to approach that information critically. Any question of bias, authorial intent, or organizational aim, is ignored. The fact that someone took the time to produce this information is enough—no further critical thought is needed.

In some ways, my students seem almost painfully naive on this subject. It's easy to see that critical analysis is not just something they don't do, but something that has never even occurred to them as necessary. Politically and personally, they take information at face value. Using the skills I learned in my political journalism class, I try to help them learn why this is important not only for their success in class, but also for greater understanding in their day-to-day lives. They are more than willing to accept whatever the first link produced by a search engine is, as accurate and sufficient—without ever questioning whether it is sponsored, or a placed ad. What I struggle with is not only teaching them to look for that information, but teaching them why that information matters.

I try to take the things I learned from my journalism classes, and from library school; to teach them about the importance of information. I talk to them about what we use information for and why it matters. They don't understand how dependent they are on it. Checking the weather so you know what to wear is information-gathering. So is looking-up the reviews for the best running shoes. So is looking up an article on the effect of wind farms on local bird populations for a research paper. As students seem to tend to take information for granted, many times they don't differentiate between the good and the bad, when it comes to doing research for their classes, but they can all tell you how much research they put into their smartphone. I want them to understand that these are two sides of the same coin.

Information-Gathering was the second class that prepared me for a future as a librarian, and it was co-taught by a communications professor, and a librarian. What I learned in that class was a large part of what I am trying to teach my students. It was, essentially, a research immersion course. You chose a topic, and spent an entire semester researching, and taking a critical look at your sources. Many students, myself included, chose pop culture-related topics. This meant that our sources ranged from scholarly articles, to television series like *Buffy the Vampire Slayer*. The critical-thinking skills this course taught me are so important. They are a key element in what I want to share with my students, and with how I approach information on a daily basis.

Additionally, I really learned from my Information-Gathering class how important it was to know how to use library databases effectively. This was the class where I learned how much difference a properly constructed search could make. This was also where I learned about the power of a search powered by Boolean logic; using the language and terms the databases want you to use in order to get the best results. This is something I want my students to understand, doing a successful search, and getting the best results isn't just about what question you are asking; it's also about *how* you ask the question.

This is true not only in terms of finding scholarly articles but also in knowing how to choose the right source for the right project. Sometimes (the majority of the time) scholarly articles are best, but sometimes you need articles about what is happening now, and newspapers are the right source. Sometimes you want to write about the cultural impact of vampires, and you're going to have to watch *Blacula* and cite *Twilight*. Even if you don't like those sources, you still have to acknowledge the role they play. Knowing *when* to use different sources can be as important, as knowing how to find them.

Information-Gathering was also the class where the library director first suggested library school to me. It was good timing, as I was starting to think about what it was I wanted to do as a journalist, and what parts of journalism I enjoyed most—and research was a big part of the answer. These two classes together influenced me tremendously. Learning how to read and think, and research critically; didn't just change how I approached things as a journalist, or later as a librarian, they changed how I approach information as a whole. This may have made me slightly cynical, but it has also made me a better, savvier consumer of information.

I would very much like to see my students (and my friends, and my neighbors, and those nice ladies from church) apply this to their own lives. Before you forward an email, do a little research. Before you hit share on Facebook—ask yourself: Does this seem likely to be true? Is it time-sensitive? How can I verify this information? Is this information worth sharing? These are questions we should all be asking about the information we encounter, especially before we pass it on.

I enjoy doing research. The thrill of the hunt is part of the fun for me. Looking for information on a challenging topic, and finding it—even if it's not what you expect to find—is something I enjoyed as a student, and that I still enjoy today. Whether I'm doing my own research, or helping a student find the right approach to their research, it is one of my favorite parts of my job, just as it was one of my favorite aspects of studying journalism.

Something else that my journalism professors emphasized was the need to be well-informed, and to know what was going in the world. Keeping up with current events, and popular culture was important because you not only needed to understand the references, you might need to be able to make them. I find that as a librarian, adhering to this principle is still helpful in my job. Being well-read is an easy thing for librarians to do, and being well-rounded is also important. This isn't always easy. You can't know everything, or be invested in every subject, and you don't have to be. Just being aware of what is going on in the world, and what people are talking about will help both you, and your students. When a student comes in wanting to research a topic that they "heard about the other day"—having at least some slight idea what they are talking about, can help me guide them to the right place, or even just help me do a little research so I can better understand what they are looking for.

Being aware of bias

Another important thing that journalism taught me, and that I hope to pass on to my students is an awareness of bias. Many of the things I learned as a journalism student were echoed in library school—but there was little to no, talk about bias. Despite, that I feel like it is an essential concept in libraries, and something my students need to learn about. Bias is something we need to be aware of in our everyday lives, and something my students need to know to watch out for.

When I define bias for my students I tell them that it is the idea that everyone has an opinion, and that everyone believes their opinion is right. Obviously, there is some nuance to be had here, but I think it gets the point across. I talk to my students about personal bias, political bias, and academic bias, to start with. The idea that a study might have been biased: based on who funded the study, or a researcher's ideas of how a study should come out, or even someone's personal reason for doing the research has never occurred to most of my students. When librarians talk about why you choose certain articles, or what makes them more reliable than others, bias should be part of that conversation. We teach our students a lot about what makes a scholarly article, but we also need to be teaching them that even scholarly articles should be approached with scrutiny.

Journalists have to be aware of their own bias. When you approach a new subject you need to try and set aside your preconceived notions; so that you can take in all of the information presented to you with an open mind. If you go into a new project without being mindful of your biases, it will color everything you do as part of that project. By considering these things you are aware of them, and can help to mitigate the effect it has.

When I discuss this with my students I try to use real-world examples of when bias might be present, and why it might be problematic. I use myself in one example, talking about my car. Like most of my family, I drive a Chevy, and for good reason. A significant number of people in my family have been employed, or still are employed by General Motors (GM). Therefore, it's common for us to buy cars made by GM because we have a personal connection with the company that leads to familiarity. In addition, since GM pays the salaries and retirement of my family members, I want to make sure my money is going to the right place. This is bias in the real world. When I bought a car I looked at vehicles from several different manufacturers, but I started at a Chevy dealership and my feelings about them influenced my decision, almost as much as the facts did.

If, when doing research for a new car, a student came across my hypothetical blog, they might not be aware of that bias. There's no reason for me to share it, so why would I? So they need to think about what is being presented to them, and be watchful for biased information. We discuss how to avoid it by looking at opinion statements, instead of factual statements, and how even if you choose to use a biased source, you need to seek out other sources that provide a more balanced view as well.

I also talk to my students about the importance of setting aside their own biases when doing research. If you only look for information that supports the conclusion you've already drawn, you might miss out on valuable data. In some cases, if you've started out with a faulty conclusion, you might not be able to find any information at all.

Talking about bias doesn't stop with journals and databases. As more scholarly works move to the open web, and as more students come to us as digital natives we need to extend our teaching to the web. These digital natives are immersed in technology pretty much since birth. They've never known a world without the internet, and most have grown-up with a computer in their home. Since I work in a more rural area this is less universally true for me than it may be for some of my colleagues, but a student with no technology experience is still a rarity.

Most of my students have grown-up with, what seems like, all the information in the world at their fingertips. Now it's literally in their pockets as well. They don't see the need to know how to assess that information, or to know the right time; to use the right information. As part of the assignment they do for me they have to assess a website. I mentioned earlier that their assessment frequently consists of "this website is good because it has information". When they want to know why their grade on that question is subpar, I explain to them that what they have really said is "this information is good because it is information", and that they need to think about what the content is, not simply whether the content exists. They need to learn that content is not the same as quality, or depth.

I mentioned before that one of the things that began to steer me away from journalism was the growing prevalence of "talking head" journalism: where opinion seems to have begun to dominate, if not to have totally replaced, fact. Chet Collier, one of the developers of Fox News said "Viewers don't want to be informed—they want to feel informed". This attitude is pervasive in pretty much all of the cable news channels these days. Rather than reporting on the information, they bring in so-called experts to talk about what they think of the information. I want to challenge that attitude; the idea that knowing what someone tells you, is the same as knowing the facts; is a perception I want to challenge. This is why bias can thrive; people don't want to work at being informed. They want information handed to them in nice, bite-sized pieces. I want the people I help at my library to know that there is more out there for them, and that the result is worth the work.

Why information matters

Journalism taught me the value of information, and—like librarians—journalists make their living with information. Bad information can ruin your reputation, and end your career. Eventually, even the least discerning readers, and viewers will lose faith in you, and without that faith you have no audience—and without readers or viewers—you're out of a job. As a librarian, your students (or patrons, or faculty) depend on you to help them find the right information, and just like in journalism, if you can't do it, you're not doing your job.

In some ways, I feel that I learned as much, or more, about information as a journalism student, than I did in library school. As a librarian I have learned to facilitate others in their search for information. As a journalism student I learned the importance of information at large. I learned that good information can be priceless, but that even bad information can tell you something. As a librarian I try to steer my patrons towards the good information, but sometimes it turns out that the bad information is what they need. My students want to know about success rates in a particular field, but forget that sometimes looking at failure rates can give you the information you need.

Library school taught me about reference interviews, and how important it is to ask your patrons questions to help you guide them to what they are looking for, but my interview skills really come from journalism. Library school may teach you the importance of asking your patrons questions, but journalism will teach you how to ask a leading question to get the answers you really need. Students will often ask for help on topics without understanding themselves what they are really looking for. They will come in with an extremely broad topic such as "I'm interested in researching education" or an extremely narrow topic, "I'd like to research the impact of parental involvement on the success of second graders studying common core math in urban communities". In both of these cases they typically hit a wall very quickly, and get very frustrated. Getting them to the topic that they are truly interested in, takes careful questioning.

Many of the athletes that come in to the library for help are a good example of this. Whether they play football, or soccer, they always want to search for their sport. That's not a bad thing. Studying what you are interested in helps you do good research. When journalists write about what interests them they produce interesting articles. However, the football players and the soccer players are stymied from the very beginning—after all, what we call football isn't as easy to find in the databases as they expected, and searching for soccer is going to exclude a lot of results from around the world. The rest of the world is contributing to those databases, and the first thing they need to do is figure out how to get rid of all those soccer-related results, or add in results, from what the rest of the world calls football. It turns out that their sport isn't the center of the universe after all. So what do I tell them? The same thing my journalism professors told me—sometimes it's all about *how* you ask the question.

Knowing how to ask the question, can be as important, as knowing what question to ask. This is something that was taught to journalism majors, and something I think librarians often learn, if not in school, then on the job. When a journalist does an interview, knowing how to approach your subject, or in a librarian's case, your patron, can make a world of difference. For our students, knowing how to approach a database can also make a difference.

When you watch a press conference you will often see journalists ask what seems like the same question a dozen different ways. Asking a question in several different ways can provoke different responses, and different nuances, in those responses. Additionally, sometimes you manage to finally ask a question in just the right way. and you'll get the answer you were looking for all along.

Databases should be approached in the same way. The answers you are looking for are almost always there, but like a stubborn interview subject, they have to be asked in the right way. I'm sure that every librarian has dealt with the patron, or student, who wants to type in their entire thesis statement, and doesn't understand why that doesn't work for them.

When doing a reference interview you take a similar approach. Patrons will come to you struggling with a topic that is too broad, or too narrow, and your job is to ask them questions until you get them to the right topic. In the case of my football players you help them walk through it from getting to American football—still too many results—to figuring out: what part of football they are interested in. Once they figure out that what they really want to know is: what impact traumatic brain injuries in high school football players has on the academic, and athletic careers of college football players; you have a topic you can actually work with, and one they maybe didn't even know they wanted to research until that moment. Now, that you've asked them just the right questions, you can help them do the same thing in the databases. Traumatic brain injuries in high school athletes is something there is a lot of research on, they just need to know how to ask.

This is also where the importance of being informed, and keeping up-to-date can come into play. When a student has a topic that they are struggling with, you can help them if you know just a little bit about it. Even if you aren't particularly up–to-date on a particular subject, just having a little background can at least help you know where to begin looking for information.

It's easy as a librarian to get caught up in the idea that scholarly articles from library databases are always the best source—especially as so many of our students are moving online, and databases are often the easiest thing for them to access. And while I certainly don't want to steer my students away from those databases, sometimes they choose a topic that they don't know much about, or that they cannot explain clearly to me; making it hard for me to help them find good resources. When a student cannot find what they are looking for, they end up frustrated, and convinced that what they want, just doesn't exist. It can be hard to convince a student to change their research strategy when they are sure they are looking for the right thing. I have had students come to me certain that they were using the right search terms, only to find out after spending hours helping them that they were thinking of something else entirely.

This is when they finally get to take advantage of their addiction to never looking past the first three search results. Occasionally, looking at the results a search engine turns-up out on the internet at large, can help them form a better idea of what their topic is, and lets us get back to the right way to ask a question. (It might even mean accepting some information from the dreaded Wikipedia.) You might not want to cite your search results, but they can help you find the right search terms. This is why it helps to keep an open mind about where to find information. That's something that you are taught when you study journalism. I mentioned before the importance of matching your sources to your topic, and I know that sometimes that can take you to unexpected places. I once had to interview someone who believed he was a vampire; which included the practice of drinking blood. Was he a scholarly source? Absolutely not. However, he was the right source for the research I was doing at that time.

The University I currently work for has a large Education program. We want those students to use scholarly sources, of course, but sometimes they need resources that the library databases can't provide. They need to look at lesson plans, or programs from other schools. At times like that, you have to take a different approach. That can be difficult, given how much time we spend trying to teach them to actually use the databases. I think the feeling that we are undermining our own work can actually stop librarians from thinking outside the box. We put so much time, and effort into teaching them to stop relying on Google, and to start using better resources that it can feel like a self-defeating act to send them back.

In the end, I can't think of any other course of study that could have done a better job preparing me for a career as a librarian than journalism. The two fields have many skills in common, and so many other skills that complement each other. The value of information, and the importance of research is key to each field, and although I ultimately did not pursue journalism as a career I am very grateful for the time I spent studying it. I'm thankful for the lessons I learned from my professors, and their commitment to teaching the skills, and knowledge needed not only to be a journalist, but to be a skilled, and ethical one. These things are a large part of what makes me a good librarian today. The pursuit of knowledge—for work, for fun, for personal growth—was part of those lessons.

For me, these lessons are not only career skills, they are also life skills; lessons that I use every day. I believe they are skills that everyone should have. Everyone doesn't need to study journalism, or major in communications, but we should all want to be able to look thoughtfully, and critically at the information presented to us, and be able to make informed decisions. I hope that I can take the lessons that I have been taught, and bring that to the people I teach.

As more and more resources move online, people are talking about the future of libraries, and the future of librarians as if they are becoming obsolete. To me this represents a fundamental misunderstanding of the nature of libraries. Libraries aren't just places where you come to borrow the latest bestseller, or read the newspaper. Libraries are a place where you come for help, and librarians are the ones who provide that help. It's not difficult to be overwhelmed with information. A Google search for snicker doodles returns over 1,200,000 results. Bing returns nearly 500,000. How does the average-user decide which result is best? I believe that's where the future of librarians lies. Not only as a distributor of sources, and but more as a guide to finding the best sources. The best journalists strive to bring their readers accurate, timely, and concise information. The best information they can provide. Librarians strive to do the same thing, guiding their users to the best information. Journalists produce information, and librarians facilitate it, but in the end they share a common goal: an intelligent, informed, consumer.

A biologist adapts to librarianship

Susan Beth Wainscott

Introduction

My first career spanned nearly two decades as a conservation biologist in the non-profit, and government sectors. During that time I held a variety of jobs with titles such as conservation planning coordinator, coordinator of volunteers, senior environmental specialist, and senior management analyst. Over the past year, I have found that a surprising number of the skills, and aptitudes honed in the conservation biology field translate nicely into my new position as a science librarian for an advanced degree granting public university. In retrospect, it seems I was training to be a librarian all along, and my preparation began long before I entered a graduate program seeking a Master of Library and Information Science (MLIS) degree.

Adaptive management

Perhaps the most important and unexpected of my transferable skills comes from working in the arena of adaptive management within applied conservation biology, while coordinating the management, and study of several ecosystems, and at-risk plant and animal species. Adaptive management is an active learning-based decision-making approach that uses the existing scientific information and newly collected monitoring data to inform policy and practice in an iterative fashion (Lee, 1993). As ecological systems are complex and impacted by many internal (e.g. resident species, topography, and local soil types) and external (e.g. upstream pollution, Climate Change, and human impacts) factors, there is much uncertainty about the likely impact of any one management action. An adaptive management approach to conservation management of species or ecosystems requires that the managed system be analyzed, and the goals, objectives, and uncertainties regarding management actions be documented. Management actions are seen as an opportunity to learn, and reduce the uncertainties about the system, and are designed as much to gain new information as to achieve the management objectives. This can take the form of formal experiments with treatment and control areas, or comparisons of measurements made of the same area before and after a management action, or can simply involve a conscious and deliberate approach to learning by doing.

In the fields of Library and Information Science (LIS) and Education, a similar approach may be called active learning-based decision-making. A more formalized approach to active learning, action research, has many similarities to adaptive management. Action research also requires an explicit description of the system of interest, and the actions to be taken, and an effort is made to document the outcomes

Skills to Make a Librarian. http://dx.doi.org/10.1016/B978-0-08-100063-2.00007-7

of those actions in order to inform future decisions about the system, and similar actions. Both action research, and adaptive management share a practice-orientation, and motivation to improve the system under study.

My current position, a science, technology, engineering and mathematics (STEM) librarian, includes many responsibilities, including library instruction, and collection development. I find that framing measurable objectives, designing assessment, analyzing data, and recommending changes, is a regular part of my day. I was fortunate to attend an instruction assessment retreat last year that helped me build a clear crosswalk between the terminology of Education's formative, and summative assessments, and assessment tools more familiar to me from my adaptive management experience. As an outcome of that retreat I prepared a very detailed, and perhaps geeky, but useful to me, assessment plan for a first-year seminar library instruction that I provide for undergraduates in the College of Engineering. Using a planning document format; that I brought from my adaptive management experience, and the language of educational assessment, I was able to craft an assessment plan that helped me describe the instruction session's goals, objectives, current practice, and hopes for the future. This melded process helped me to understand how impactful both formative, and summative assessment techniques can be; when used in an active learning-based, decision-making process. I used this clarity to better communicate with the primary instructors of the course, my supervisor, and to craft a successful application to the Association of College and Research Libraries' Immersion Program—Teacher Track.

For collection development, when I set up a trial for a new database, or other product, I craft objectives and criteria to assess the product, and create questions for faculty and staff, to address in their review of the product. Also, as a new librarian, a criteria-based approach to weeding was necessary for me to overcome my decision paralysis. I am thankfully able to take advantage of use data collected by the vendors, WorldCat, Document Delivery Services, and our integrated library system to make weeding decisions that I can confidently justify. My current employer uses assessment data, and several forms of process improvement from the corporate world, to continuously improve services, and find cost-efficiencies. I am fortunate to have found such a perfect fit for my analytical side. After several years using an adaptive management approach, it is now second nature to me to formulate objectives, determine measurable criteria to gauge progress or success, and try to make time to reflect on earlier lessons learned: before starting a similar, new project.

Another method that is often used in adaptive management, and indeed all of the sciences, is to develop a model of a system in order to describe the variables in the system in such a way that their interactions, and the potential outcomes of an action can be predicted. This model can be documented using flowcharts, other graphics, and/or a narrative description for a conceptual model, or using equations, and measured values for a quantitative model. The model is then tested by measuring the actual system, and the fit of the model to the measured data is reviewed for potential improvement, or discard of the model. While I have yet to document a predictive model for a library-related question, I do use some of the techniques I learned while working with ecological models. In particular, I use the document, test, and review pattern of model development to test my intuition or *Gestalt* understanding of a situation in order to yield additional insight into my, and others' conceptual models, of common practices and politics in the library and university. When I am about to navigate new political territory, I ask my more seasoned colleagues, "What do you think would happen if X, Y, and then Z?" With their experience-informed predictions, and any observations I may have made; I formulate a mental, undocumented conceptual model, and then test my model in a low-risk fashion to see if there is any insight to be gained. This spirit of inquiry keeps me from simply accepting conventional wisdom, and allows me to test the waters in a manner that respects the experiences, and wisdom of my colleagues who have "been there, done that".

Evaluating and writing grant proposals

While completing my Biology graduate program, I served on the board and grant review committee for a graduate student honor society, and participated in a rewrite of the grant application, and review rules to better emulate National Science Foundation grant application process (c.1994). We instituted a peer-review process that followed more explicit evaluation criteria that were provided to applicants as part of the application instructions. We also implemented a blind peer-review process that required reviewers to maintain confidentiality about which proposals they reviewed, and about the content of their reviews. This experience provided insights when I assisted in several revisions of request for proposals processes, by the local government agency I worked for, where blind peer-review was precluded by local government laws that require transparency of both reviewer identities, and their review comments.

I also experienced the rather unique challenge of crafting several requests for proposals for design, and implementation of scientific research projects within the context of local government purchasing policies, and laws that are generally more robust for use to purchase widgets, or select a vendor using construction project bid processes. Imagine the confusion when our agency needed to craft a procurement document to select a vendor who would "plant" dead desert shrubs to camouflage closed vehicle tracks within a conservation area. We were asked questions such as: why weren't we requiring a sprinkler system or fertilizer application, and was this more similar to constructing a fence? The resulting requests for proposals, or bids often contained requirements for potential vendors that were seemingly unrelated to the work our agency wanted the successful vendor to perform, but were a requirement of the procurement process that was prescribed by our purchasing department. I tap these experiences when preparing applications for funding, as I now know that the instructions in a request for proposals, no matter how odd, or inconvenient they may seem to the applicant, are important to the people who will process, or review my application. I also know that it is better to ask early for clarification of an unfamiliar application requirement, rather than to make presumptions, and guess incorrectly. I know that a failure to follow those instructions can be interpreted as a sign of disrespect, and may result in outright rejection of the proposal without regard to the merit of the proposed project. I share this perspective with colleagues, and patrons when assisting them in grant-funding applications.

While working for the nonprofit organization, and the local government agency, I was involved in preparing, and writing several grant proposals, and drafting budget estimates. Interpreting each request for proposals, even from the same agency, was a new adventure in bureaucracy as those agencies were constantly receiving, and implementing new instructions from their legal, and finance departments. Frequently each subsequent request for proposals had different requirements than in the past. Building upon my grant-reviewing experiences, I learned to carefully read, and analyze each request for proposals with fresh eyes, to ask for clarification early, and to convey respect for the agency, and the contact person assigned to answer all of those questions. I also learned to ask for constructive feedback from the contact person when a proposal was not funded, or not fully-funded.

Defining research data management plans and metadata guidelines

One increasingly common requirement for many requests for proposals, or grant applications, is a data management plan that describes the types of data to be collected with the grant funds, and how or if, any of those data will be made available to other researchers, or to the general public. In my most recent non-library position at the local government agency, my ability to make good decisions was reliant upon access to data collected by others, and often those data were collected for purposes different than my agency's current need. Only if the data, and sufficient metadata describing the collection, and limitations of those data, were available to me could I hope to responsibly use the fruits of those earlier efforts to inform our current questions. I quickly learned that what seems to the original researcher to be too obvious to write down, is often the most critical metadata for those who hope to review the data in the future. Consequently, in my former position as a senior environmental specialist, I was involved in an effort to require written data management plans with applications for research funding, and to define research data management, and metadata guidelines. Our local government agency began to require metadata for all of the research, species inventory, and biological monitoring projects that we funded in the mid-2000s, implementing policies that federal government agencies were beginning to discuss, and would soon also implement. I have also been an advocate for data quality, and assurance planning, and led the design of a catalog for the agency's many and varied species datasets. I can now speak from experience to faculty, and other researchers who struggle to comprehend why a grant agency cares so deeply about their metadata, and file storage formats. This experience also allows me to assist faculty, and students to seek out the appropriate resources, and expertise to address funding entity mandates for data management plans, and data sharing.

Sciences content knowledge

While I have collected little original research, or monitoring data in my career, I have had the pleasure of collaboratively designing, reviewing, and assisting with a wide variety of science studies using measurements in the field, as well as geographic information system (GIS) data analyses. I have been a consumer of the scientific literature, and the wealth of information found in the grey literature—the technical reports, and other documents that are prepared by scientists, or other experts for inter- or intra-agency purposes. I worked within the interface between pure and applied science, and have felt firsthand the tension that occurs when there is a desire to research a purely scientific question, and the funding available requires the research to be applicable to a practical, and immediate human need. Engineering research tends to occur in this tension zone, and I enjoy the creative process that occurs when scientists attempt to address both pure, and applied questions within a research program.

Scholarly publishing

While completing my MLIS program, I had the incredible opportunity to serve as the managing editor for an open access scholarly Library and Information Science journal for two semesters. I experienced the process of scholarly publishing from the publisher's side, coordinating double-blind peer-reviews, and consolidating reviewer comments, and recommendations to make final decisions with the editor-in-chief about which manuscripts would move forward, and which would be rejected. With this knowledge, I hope I am now a better author, and I understand the importance of completing a copy-edit of my work before submitting my manuscripts to editors for their consideration. Many of the skills and experience I gained in grant writing, and evaluation were useful and relevant to publishing: as submission, or revision requirements can often seem odd, or inconvenient to authors, but are critical to maintain some semblance of efficiency and coherence on the editorial side of the publishing relationship. Experiencing the amount of effort that is required to produce a quality peer-reviewed journal, also gave me insights into the open access movement, and the phenomenon of predatory publishers who seek to take advantage of authors, and readers by skipping or minimizing key components of the scholarly review, editing, and publishing process. This experience improves my ability to assist scientists as they consider where to publish their manuscripts, and helps me to navigate LIS publishing opportunities for my work.

Writing and finding technical reports

In my previous career, my salary was funded by a series of grants that required periodic progress report, and culminating project reports to describe the outcomes of the grant funding. I also used the information within many grant reports in my applied conservation biology work. Additionally, I wrote, edited, and used many grant reports, environmental regulation compliance plans, and other technical documents while implementing species, and land-use management plans. Along the way I learned the value of standardized report structure, use of parallelism in technical writing, inclusion of a glossary to define jargon, and consistent use of technical terms throughout the narrative to assist the reader. I also learned to create templates of each recurring report to make the tedious work of report writing more efficient. This experience allows me to provide new faculty, graduate students, and upper-level undergraduate students with my lessons learned, and useful technical writing resources.

Also, as a former agency employee, I am keenly aware of the vast, and often unseen treasure trove of information held in unpublished agency reports, environmental compliance documents, and datasets. These resources are often not discoverable using vendor databases, or internet search engines. I use my knowledge of the roles of various government agencies to search for datasets that may not be deposited in searchable data archives, and I am not shy about contacting agency staff to ask about the information they may potentially be able to share with our researchers. I also know from experience that there is little harm in placing a public records request, or Freedom of Information Act 1996 (FoIA) request if it is carefully crafted to target what is wanted, and excludes reams of non-relevant articles. Having a conversation with an agency staff person about how to best describe a desired document, or dataset, and to narrow a records request can lead to a greater understanding of the agency, and how it operates, and build a good working relationship; rather than damage one, with a hastily crafted, and overly broad request for records.

Public speaking experience

In my current role, I provide instruction, and speak to groups of students, and faculty in a wide variety of settings, and to groups large and small. Public speaking did not come easily to my skill set. I explored teaching while an undergraduate, but selected another path, in part due to my intense fear of speaking in front of groups. Little did I know, that I would one day teach critical-thinking, information literacy, and other topics to students, and peers in a university setting. In high school I would try to bargain with teachers, and offer to accept scores of zero, in order to avoid any type of presentation, or speech to any sized group. In middle school, I even made myself physically ill with worry, and avoided participating in a puppet show (where I would be hidden from the audience behind a puppet stage) for the then Governor Thompson of Illinois. Over time, I learned some tricks to calm my nerves.

At first, I would imagine that most of the audience wasn't paying any attention to me, and I would present to the wall at the back of the room, or one or two friendly faces in the audience. As time passed, and I was forced to present more frequently for my jobs, I would try to make the presentation more of a conversation with those few friendly faces, and use their reactions to add, or delete detail, or even pose a question to the audience. This more conversational tone suits my personality, and willingness to ask or even take questions in the middle of my presentation as time allows. I have now presented or provided instruction to groups as small as 1 and as large as 200, and have also served on panels at conferences *apropos* endangered species management, and regulations—where the questions occasionally provoked conflict, and controversy among audience, and panel members. Student feedback, and assessment data suggests that some appreciate my more informal, and conversational lecture style, and feel willing to ask questions because of it. I also strive to incorporate more active-learning techniques in instruction, which can involve facilitating discussions among several groups of students with limited instructor lecturing.

Meeting facilitation

As anyone at an academic library can attest, meetings are a big part of my work. Within academic settings, executive managers, and administrators tend to engage in some level of shared governance with faculty, and this atmosphere permeates much of the campus. Shared governance leads to an emphasis on collaborative decision-making, many committees, and even more meetings. I was very fortunate to receive training in meeting planning, and facilitation, as well as, many opportunities to practice my skills with my former employer. I learned a style of meeting design, and facilitation that is focused on consensus-based decision-making, and ensuring a more equalized power structure among group members. I also experienced open public meeting facilitation, that requires pre-planning, and public posting of meeting agenda: several days in advance of the meeting, as well as formal documentation of meeting discussions, and decisions. I learned how to break down a discussion, and decision-making process into agenda topics that provide ample opportunity for participation by group members, and clear documentation of decisions. I also learned, and practiced a variety of techniques to assist all group members to participate equally, and to express, clarify, and explore commonalities, among their interests rather than simply state their formal, initial positions about the topic. My facilitation mentor emphasized the need to work with each group to establish, and enforce group rules, or norms, to plan for alternative approaches to potentially difficult agenda items, and to remain neutral while serving in the role of facilitator. These skills and the knowledge that there are many guides, handbooks, and websites dedicated to meeting design and facilitation (e.g. Schwarz, 2002; Office of Quality Management, 2000; Hunter, Bailey & Taylor, 1995) allow me to more successfully lead productive meetings with library colleagues, faculty, administrators, and staff. These skills also assist with my community service roles, influence my instruction design, and how I manage in-class discussions, and the incorporation of small group discussions among students.

Negotiation

My previous employer also provided me with several professional development opportunities to learn negotiation techniques, and I find most useful a negotiation style best described by Fisher, Ury and Patton (2011). This style is focused on building the opportunity for a series of mutually-beneficial agreements between negotiation parties. This style happens to suit my personality, and is recommended for relationships that may approach partnerships. The style requires an investigation of the other party's potential goals, and objectives for the negotiation, and finding low-cost or low-risk opportunities to meet those objectives; in exchange for receiving what it is your party values. This style is ideal when negotiating within an organization, where all parties will be working together for the long-term. It can also be appropriate when a series of agreements are anticipated with a vendor over a long period of time. I also received training and experience in negotiations relating to environmental conflicts, where legal requirements, people's livelihoods or traditions, and passionate advocacy interests are involved. In these situations, emotions can run high, leading to deep-seated, and seemingly intractable positions, and disagreements. This training and experience helps me to be more compassionate when library patrons or stakeholders, are advocating for a service, or resource that has an overall high-cost per use, compared to more broadly used resources, yet is critical for their research program, and thus their career development, and livelihood.

Also while working for the local government agency, I was involved in negotiations with the offices of sponsored projects for several research universities. These negotiations revealed to me some of the fundamental cultural values of an academic institution, where intellectual property rights (IPRs) of researchers are at least as important, as fiduciary responsibilities to the institution. During these negotiations my colleagues at the agency and I, struggled to find a balance between these values and our employer's need to own, and use the outcomes of the research we were funding for the purposes of our adaptive management program. We also had to balance the desire of the faculty for exclusive use of the data for an adequate period of time to allow them to publish their results with our employer's desire for timely access to the data. We also had to navigate a legal (State law) requirement that the public be allowed to inspect, and even make copies of the outcomes of this public funding. While some university researchers desired to have only peer-reviewed publications as final outcomes of the grant-funded project, in lieu of final project reports, copyright restrictions of likely publishers were problematic in light of the State law requiring the public's right to copy: grant products. We also had to consider whether or not the written outcomes of the grant funding were works for hire, implying that the copyrights would belong to the local (i.e. not federal) agency, and not the researcher, thus impeding their ability to reuse portions of the final report document in their publications. These experiences provided me with interesting scenarios for discussion, and debate in the copyright seminar course I completed for my MLIS degree program.

Project management

Project management training is surprisingly useful in an academic library setting. Project management tools are used to reduce each phase of a project into discrete tasks, schedule, and estimate the cost of each task (Portny, 2013). I used these tools to create, monitor, and modify plans for ecological restoration, or species monitoring projects in my former career. I find that these techniques are equally valuable when planning instruction, research project design, collaborative writing projects, and complex reference assignments. Project management scheduling tools such as Gantt charts (Portny, 2013) allow me to analyze, and graphically describe which tasks are reliant upon earlier steps, and which tasks can be accomplished out of sequence, and perhaps simultaneously. This skill helps me immensely when working with a team to track overall progress, and estimate likely completion as each team member completes their assigned tasks. When a project is broken down into a set of steps in a sequence such as in a Gantt chart; it is easier to see the scheduling flexibility of deadlines, internal to that project. This allows me to better strategically synchronize the schedules for several projects, as well as, my daily operational responsibilities within the library, and campus, or other service responsibilities.

I also use project management skills to create my personal "to do" list, and allocate my mental energy to each item on the list. For instance, I break down more complex items into chunks that are achievable, and may require different levels of my mental energy. Instead, I allocate my mental resources according to their best availability, as if they were team members on a project team. Seldom, do I spend an entire day writing, analyzing assessment or collection data, or completing a set of short, and simple tasks. Instead, I try to achieve at least one hour of writing each afternoon, or evening, and work on simpler tasks in the morning when I, a night owl, am not yet fully awake. More complex analyses, or research are best accomplished midday. Of course, library and campus administrators', or patrons' requests, disrupt these plans in delightfully unexpected ways, but my plan is ready for me when I can return to my routine tasks.

Local government agency culture

Last, but certainly not least, familiarity with government budget cycles, purchasing rules, and policy-making allows me to navigate the complex landscape of purchase options, and funds available for the collection development. Our State has a two-year or biennial budget cycle, and this makes it difficult to enter into subscriptions, or other service agreements longer than two years in length, unless we can use grant funds. Some publishers, and other vendors find this situation challenging, and are loathe to modify their standard contracts, to accommodate our requirements. Fortunately, our collection development group is very creative, and our library leadership is supportive of innovation. They are able to suggest new contract terms to try, and accommodate the needs of our patrons, vendors, and our purchasing policies, and legal regulations. Based upon my prior years within a local agency that was also subject to this biennial budget cycle restriction, I was not at all surprised to discover that the university library had to spend time, and effort to negotiate solutions to this situation, and I now look for compliant, or flexible purchasing terms when evaluating potential vendors.

Another unexpected similarity to my former place of employment, is the distributed nature of information technology (IT) support within a university, where the library has its own IT group supporting the unique to libraries' systems, or inhouse developed tools; with the enterprise IT group remaining in control of systems such as email, human resources systems, productivity software, and the learning management system. Such arrangements may not be readily apparent in new employee orientation programs. As I was familiar with such a support relationship, I was able to remain outwardly calm in front of students, and course instructors while being bounced back and forth between both IT groups; while seeking a solution to a classroom software issue. Also from this experience, I learned to never, ever underestimate Murphy's Law when teaching a new instruction session for Faculty you hope will become your best word-of-mouth marketers for university library services.

Conclusion

Finally, as I continue in my transition to a LIS career, I have been fortunate in ways to stay involved in the conservation biology field through community service activities that also count towards my service responsibilities as a Faculty member. As a library often is, or operates within, a large organization, many of the lessons learned in other workplaces can translate well to a library career. Those considering a career change can seek out professional development opportunities, or volunteer for community service organizations, to gain the requisite transferable skills, and ease the transition. Those who have already worked within the public sector may find that they are already primed to successfully navigate some of the subtle nuances of public library systems, or academic libraries. I find that many of my seemingly disparate experiences and skills are directly transferable to my new career, and build credibility with both Faculty, and graduate students. I remember that a high school career interest, and aptitude survey instrument, predicted librarianship as a good fit for me when I was a shy, insecure bookworm. I smile as I realize that librarianship is a much better fit for me—now that I am a confident public speaker with precious little time to read. I could not have designed a better program for my preparation to be an academic science librarian.

References

Fisher, R., Ury, B., & Patton, W. (2011). *Getting to yes: negotiating agreement without giving in* (3rd ed.). New York: Penguin.

Hunter, D., Bailey, A., & Taylor, B. (1995). *The art of facilitation: how to create group synergy.* Tucson: Fisher Books.

Lee, K. N. (1993). *Compass and gyroscope: integrating science and politics for the environment.* Washington DC: Island Press.

Office of Quality Management (2000). *Facilitator's tool kit.* Available from, http://www.uspto. gov/web/offices/com/oqm-old/Facilitation.pdf, Accessed 30.03.14.

Portny, S. E. (2013). *Project management for dummies* (4th ed.). Hoboken: Wiley.

Schwarz, R. (2002). *The skilled facilitator: a comprehensive resource for consultants, facilitators, managers, trainers and coaches.* San Francisco: Jossey-Bass.

A librarian prepares: strengthening job performance through theatre practice

Michael Saar

Introduction

You are filled with a nervous energy. Will all your preparation pay-off? What if you forget something? What if they just aren't receptive? You step forward as the chatter starts to dim down. Suddenly you realize it is just you, and a roomful of expectant eyes upon you. You gather up your courage and speak your lines, "Hello my name is _____, I am a librarian here and today I will show you how to . . .".

The above description of a librarian beginning an information literacy session could easily describe an actor preparing for a performance. It certainly is not difficult to see the similarities in this scenario; both situations involve an individual preparing to put him or herself in front of an "audience"—a very vulnerable position. The idea of instruction as "performance" is definitely not a new one. However, given this similarity, it may be surprising to hear that thespians, and librarians are often considered antithetical entities. Stereotypically, theatre people are viewed as boisterous, gregarious, overly emotional individuals who love to be the center of attention. Whereas depictions of librarians in popular culture typically focus on the idea of the introverted, strict, "spinster". Of course, as any librarian will tell you, this perception is often quite far from the truth. The same holds true for thespians. Being both an academic librarian, and an actor/director; I have certainly faced surprise, and misconceptions about what my personality should be like from people in both professions. In this chapter, I hope to demonstrate that despite these apparent differences, there is a surprising amount of crossover between the two professions' skill sets and in fact, many of the skills that are useful to theatre can also be applied effectively to librarianship.

Background

Perhaps some personal background would be appropriate here. For as long as I can remember, I have had two great passions in one form or another: theatre and libraries. My first regular trips to the public library began around the same age as my first participation in community theatre. To a young seven-year-old both areas provided access to exciting and magical worlds: theatre through productions, and libraries through books. As I grew older, I continued to be active in local theatre, and a

Skills to Make a Librarian. http://dx.doi.org/10.1016/B978-0-08-100063-2.00008-9

regular-user of local libraries. Upon entering college, I chose to pursue an education in theatre (specifically directing) and while I would not receive formal training in librarianship until enrolling in a library science graduate program years later, I not only continued to utilize libraries but became more interested, and invested in the process, and the activity of library research. This interest was most apparent as I taught introductory theatre courses while obtaining my first Master's degree in Theatre Historiography. I emphasized the research assignment as much as the class' theatrical performance work. I highlighted this aspect in the course so the students could discover how investigating a work more critically through vigorous research would illuminate the themes, and atmosphere of a play that might otherwise remain undetected. While the context may have shifted, libraries continued to provide access to different, exciting worlds, and possibilities.

The title of this chapter, is a reference to the seminal work of the famous Russian director, and pioneer in acting theory, Constantin Stanislavsky. Before Stanislavsky began to implement, and share the approach to acting initiated in the Moscow Art Theatre, and outlined in three books beginning with, *An Actor Prepares*, acting did not typically replicate "realistic" human behavior. Instead, actors were much more presentational, and formalized in their approach; directly addressing the audience and portraying characters through gesture, and expression instead of the more psychological-based approach prevalent in most Western theatre, movies, and television today. The work laid-out in Stanislavsky's books, especially *An Actor Prepares*, were intended to lay the groundwork for creating naturalistic portrayals of character. I allude to Stanislavsky's work because in a similar vein, my experience in the theatre has laid much of the groundwork responsible for my future success as a librarian (naturally in conjunction with my training in library school and on the job). In the remaining pages, I would like to explore how the skills, and techniques of acting, and directing have found application in my work as an academic librarian. This chapter will focus on my personal experiences, and as a result, deal mainly with the areas of reference services, and library instruction. However, these skills can be useful to just about any aspect of librarianship. As I continue to work in the theatre, I have found the skills, and techniques I have picked up as a librarian have been equally useful in my theatre practice. The latter part of this chapter briefly examines the application of library skills to theatre. Finally, I discuss the ways those interested in participating in theatre can get involved.

General skills

While the majority of this chapter will examine the application of theatre skills to specific areas of librarianship, I would like to take a moment to discuss some of the broader areas that may benefit from a theatre background. Indeed these traits, are useful not only to any area of librarianship, but pretty much any professional job.

Both communication, and the ability to work successfully with others are qualities that are valued, and needed in just about any professional position today. Many professional projects are completed collaboratively with individuals from a variety of backgrounds to achieve organizational goals. Likewise, conveying information to clients, either internal or external, requires efficient, and clear communication. The importance of these skills in any work environment are clear, however, theatre may be unmatched in the extent to which these traits are ingrained in every aspect of the field.

Theatre does not occur in isolation. For every production there are a number of different people involved in ensuring the show's success. Their roles range from onstage talent (acting leads, supporting roles, ensemble) to production crew (directors, designers, stage crew) and various other individuals including: producers, theatre staff, etc. These entities often have their own specific concerns, and focuses with each project. Aside from the idiosyncrasies resulting from their role in a production, they may have their own unique perspectives on how to achieve their role. For example, a group of five actors may have vastly different educational, and training backgrounds, approaches to creating a character, and even styles of acting. It is typically the director's job to take these disparate views, and goals, and unify them around a singular vision for a project. In order to achieve this a director has to quickly become adept at balancing differing (and at times volatile) personalities, schedules, needs, and desires. Failure to do so can turn even the most promising production into a horrible experience (both for the artists working on the project, and the audience viewing the results). Even in the rare instances where an individual produces a theatrical piece without any additional assistance (directing, writing, designing, performing, promoting, etc.) the incorporation of an audience to see the show involves a unique form of collaboration. A good performer will always be aware of how a specific audience is responding to a show, and make various adjustments based on that input ranging from simply holding for laughs, to performing more energetically, or even adjusting the character, or style of performance.

One critical element to working effectively in a collaborative environment is the ability to communicate well. As a visual, and auditory medium, theatre is judged on the efficacy of its communication. Failing to correctly convey the artistic team's intent of a production, risks leaving the audience with a misinterpretation of a production's characters and/or themes at best, or flat out rejecting the production at worst. The quality of a production's communication begins in production meetings and rehearsal rooms. Once again, while everyone is a crucial component in the process, it is typically the director's responsibility to ensure everyone is on the same page artistically. A good director will quickly become adept at concisely, and clearly conveying her vision, and often has to convey different ideas to several different parties at the same time. The hectic pace of the final rehearsals before opening night where a director must relay a lighting effect to the designer, immediately before telling a performer where to move on the stage, and then responding to another actor's question about the interpretation of line, is more the rule than the exception. This turn-on-a-dime style of communication provides useful practice for working a busy reference desk where patrons with vastly different information needs are clamoring for the librarian's attention.

Reference

Strong communication skills are key to success in the theatre, and at the reference desk as well. Unfortunately for reference librarians, patrons don't often have the same strength in communication. Many times a patron comes to the information desk without a clear idea of what it is they are actually looking for. More often than not their *stated* information need, is not the same as their *actual* need, and it is part of the librarian's job to dig deeper and find the *real* reason the patron came to us for help. Additionally, part of what makes reference work so exciting is the unpredictability of questions received. Inquiries may range from relatively straightforward requests such as known item searches, or assistance with computer software to highly idiosyncratic requests (e.g. the per cent of recycled material in the US dollar, bird species inhabiting in a local river—provide just two examples of the various unique questions I have received while working the reference desk). Common requests are quite easy to respond to, and become almost routine for any librarian after a while, whereas these more obscure questions sometimes seem to be equally challenging for the librarian, as it was for the patron. Both the ambiguity behind patrons' questions, and the uniqueness of many requests mean that interactions between reference librarians, and patrons can rarely follow a repeatable pattern. To put this in a theatre parlance, these patron interactions are more akin to improvisation than following a script.

Improvisation is an area of performance that taps into some different skills than performing a scripted play, and has a history almost as long and varied, as scripted drama. The art of improvisation revolves around creating character, plot, dialogue and/or movement extemporaneously without the benefit of a pre-written text. The most notable early existence of improvised theatre is the notorious *Commedia dell'arte* of sixteenth century Italy. *Commedia* performances were typically short comedic sketches using stereotypical, or stock characters. The sketches were based on loosely constructed plots around which performers were free to make-up dialogue, and movement (often incorporating local references for added comedic effect). Today, we most commonly think of improvisation as carrying on the *Commedia* tradition through short-form sketches seen in "improv games" at comedy clubs, or on television shows such as *Whose Line Is It Anyway*. While this is certainly the most popular form of improv, it is by no means the only. Any form of performance consisting of speech, characterization, or story primarily made-up in the moment, is improvisation. This style can range from short form comedic works to longer, dramatic improvisations.

Looking at reference services through the lens of improvisation theatre can offer some valuable skills and tips. One of the most important skills in improvisation (equally important in any type of theatre, and any aspect of communication in general for that matter) is the ability to actively listen to the person you are working with. This is not as easy as it may seem. One of the biggest temptations when performing an improvised scene, especially if it is a comedic one, is to try, and formulate the perfect one-liner, or comedic response while a scene partner is speaking. The reference desk equivalent would be determining the nature of a patron's reference question before they have even finished asking it. In either scenario, this is clearly a bad practice. Focusing on the performer's own thoughts at the expense of listening to the scene partner can result in the performer missing an important piece of character, or story information. Often the result is that the perfectly witty statement the performer has been crafting internally, will fail to achieve its effect because it is no longer relevant to what is happening in the scene. Likewise, deciding what a patron wants without completely listening to their question, may prevent the librarian from picking-up on the subtle clues that are often present when a patron's information need, is not the need stated explicitly, in the question!

A common trope in modern improvisation is the concept of "yes and . . .". In practice, this means the performer takes whatever information the scene partner is giving, accepts it, and builds upon it. This is a crucial aspect of improvisation, because it allows a scene to continue, and build whereas rejecting someone's ideas can prematurely end a scene. Let's look at an example. Suppose you enter a scene and your partner says to you, "Thank God you are here doctor, the patient is right inside!" Now the appropriate response would be to accept this information, that you are the doctor, and build upon it. Even if just prior to entering the stage you put on a chef's hat and apron. If you corrected the scene partner by saying, "I'm not a doctor, I am a world famous cook!" The scene then runs the risk of an abrupt ending. Whereas, if you accept this information, and incorporate it with your own information, to build upon the scene: the results would be much more productive, and entertaining ("Let's get to work on the heart transplant, I only have ten minutes until my muffins are done!").

The concept of "yes and . . ." is a useful tool to keep in mind during reference interviews. Patrons are often indirect at stating their actual information need. This is not because patrons like to be coy, but may actually not fully understand what information they actually need. A student may come to the reference desk saying they need "plays by the person who wrote *Hamlet*", when further investigation may reveal they are actually researching the Shakespeare authorship debate. Going through repeated exchanges from various students, or patrons that are on similar topics may tempt the librarian to make assumptions about the nature of an information request, particularly in an academic library where there is a research assignment many students are working on. However, it is important to be receptive to each individual transaction, and not try to preempt the patron's request. Instead, build upon the information given by the patron with probing questions further investigating their need. Rather than make assumptions about the patron's request ask questions that may elicit further information ("What is your interest in Hamlet?" and, "What would you like to know about the author?" etc.). This process will not only increase the likelihood of discovering the patron's actual need, it will also leave our mind open to exploring all possibilities. In both improvisation, and conducting reference interviews making preemptive decisions leads to a tendency to edit out responses, and focus on a single (perhaps familiar) solution rather than allowing for a range of possible solutions. I continually find the unpredictable, and spontaneous nature of reference questions to be one of the most enjoyable aspects of working the reference desk. Business might go from slow and calm one moment, to frantic and buzzing the next. It is not unheard of to quickly shift from the slow pace of a single, basic question ("Where's the circulation desk?") in an hour, to three complex reference questions in the span of minutes. By taking the approach of accepting, and building within the reference interview through ("yes and . . .") I have not only been more effective in helping the patrons articulate their information need, but I have been more open to viewing a seemingly routine question from new angles, and sometimes discovering newer, and better resources, and results.

Instruction

Continuing with the performance analogy, if a reference interview is akin to improvisation, surely the metaphor for library instruction would be a scripted production.
From the perspective of the librarian this comparison seems clear, and in many ways
accurate. As the paragraph introducing this chapter suggested, stepping in front of a
classroom full of students is not far removed from a performer stepping onstage in
front of an expectant audience. The instructor, like an actor, is responsible for communicating information to her audience, holding the class' attention, and maintaining
an engaging environment. The instructor arguably has a much more challenging task
because she does so without the benefit of a script written by a talented playwright.

Obviously, a background in performance can benefit instructors with the more
performative aspects of pedagogy. Skills that are necessary on stage translate very
well to the classroom. As an actor you quickly learn to project one's voice so that
people in the very back of the auditorium can hear what you are saying. Additionally,
infusing your words, and actions with a constant flow of energy will help maintain an
engaging presence for your character, whether you are playing "Romeo" or the
"English 101 library instructor".

Beyond these basic skills, theatre practice, and performance in particular, offer
some less apparent techniques that can serve instructors well. While the need to speak
clearly and audibly, and with an energetic persona are easily recognizable in a quality
performance; there are many other elements beyond voice, and presence. Effective
performance also necessitates cognizance of one's position in the space, the response
from the audience, the relation to the set, and fellow performers, among other factors.
There are many different ways these elements have been explored in various acting
theories, but one that I have found very informative both on stage, and carrying over
into the classroom, is director Anne Bogart's concept of viewpoints. Bogart's work on
a basic level, experimented with breaking down the various components that create a
whole performance into their individual parts. Rather than trying to focus on every
aspect at once, performers using viewpoints might just concentrate on a single element
in rehearsal (their relation to the audience, or their use of high, or low space, for example). Eventually these items are typically incorporated into a whole, but focusing on
the elements on an individual level allows the actor to maintain an awareness of these
different qualities throughout the performance. In the classroom, this awareness is
valuable as well. In addition, to being energetic and eloquent, I make a point to
position myself in a way that draws focus on myself without interfering with the view
of any projections, for example. Perhaps the most important viewpoint element
I incorporate into my teaching is an awareness of the audience. Considering one's
audience is probably not new to anyone reading this chapter, indeed any of us who
have taught a writing class before have probably taught our students to do just that.
Still, thinking about it in the context of performance has been enlightening to my
teaching practice. First, it caused me to give even more focus to the content of my
instruction materials, and the context of the class: Am I being asked to demonstrate
database search strategies? If so, is it for a graduate or undergraduate class? Is it in the
humanities or the sciences? History or music? Which professor? Every group is

different, and a one-size fits all approach is not the most effective way to teach material. Second, maintaining an awareness of your audience, or in this case classroom, will allow you to make important adjustments throughout a class session. As much as instructors may wish, students are not always forthcoming in letting instructors know when they are having trouble grasping material. Keeping a degree of your attention on the students at all times helps you pick up on subtle cues that they might not be understanding something (attention is waning, a confused expression, staring at their computer screen in frustration, etc.). Similarly, this awareness can help the instructor sense the "temperature" of the room overall, determining when a bit of levity is needed to relax the students, or an impromptu group exercise might help reinforce what was just covered, and refocus the group.

Of course, with this comparison of instruction to production it is crucial to note that no successful theatre production occurs without a great deal of rehearsal beforehand. Similarly, effective instruction requires a great deal of preparatory work. Not only should a librarian outline the desired test objectives for each instruction session, but it is a smart idea to rehearse the session whenever possible. Going through a session in front of an imaginary audience, or even willing colleagues, can help an instructor become more comfortable with speaking in front of a group, and highlight areas that might need some tweaking before "opening the show". Even if you don't have the time, or inclination, to rehearse an instruction session in advance, a mental rehearse can provide a solid idea of some of the challenges that may arise during the session, and approximate lengths of each element of the class.

It is worth reiterating the importance of rehearsal to creating a production. No production is created overnight. Even improv troupes spend a great deal of time rehearsing their timing, and chemistry with each other before performing. Rehearsal is a lengthy process necessary for achieving a quality production. When thinking of information literacy especially in the context of a semester-long course, or repeated visits to a class, the metaphor of the rehearsal process is apt. Just as in the theatre the objectives of a course do not happen suddenly, it is a series of slow steps that build from a base of knowledge, and continuously refines until the aims are reached, (whether these aims are creating an audience-worthy production, or building students' information literacy). The process requires patience, understanding, and effort from all parties involved. One of the best things a director or instructor can do is create an environment that is a safe space for working. In the theatre this means creating a space where actors can feel comfortable experimenting with their characters, and taking risks with their performance. Not all the choices they make may work in this process. In fact many may not, but through trying different approaches, and ideas the actors can gain a greater understanding of who their characters are, and how they fit within the world of the play. In the classroom setting this approach is invaluable. Anyone who has taught an information literacy course or even an introductory library one shot, is acutely aware at how rudimentary students' research skills often are. Just as actors may begin a process uncertain, and uncomfortable in the skin of their characters; students are nervous, and anxious about playing their new role of scholarly researchers. One of the instructor's chief roles in this process is creating an environment where the students feel comfortable with the skills they are using to the point that they feel free to experiment, and try new approaches in their research. Creating a supportive atmosphere will help students feel safer in synthesizing their knowledge.

The notion of process is a useful conceptual tool for the act of research itself. In the theatre, rehearsals don't go from beginning to end in a direct line. Moments are staged, then revisited repeatedly. After the initial stage movement (blocking) is constructed, the scene is reworked repeatedly adding in new performance layers, design elements (e.g. lighting, costumes, etc.) until finally the production is in a place where it can be run through in its entirety from beginning to end. Likewise the act of research is rarely, if ever, linear. Scholars begin with a hypothesis, or research question, conduct basic research, and use those findings to revise the research strategy. Beginning researchers often resist this approach hoping to find the sources they need as quickly, and easily as possible. Part of our task as instructors is to instill in students the benefits of viewing research as a nonlinear process where each iteration of a search can yield newer more fruitful results. The concept of the rehearsal process as a metaphor for both research, and pedagogy is a useful tool to incorporate into bibliographic instruction.

Library skills in theatre practice

Thus far, I have discussed the ways my theatre background has enriched my professional development as a librarian. As a continuing theatre practitioner I am happy to say the exchange was not unilateral. The skills and techniques I have learned in obtaining my library science degree, and working as an academic librarian; have strengthened my work as a director and actor. A great deal of the director's work before rehearsals begin typically involves frequent trips to the library. To differing degrees (based on an individual production) the director is responsible for the following tasks: advocating for and expressing the playwright's intentions, creating a unified, and coherent world of the play, elucidating and communicating the specific production's own interpretation of the play and message. Any of these tasks benefit from thorough research. If the director does not have the benefit of having the playwright present in the rehearsal process, a critical analysis of her works (especially the play being produced) and any interviews with the author, or reviews of previous productions might be helpful. Even for the large number of directors who do not want their vision influenced by other people's interpretations, successful research offstage can yield great results on stage. Few theatres have the budget to send directors out to locations that plays are set in (and no theatre to my knowledge has developed a working time-machine to send director's back to specific historical eras). Research can help flesh out these worlds by providing details on what society and culture was like in a specific time and place, what people wore, how they spoke and other important details. Additionally, taking advantage of a library's archives, and special collections may provide those unique details that really make a show come alive. For example, in a recent production at a local theatre, the director was doing research for a play set in the army barracks in the Southern US during the Second World War. She discovered a photo that was taken from both the time, and place of the play that became the inspiration for the scenic design. The skills I have learned as a librarian have been especially helpful in tracking down more esoteric information. For a play I recently directed, I needed to create a great deal of fake meat as a stage prop. Since this is relatively obscure information, I was only able to find some documentation on how to do this after executing a well-crafted search strategy. Without my training, I might not have had the skill set to success-fully satisfy this information need. This is just one example of the hundreds of times research skills have aided my work as a theatre director. These skills are an essential, and are often a misunderstood aspect of theatre production.

Perhaps nothing better underscores how simultaneously important, and misunder-stood the role of research is in the artistic process than the existence of the dramaturge. The role of the dramaturge is a bit nebulous, and often varies depending on the company (further emphasizing the lack of appreciation some in the theatre world have for rigorous research) but one of the most common duties entail handling the research duties for a production. For a pre-existing script the dramaturge often takes on the research tasks described for the director above, and shares this information with the production cast and crew. In many ways the dramaturge is the theatre's equivalent of a librarian. The dramaturge typically serves as the advocate for the absent playwright, ensuring both the historical, and cultural research necessary to create the world of the play, and the critical research on the play's style, and themes necessary to interpret the work have been conducted. This information is shared with the production team, and they can choose to use as much or as little of it as they like in their production, but they at least have the information at hand. In more recent years, the dramaturge has taken more active artistic duties in selecting a well-balanced season, and assisting new playwrights in developing work. Sadly, this position is not common in American theatres, but those companies lucky enough to have a dramaturge, are appreciative of their value.

While not often as academic as dramaturges and directors, actors usually conduct their own research when developing a role. This process varies from conventional library research to more esoteric notions of the concept. For example, I am currently working on a character for Tennessee Williams' *A Streetcar Named Desire*. As part of my preparation for my character, Mitch (a Second World War veteran) I conducted research on specific battles that were referenced in the play, symptoms of post-traumatic stress disorder, and other details such as the specific New Orleans dialect he speaks. The library and research skills I have picked up in my job have been quite valuable in these matters. In addition, to conventional research approaches, actors often look for inspiration outside of texts, and other library resources. Books, articles, and other scholarly resources are helpful for determining the factual circumstances for the character (e.g. location, time period, occupation, etc.) but may not be as useful for the more affective aspects of performance. Libraries certainly house resources that may help actors discover the emotional core of their character through video, audio, other literary works, but many actors make these discoveries by observing, and emu-lating aspects found in the outside world (people, animals and even inanimate objects). The materials may be different, but one might be surprised at how similar the process is to traditional library research. An actor may focus on a few actions and/or qualities. For example, "How does Mitch, a big, shy person conduct himself around a woman he is attracted to?" To discover this, an actor may search for these qualities in the everyday world, discover them in an individual, and use that information to further refine the search before conducting it again. By the end of this process the actor would have a much stronger idea of how to portray that moment on stage.

Getting involved

As I have demonstrated, not only do librarians have skills that are quite useful in theatre practice, but participating in theatre can be beneficial to our professional development as well. Hopefully, this chapter has encouraged the reader to become involved in theatre. Thankfully there are many opportunities to participate for those who are interested. Perhaps the easiest way may be getting involved in your local theatre group. Almost every community has a theatre troupe that often utilizes the local talent. Community theatres such as these are typically quite welcoming to newcomers, and accommodating to people's hectic work schedules. For those who may have trepidations about stepping on the stage there are plenty of roles available backstage as well. Most theatre groups have websites that list performance dates, and opportunities for working onstage or off.

For those interested in a more structured approach, local theatre companies, and private instructors often offer classes, or workshops on various aspects of theatre practice. These may vary in both time commitment, and price but are a great introduction for people who may be nervous working on a production without any prior experience.

Depending on the size of the local college or university, there may be a need for community actors to fill in on departmental production. This is especially likely for older actors, as most students are not age-appropriate for older characters. Participating in departmental productions cannot only be a nice artistic experience, but could also serve an effective outreach role for librarians working on campus. As theatre production is by definition a social activity, students involved in the production will most likely become more comfortable, and familiar with the librarian involved. This should translate to a greater likelihood of their approaching the librarian for research help throughout their academic career.

As this chapter has shown, getting involved in theatre can be rewarding artistically, socially, and professionally. Theatre participation can increase skills in communication, and working collaboratively. Additionally, reference work can be improved by approaching it as an improvisation, and opening the librarian up, to the patron's specific information needs, and discovering new approaches to resources. In the classroom, theatre skills can translate to greater comfort in front of the class, as well as providing a greater understanding of the subtle shifts in energy, and attention the class goes through, by considering them as an audience. A theatre perspective helps stress the notion of research as a process, and can help instill in students the idea that research occurs over multiple iterations of refinement. Librarians have many useful skills to bring to the theatre as well, particularly in their efficacy in research and strategic approaches to information discovery. For those interested in getting involved in the theatre there are many opportunities. Show up to an audition, or check out a production, and introduce yourself. You may soon find a second home!

Why a marketing background is a good fit for the library profession

Beth R. Canzoneri

Introduction

Entering the library profession after years of honing skills applicable to another field—marketing and communications—I wondered how difficult it would be to make the transition. What I found surprised and encouraged me: Marketing skills not only can provide a solid base for a library career, they are essential.

The seeds of my library career were planted during a student job in my college library. However, armed with an English degree, and the necessity of finding a job after college, I began a 25-year career in marketing and communications. During those years, I marketed the services of a professional association, a state agency, and finally, an architecture firm. I had a successful career, but I was always aware that it was only a job, and not a passion.

The economic downturn of the last decade gave me a reason to take stock of my career choice, and work/life balance. I decided to chase a long-time dream to work as a librarian, and applied to library school—a goal I had wanted to pursue since those days in my college library. Two years later, after continuing to work full-time as a marketer, I completed my MLIS degree, focusing on providing reference services, and bibliographic instruction in an academic library.

A month after graduation, an introduction to an academic librarian at the American Library Association (ALA) Annual Conference proved fortuitous. After a brief conversation, I handed him my resume. A marketing and communications position had just been created in his library, and I knew I had to apply; the position was a unique blend of my marketing background, MLIS degree, and enthusiasm for academic libraries. When the job offer arrived, I didn't hesitate to accept. A year later I received the opportunity I had hoped for—a reference, and instruction librarian position that incorporates marketing responsibilities.

Many like me are entering the library profession as a second career. If you have a business marketing background, and are wondering if the leap to librarianship is too big a stretch, take a look at your background. If you have experience:

- developing presentations;
- designing promotional materials;
- writing press releases;
- editing publications;
- coordinating special events;

Skills to Make a Librarian. http://dx.doi.org/10.1016/B978-0-08-100063-2.00009-0

- website design and development;
- creating a social media presence; and
- maintaining positive relations with donors.

Libraries need that type of experience. The notion that libraries would always be perceived as relevant is no longer true. Library marketing is vital to the success, and existence of libraries, and a librarian with marketing skills is a valued commodity.

Marketing and libraries

What is marketing, and how do you define the concept as it relates to libraries? The business world defines marketing as 'the process of planning and executing conception, pricing, promotion, and distribution of ideas, goods, and services to create exchanges that satisfy individual and organizational objectives' (Bennett, 1995). Translated to the library world, marketing is much like in any other service organization, and it can be defined in the same terms; simply change the words "individual and organizational objectives" to "user and library objectives". In essence, marketing is the link between the user's needs, and the library's resources and services.

Reasons to market libraries

Library marketing is not new. Historically, knowledge of the need to market libraries can be traced back to the late nineteenth century when leaders in the field promoted their library's resources and services, and interacted with users—not only as a means of elevating the library's status in the community, but as a way to learn about their users' preferences. Samuel Green, one of the chief founders of the public library in our country, and President of ALA in 1891, believed that it was a library's duty to respond to the needs of its users, and he advocated librarians forming personal relationships with their users. His early attempts to connect the library's users to its services were some of the first forays into library marketing (Renborg, 1997).

Green's philosophy became more prevalent in the first half of the twentieth century when library leaders such as John Cotton Dana, also an ALA President, began promoting their libraries to influential citizens, and cultivating civic partnerships to increase funding sources (Giuliano, 2009). In the later half of the twentieth century when the advent of computers, and the rise of the internet gave libraries greater competition for information-seeking, this type of marketing technique would prove essential. In the first decade of the twenty-first century, the crisis in the American economy, and resulting budget cuts put still more pressure on libraries to market both their resources, and services.

Through the efforts of our forebearers in the profession, libraries became widely acknowledged as an indispensable part of any community. However, today that axiom is being challenged. Changes within the social, economic, and technological realm have lowered the public perception of the library's value. Consequently, libraries are charged with defending, and promoting their services to dispel misconceptions about their demise. A call to action on the Association of College and Research Libraries (ACRL) website states this well: 'In today's complex information environment, we have a greater responsibility to communicate the resources and expertise our libraries and librarians provide, both on our campuses and in society'. (Association of College and Research Libraries, 2009).

The library world's professional organizations are supporting its members in facing the challenge. The ALA's "Campaign for America's Libraries" provides resources to all types of libraries to help them meet the challenge of proving their importance. The campaign acknowledges that: **'While libraries are popular, they are often taken for granted; while libraries are ubiquitous, they are not often visible; while libraries are unique, they are facing new challenges'.** The ALA directs libraries to communicate their value by marketing themselves as 'changing and dynamic places of opportunity that change communities and the lives of individuals' (*http://www.ALA.org* [Accessed 10 August 2014]).

Libraries need marketing for the same reasons as businesses, and they must view themselves from this perspective. Like businesses, libraries need to market to educate potential customers, or clients (library users) about their value; to grow their customer or client base (library usage); to strengthen partnerships with stakeholders (the library community); and to increase profit (library funding).

Educate and inform users and potential users

With competition at a fever pitch from a host of other information providers, libraries must be their own advocates. They need to strongly communicate the reasons why they can meet their users', and potential users' needs better than other information providers. Libraries have to educate, and inform their users, and potential users about the resources, and services that match their needs, and interests; many of whom may not even be aware or have limited understanding of what is offered.

Create and strengthen partnerships

Raising public awareness of the library's role in the community builds relationships, and creates new partnerships within its community of users. Stronger community partnerships can provide vital support for the library. Building allegiances within the community is not just good practice, it is vital for it to survive, and thrive in today's economy.

Increase funding and variety of funding sources

Increasing funding, and funding sources may be the most important reason of all to market libraries. In today's economy as the cost of library resources, and services steadily increases, financial support is more critical than ever. Marketing to potential donors throughout the library's immediate, and larger community is necessary to sustain the library with vital, and cutting-edge resources and services.

The need for librarians with marketing skills

The library profession needs librarians with marketing skills. In fact, marketing is now widely considered one of the competencies of professional librarians. However, unfortunately, since 1963 when the first course on library public relations was introduced at Columbia University (Renborg, 1997), library schools have been lax in equipping new librarians with marketing skills. A brief introduction to marketing is often covered in LIS courses like Library Administration, or Library Management, but reports published in 2001 and 2003 stated that less than half of all ALA-accredited library schools offered a course in marketing as a requirement or elective (Winston & Hazlin, 2003; Bouthillier, 2001).

However, a survey of library job advertisements in the US and Canada between 2000 and 2010 revealed that the number of ads listing marketing, promotional, and outreach responsibilities had grown by more than 500 per cent (Okamoto & Polger, 2012) vividly substantiating the claim that the importance of librarians with marketing and communications skills has increased in importance in recent years.

One reason for the elevated interest in hiring librarians with marketing and communications skills can be attributed to our nation's economic downturn, and the funding effect on libraries. Many are still experiencing budget cuts, and cannot afford to hire a dedicated marketer. When funding is available for new positions, the job advertisement will often be wrapped into a librarian position, and include the word "marketing" in the position title. Examples of these job titles include marketing & communications librarian, development & marketing librarian, or public relations & marketing librarian. Sometimes, marketing skills are simply implied in such titles as Outreach or Community Engagement Librarian (Okamoto & Polger, 2012). Other libraries form committees to handle marketing tasks, and initiatives (Carter & Seaman, 2011). Ideally, a librarian with marketing experience would provide leadership for such collaborations.

Although all libraries, no matter the type, are aware that they must market their value in order to survive and thrive, reduced funding has dramatically affected the hiring of skilled new professionals to carry out these tasks. Many smaller, and underfunded libraries must make the best use of their limited resources by assigning the function to librarians, and staff members. If they have limited or no previous experience or training, they may struggle to wrap their minds around the unfamiliar process of marketing.

Recent studies of how academic libraries handle their marketing responsibilities revealed that when libraries do fund marketing, and outreach positions, most are half-time, or divided between librarianship, and marketing duties. The study also found that of professional librarians, it is often reference librarians who have gained marketing skills on the job, or in a previous career, and are therefore the ones filling marketing and outreach positions (Carter & Seaman, 2011).

If they lack previous marketing experience, reference librarians may struggle to meet the task. A recent study of more than 200 academic reference librarians who were charged with marketing their libraries asked them to describe the duties of their position, their background and previous experience, and their challenges in meeting the responsibilities of their jobs. The study revealed their challenges were with time restraints, lack of training, and limited support from the library (Polger & Okamoto, 2013).

The majority of librarians with marketing responsibilities have no previous marketing experience at all. A 2010 UK study of librarians' attitudes toward marketing reported that although 60 per cent of the respondents perceived of marketing as useful in their jobs as librarians, only 40 per cent said they had previously studied it, or had received training (Estall & Stephens, 2011).

New librarians must be cognizant of these facts and figures as they enter the field. Clearly, training and competence as a marketer are an advantage to those starting out in the library profession. Marketing skills allow a new librarian to confidently face the current library environment.

Marketing skills to bring to the library profession

In library school, you may have been told, 'Don't discount your years of marketing experience", but you questioned whether this would actually be true when it came to finding a job as a new librarian. The good news is that all types of libraries are now seeking librarians with enhanced skill sets.

Marketing skills add value to your resume

Marketing experience adds value to your resume as you seek a library job in a tight job market. Your marketing experience will be a huge asset when you apply for your first library job, and can increase your chances of landing it.

Whether you apply for a job as reference librarian, or other public services position, in addition to your library skills, and experience your resume will be noticed for your marketing skills. Instead of burying skills from your former career, be sure to highlight them on your resume. That may be enough to bring your resume to the top of the stack.

Once you have been hired, marketing skills will add value to your stock as a newly minted librarian, and will make you a valued commodity as you move into the profession. You will simply be using your marketing skills from a new perspective. For example, in my new library job, prior experience developing proposals, and presentations—easily converted to classroom instruction; member services experience was helpful in overseeing library donor relations; utilizing social media as a tool for business purposes was helpful in promoting library initiatives, news and events; conducting interviews; and writing feature stories immediately transitioned to my new task of editing the donor newsletter.

Marketing skills for your professional toolkit

In your previous career as a marketer, you have amassed a broad mix of skills including effective communication, networking, organization, persuasion, innovation and strategic thinking. You will be required to apply these same skills and methodologies as a library marketer.

Communicate effectively

Because you have worked in the marketing field, it is taken for granted that your written and oral communication skills are first rate. As your library's designated marketer and advocate, you will likely be asked to write and edit information for newsletters, press releases, fund raising and social media.

You will also be asked to present information orally in many aspects of your new job. Communicating effectively extends to the ability to clearly and professionally present information to groups. Your marketing background has probably included experience as a presenter and you are already equipped with this skill. If you enter the profession as a reference librarian in any type of library, your position will require some type of bibliographic instruction. Your presentation skills will help you meet this requirement.

Your ability to communicate interpersonally is another key factor. Because you have a marketing background, your interpersonal skills will help you be successful at communicating your library's message and value in one-to-one situations. As the dedicated marketer for your library, you will be meeting with stakeholders and or donors. If you work in an academic library, you will also be interacting with administrators and faculty from various disciplines.

Effective communication skills include negotiation skills. As a marketer, you most likely have negotiations experience, and this will help within the library among your colleagues as you serve as a team member. You may also serve on committees within your library's broader community. When you share responsibility for the outcome of a team project, your negotiation skills will be essential.

Comprehend and assimilate new information

Marketing requires the ability to comprehend and assimilate new information. Being able to 'hit the ground running' is a valuable trait for a new librarian. Your marketing experience has taught you to be enthusiastic and thorough when approaching a new client. You can approach your new library job in the same way.

From your first day of work, you will be challenged to quickly learn your library's policies, its services, collection, and other resources. Soon after, you will need to grasp the scope of its user community and other stakeholders. Once you have fully comprehended your new knowledge of all these elements, you can begin to integrate this with the library's mission and vision.

Network

From the marketing world, you have already learned the importance of networking. Whether it came to you naturally or not, you have been required to be outgoing and constantly seek new contacts and clients. This valuable skill will serve you well in any type of library. If you work as a public librarian, connecting with your community is essential; if you are employed in a special library, making contacts within that area of knowledge will serve you well; if you are an academic librarian, reaching out to the various departments within your institution will be instrumental in your success. In fact, you may have used your networking skills to find your first library job. You will continue to use this skill as you progress in your career.

As a new librarian, you will be building a new network in your library community. Building a network takes time, and your must keep your eyes and ears open for opportunities as they present themselves. You will network with your colleagues in the library where you work, with members of the community or larger organization of your particular type of library (academic institution, public library, special library, etc.), and professional organizations. As a business marketer you already know the importance of keeping track of your network and contact information and specific details about those contacts. Your networking abilities will help you build partnerships and alliances for your library.

Persuade

Marketing also requires the ability to persuade. As a new library marketer, you can use that ability to carefully craft and deliver the library's message to its target audiences. During my marketing career in the business world, I developed persuasive skills to help attract and maintain clients. I employed those skills in presentations and in print. Not unlike private business, libraries also need to attract and maintain clients, i.e. their users or patrons.

Advocacy will be a big part of your role as a library marketer. In order to serve as a strong advocate for your library, you will use your knowledge of your library's strengths, weaknesses, opportunities and threats (SWOT). Your experience conducting thorough SWOT analysis will help you understand your library's position in the marketplace and enable you to make good decisions on how to educate your library's users and potential users and promote its resources and services.

Organize and categorize information

Your marketing skill set includes the ability to organize and categorize information. Those abilities are at the heart of librarianship in general. It even could be one of the reasons you were drawn to the library profession. Just as you applied this skill in your corporate job, your organizational skills will help you as you oversee the very important role of marketer for your library. The types of information and organizational tools may be different, but the same concepts apply to tasks such as grouping your users into segments as you research your library's diverse audiences.

Perhaps you have compiled an annual report in your work as a business marketer; that experience is applicable in a library setting. Coordinating the information for my library's annual report was one of the first tasks I was asked to undertake as a library marketer. Organizational skills gained in my marketing career helped simplify what might have been a complex process of gathering and compiling material from every department, units, and task forces in our library.

Innovate and create

Your marketing experience has taught you to think creatively. You know that to keep ahead of the competition, you must use innovative techniques. Often when marketing tasks fall as an added responsibility of already overloaded library staff, the tendency can be to get by with what is necessary and easiest. Your marketing experience will bring a new perspective on old ideas as you evaluate your library's marketing needs and strategies for accomplishing them. In a public library, new initiatives could draw an overlooked segment of the community; in an academic library, new ideas could transform your library's outreach to students.

Think strategically

Your marketing experience also has taught you to think strategically. This is a trait shared universally by all information professionals. The Special Library Association, a professional organization for librarians in corporate, law, museum, medical and similar institutions, defines an information professional as someone who 'strategically uses information in his/her job to advance the mission of the organization' (Abels et al., 2003).

From your background in marketing for a business organization, you have experience creating a marketing plan. You already know how to analyze and apply your knowledge of your organization's resources, services and users to communicate the value of your product in a calculated fashion to reach your customers.

The marketing and communications process for libraries

As the professional marketer knows, marketing is not just public relations and promotions; it involves creating a marketing plan. Your experience creating a marketing plan for a business will be priceless in your new library job. A library marketing plan is based on the same concepts as a business marketing plan – adapting goods and services to meet the current and potential users' needs. User research gauges this, and promotions get the word to users that the library can meet those needs.

The marketing plan

To create a plan, you will be looking at your library through the same kind of critical lens. The Online Dictionary for Library and Information Science (ODLIS) defines a marketing plan as a 'series of actions to be undertaken by a company or organization to successfully interest potential customers or clients in a product or service and to persuade them to buy or use it. Often based on *market research*, such a plan is specifically designed to systematically implement a set of goals known as a *marketing strategy*, through promotion and outreach' (Reitz, nd).

And from the business world, you also already know that a marketing plan is not a static document. Neither is the strategic alignment process. This is especially true in a library. Your plan will be an ongoing and dynamic process, because user needs and library products and services are constantly changing.

The process of creating a strategically-aligned marketing plan for your library will begin by examining the library's mission and values. Then you will conduct a thorough audit of its resources and services and research its users and potential users. The results will help you set goals for your marketing and create strategies for achieving them. You will end by assessing the outcomes of your marketing strategies. Ideally, the process will be just that—a process, one that you will continually reassess and start over again.

Examine values

You will begin the process by examining your library's mission and aspirational goals, which will serve as the vision for all other steps of your marketing plan. Your marketing plan should align and complement the values that form the core reason for all the library's resources and services.

Audit resources and services

Next, you will conduct an internal audit of the library's resources and services. Make a list of every resource in the library, as well as every service currently offered to users. Further in the process, you will be looking at how those resources and services match the users' needs and expectations. Your internal audit should include a SWOT analysis, with which, as a former business marketer, you are already familiar.

Research users

In the business world, goods and services cannot reach users without promotion; the same is true in the world of libraries. The challenge for businesses is first to understand how their customers or clients perceive their product before they begin to promote it. In the same way, libraries must also initially seek to understand their users.

You can adapt your experience researching your business competitors to the tasks of researching your library's current and potential users. In fact, your experience with research as a marketer might be one of the reasons that lead you to the library profession as a second career. As in business marketing, library marketing cannot truly begin without an understanding of where to direct the marketing message. You will use your research skills to uncover who your library's users and potential users (audiences) are and understand their needs and wants.

User research can help reveal what your community really thinks about your library. You will learn whether they find it an inviting environment; whether they view the librarians and staff as helpful, friendly and efficient; whether they are aware of the library's electronic resources and services.

There are two steps involved in user research: The first is demographics. Who are they; where do they live; what are their ages? As in business, a library needs this information to know how and where to reach its audiences. By gaining an understanding of your library's user demographics, you are much better equipped to reach out to the people you currently serve and seek to serve.

Once you have knowledge of your audiences' demographics, you are ready for the second step: Defining their needs and wants; determining how they perceive the library's resources and services and what they really want and need from their library. You will then use your list of resources and services to match the users' needs and expectations. You might employ surveys or focus groups. You may even offer incentives to persuade your users to participate in your information-gathering.

Part of conducting user research is dividing them into groups to more directly target them with marketing strategies. For example, if you work in an academic library, you could break your groups into students, faculty and community; those groups could be further divided into undergrads, grad students, international students, physically challenged students, high school students, local business or government agencies, and others. If you work in a public library, those groups might be children, young adults, retired adults; those groups could be further divided as well. How you divide your users into groups will depend not only on your type of library, but also on the size of its community.

Organizing users into groups, or segments, will allow you to focus on your users rather than your resources and services. Knowing what specific groups comprise your community of users will uncover the characteristics of each group; then you can decide upon the best methods of communicating your message to each group. A broad picture of your community of users will be your guide as you develop goals and objectives for your marketing strategy, always keeping in mind that the users' needs are what drive the marketing process.

Now that you understand your users – their demographics, wants and needs, and perceptions of the library – you will be ready to move on to the final part of your plan, developing goals and objectives for your marketing. You can now connect the dots between your users and your resources and services. You are one step closer to putting your plan into action.

Establish goals, objectives, and strategies

At this stage of your marketing plan, you will reflect back on the reasons that libraries need marketing: To educate, inform and users and potential users; to increase funding and variety of funding sources; to create and strengthen partnerships. Your goals and objectives should be fashioned around those reasons. Strategies for accomplishing your goals and objectives might include reviewing your library's brand identity, reworking your website, coordinating your social media profile, developing a donor newsletter, creating print and electronic promotional materials, and hosting special events and programs.

If your first goal is to educate your current and potential users, then you will want to focus on your library's brand identity. When your users recognize your brand, they pay attention to your message. Establishing a brand is the key to consistency in your marketing program. You will also want to focus on your online presence. This includes your website and social media. Social media marketing is designed to be interactive and engaging to your users. When their friends "like" your library or share its social media content, the added attention will create a greater user base, and hopefully a more diverse one.

Another strategy for increasing users is hosting special events. The type of event or program will depend on your type of library and its community. This is a great way to get potential users – and donors – in the door and show off your library's collections and amenities, as well as to demonstrate commitment to your community. Creative fund raising ideas that you bring to your new library job from your previous career in marketing will be an asset.

If your second goal is to create and strengthen partnerships, then you will need to get outside of the library to develop relationships with community organizations. As your library's marketer, you will be the public face of the library, whether your library community is an academic institution, a town or city, or a large corporation. Get to know your community members, and seize every opportunity to interact with them through participating on local committees and attending community events. Your networking skills will be important as you meet and greet your public.

If your third goal is to increase funding and variety of funding sources, then you will definitely want to develop a donor newsletter, print and/or electronic. Direct mail is another option, but this can be costly. And don't neglect media coverage. Spread the word about your library's success. Press coverage in the local media is vital to cultivating interest in your library, as well as support from new donors.

Once you have carried out your strategies to market the library's resources and services to all its audiences, the marketing cycle is nearly complete. Finally you will gather user feedback to your marketing.

Assess outcomes

The final step in the marketing process, and one not to be ignored, is to measure your efforts to see how well your plan is working. Assessment will provide you with user feedback on your marketing strategies and reveal a great deal about the wants and needs of your library's users. Assessment does not need to be complicated. But it may be uncomfortable, which explains why many libraries overlook this step. Library staff may not want to hear the results. But assessment is absolutely necessary to tailoring your library's resources and service to reflect your users' needs and desires.

Assessment can be as simple as measuring how many or what percentage. If your objective was to have 50 attendees, evaluation is easy: Simply count them. If your measure of evaluation is customer satisfaction, you will need another method –a survey form or focus group meeting for example. Or you might find that some of your library services simply cannot be measured.

Assessment is not simply about listing your successes; it also involves coming face to face with your failures. Evaluation may reveal that some of your library's services simply fail to meet the perceived needs of its users. If your efforts have been met with little fanfare and your promotions have been poorly received, you will need to change your mix of marketing strategies as needed to improve the results.

Most importantly, assessment will help your library plan how to increase user satisfaction and adjust the library's services to better address their perceived needs. You may even discover that what is actually needed is to revamp your marketing plan. And so, the marketing cycle continues.

Conclusion

Library marketing is vital to keeping our users and potential users informed and educated about the resources and services that match their needs and interests. Effective marketing skills are needed to increase awareness of the library's value and to expand its user base. With these skills in hand as you enter the library profession, you are holding the keys to your new career.

Marketing is the link between the library user's needs and its resources and services; as a library marketer, you create that link. Your skills will help connect the library to its users, who know that they can get information many other ways without even coming to the library building or interacting with a librarian. With constant competition from other information providers, librarians need to communicate to their users that they can meet their needs better than other providers. As librarians, we know that libraries are so much more than traditional print books and shushing librarians; we just need to change that stereotype. Library marketing reminds users that their library is still a great choice for meeting their information needs in today's world.

A marketing background is an excellent fit for the library profession. Marketing experience prior to entering the library profession is a highly valuable asset; in fact, it can be the deciding factor for a hiring committee. No matter the type of library in which you desire to work in the type of position you are seeking, your marketing experience can help you get the job. Use it to your advantage. Libraries need professionals like you.

References

Abels, E., Jones, R., Latham, J., Magnoni, D., & Marshall, J. D. (2003). *Special Libraries Association competencies.* Available from: <http://www.sla.org/about-sla/competencies/>, Accessed 7 March 2014.

Association of College and Research Libraries. (2009). *Marketing @ your library.* Available from: <http://www.ala.org/acrl/issues/marketing>, Accessed 2 March 2014.

Bennett, P. D. (1995). *Dictionary of marketing terms.* Lincolnwood, IL: NTC Business Books.

Bouthillier, F. (2001). The teaching of marketing and quality management in schools of library and information studies: the case of North America. In S. Koopman (Ed.), *Education and research for marketing and quality management in libraries* (pp. 21–30). The Hague, Netherlands: International Federation of Library Associations and Institutions, Available from: Google Books, Accessed 2 March 2014.

Carter, T. M., & Seaman, P. (2011). The management and support of outreach in academic libraries. *Reference and User Services Quarterly, 51*(2), 163–171, Accessed 17 March 2014.

Estall, C., & Stephens, D. (2011). A study of the variables influencing academic library staff's attitudes toward marketing. *New Review of Academic Librarianship, 17*(2), 185–208, Available from: Library, Information Science and Technology Abstracts, Accessed 17 February 2014.

Giuliano, S. J. (2009). We have books and computers: libraries and the importance of marketing. *Library Student Journal, 4,* Available from: Library, Information Science and Technology Abstracts, Accessed 21 February 2014.

Okamoto, K., & Polger, M. A. (2012). Off to market we go. *Library Leadership and Management, 26*(2), 1–20, Available from: Library, Information Science and Technology Abstracts, Accessed 21 February 2014.

Polger, M. A., & Okamoto, K. (2013). Who's spinning the library? Responsibilities of academic librarians who promote. *Library Management, 34*(3), 236–253, Available from: Library, Information Science and Technology Abstracts, Accessed 25 February 2014.

Reitz, J. n.d., *Online Dictionary for Library and Information Science*. Available from: http://www.abc-clio.com/ODLIS/odlis_A.aspx, Accessed 7 March 2014.

Renborg, G. (1997). *Marketing library services. How it all began*. Available from: http://archive.ifla.org/IV/ifla63/63reng.htm, Accessed 18 March 2014.

Winston, M., & Hazlin, G. E. (2003). Leadership competencies in library and information science: Marketing as a component of LIS curricula. *Journal of Education for Library and Information Science*, 28(2), 177–187, Available from: Library, Information Science and Technology Abstracts, Accessed 12 February 2014.

Bibliography

Bates, M. E. (1998). The newly minted MLS: What do we need to know today? *Searcher*, 6(5), 30–34, Available from: Library, Information Science and Technology Abstracts, Accessed 17 February 2014.

Dempsey, K. (2009). *The accidental library marketer*. Medford, N.J: Information Today.

Marshall, N. J. (2001). Public relations in academic libraries: A descriptive analysis. *Journal Of Academic Librarianship*, 27(2), 116–122, Available from: Library, Information Science and Technology Abstracts, Accessed 17 February 2014.

Matthews, B. (2009). *Marketing today's academic library: A bold new approach to communicating with students*. Chicago, IL: American Library Association.

Nowak, D. (2003). *Marketing the library, staff training from Ohio Library Council*. Available from: http://www.olc.org/marketing/index.html [Accessed 9 March 2014].

Shontz, M. L., Parker, J. C., & Parker, R. (2004). What do librarians think about marketing? A survey of public librarians' attitudes toward the marketing of library services. *The Library Quarterly: Information, Community, Policy*, 74(1), 63–84, Available from: Library, Information Science and Technology Abstracts [Accessed 17 February 2014].

Siess, J. A. (2003). *The visible librarian: Asserting your value with marketing and advocacy*. Chicago, IL: American Library Association.

My journey from certified bra fitter to reference librarian

10

Robin L. Ewing

Introduction

I currently serve as the Reference Workgroup leader, and the assessment librarian at St Cloud State University (SCSU). I have worked at SCSU in one capacity or another since 2003, and I was awarded tenure in 2009. My library is organized around workgroups. Other workgroups include both faculty librarians, and paraprofessional staff while the Reference Workgroup includes faculty librarians only. Workgroup leader is a position with responsibility but limited formal authority. At St Cloud State University faculty do not supervise other faculty due to our contract. As one of my colleagues described it several years ago, "library workgroup leaders often have all of the responsibility to see a task fulfilled, but rarely any of the authority" (M. K. Ewing, personal communication, 19 April 2010). As a member of the Reference Workgroup, I provide in-person, e-mail, and telephone reference service. I also develop and teach course-integrated library instruction classes for which I create course guides. As the Reference Workgroup Leader, I facilitate workgroup meetings, coordinate the Reference Desk schedule, represent the Reference Workgroup at the Dean's Council, and provide leadership in the prioritization and revision of services.

As the Assessment Librarian, I chair the library's Assessment Committee, represent the library on the University Assessment Steering Committee, counsel library workgroups on assessment issues, and oversee library-wide assessment efforts such as the administration of the LibQUAL+ survey. Our main focus this spring has been the LibQUAL+ survey and the creation of an infographic to communicate the value of our interlibrary loan service to students.

Prior to working at SCSU, I spent a year at Texas A & M University in a non-tenure track position: I worked at the West Campus Library which is the business and agriculture branch library. My duties primarily consisted of providing reference assistance to students, faculty, staff, and other patrons and hiring, training, and supervising the 10–15 reference student workers. At the West Campus Library, student workers and librarians jointly staffed the Reference Desk. This position was my first professional librarian position. I was fortunate to start work there as I would have flailed around; if I had started in a tenure-track position immediately after library school. Here, I acquired an understanding of the work performed by professional librarians.

In my previous life, I spent over 14 years in retail and that experience informs my work today as a librarian particularly my interactions with students at the Reference Desk. I worked for three different companies, J. Brannam, Dillard's, and the Army and Air Force Exchange Service. Each of my retail positions contributes to the

Skills to Make a Librarian. http://dx.doi.org/10.1016/B978-0-08-100063-2.00010-7

Reference Desk service I provide every day to SCSU students, faculty, and staff. I'll describe my employment at each of these companies, the influence each position has had on me, and how my retail experience provided many of the skills expected of a reference librarian. Davis (2006) views the retail sector as a negative influence on reference work. Davis is particularly concerned that the incorporation of retail aspects into reference will spell the end of the reference interview. However, I firmly believe that my retail jobs have allowed me to be successful in my vocation as a reference librarian.

J. Brannam

I grew up in Oklahoma City, graduated from Del City High School, and attended the University of Oklahoma for my undergraduate degree. The first store I worked at was a J. Brannam's store in an outlet mall in Moore, Oklahoma. J. Brannam was a discount clothing retailer owned by the Woolworth Company. My sister was the assistant manager of the store. The store was closing because the company was going out of business (Gilman, 1985). They hired temporary employees to assist in the process of liquidating inventory. I worked part-time at the store during the fall semester of my freshman year. My interactions with customers were limited though I did answer many directional questions. Anyone working a service point in a store or a library needs to know where resources, merchandise, and, where people are located. My position at J. Brannam was just my second job. I had worked as a part-time janitor on the weekends during my junior and senior years of high school. J. Brannam's was the first time I had to interact with other people on a job.

Dillard's Department Stores

At the end of my freshman year, I was in dire need of employment and my sister came through for me again. After her J. Brannam store closed, my sister went to work at the Dillard's Department Store in Crossroads Mall in Oklahoma City, and she arranged an interview for me with the assistant store manager. Dillard's is a family-owned business with its headquarters in Little Rock, Arkansas. Founded in 1938 by William Dillard, Dillard's is still run by the Dillard family, and the current chairman and CEO is William T. Dillard II. At the end of 2013, Dillard's had 302 stores in 29 states, mainly located in the South and Southwest (MarketLine, 2013). My sister still works for Dillard's, and I shop there whenever we visit Oklahoma.

I was hired to work in the lingerie department, and I worked there from 1986 to 1991 while completing my undergraduate degree in management at the University of Oklahoma. This position was my first real job and the work experience that has influenced my library career the most. Basically, I learned how to work. I experienced job stress for the first time. Retail can be especially stressful during the Christmas season and inventory. Research has shown that a large portion of the stress experienced by frontline retail employees is due to the tension between satisfying managers and customers (Wetzels, Ruyter & Bloemer, 2000). The crush of the Christmas retail season is remarkably similar to the last weeks of the semester. The Christmas shopping season fills stores with stressed-out customers; much like the end of the semester fills college libraries with panicked students. I joke that you can smell the tension in the building.

Another stressful aspect of working at Dillard's was the need to maintain a certain selling cost. Employees in the lingerie department did not work on commission but were expected to sell at least $110 an hour. Sales associates that fell below their sales target were put on probation, and could end-up fired from the company. I was put on probation once but a strong Christmas season saved me. I gained familiarity with working in the evening, and on weekends during my time at Dillard's. My library's reference desk is open seven days a week, and the librarians do have to cover weekends and evenings (though nowhere near as many as I did during my days at Dillard's). Most importantly for my future library career, I learned how to work with customers, and how to consistently deliver excellent service to those customers.

I initially worked part time for a couple of years before eventually moving to full-time as the lingerie department manager. A position remarkably similar to what I currently do as Workgroup leader. I had no real authority over the other people in the department but I was to take the lead on completing projects such as markdowns or inventory preparation. The lingerie department at my store included: bras, panties, sleepwear, and loungewear. The area sales manager was the supervisor for everyone in the department. However, because of the added responsibility expected of a department manager, I was given a slight break on my selling cost.

After I worked there a couple of years, Dillard's started a program for lingerie sales associates to become certified bra fitters and I was one of the first employees in the Oklahoma City area to be certified. At the time I worked for Dillard's there were six stores in the Oklahoma City area though restructuring and consolidations have reduced that to three stores now. In order to become a certified bra fitter, I first attended training, and then I had to pass two tests. One was a written test on general knowledge about bra fitting while the second test was to actually perform a bra fitting while being observed by the regional expert. After I passed both tests, I received a slight increase in pay and my photo was displayed in the department. I also wore a tape measure around my neck so I was prepared for a fitting at all times. Susan Nethero (2005: 36) describes what a woman can expect from a professional bra fitter:

> " — She'll educate you about your correct size.
> — She'll show you which styles are good for your body type and shape.
> — She'll recommend specific bras designed for your individual lifestyle.
> — She'll teach you how to take care of your bra so it stays in great condition."

Certified bra fitters are still a focus for Dillard's. Current chairman and CEO, William T. Dillard II, speaking to innerwear executives said, "the company is diligent about the experience of its bra-fit specialists. Some people just slap on a tape measure to try and think they're certified fitters, he said. Ours is a rigorous program that takes six months, with written tests" (Monget & Eichner, 2008: 12).

Army & Air Force Exchange Service

After I finished my undergraduate degree in 1991, I left Dillard's and Oklahoma to work for the Army & Air Force Exchange Service (AAFES). The AAFES operates department stores, gas stations, and food outlets on Air Force and Army installations serving military personnel and their families. The AAFES was founded in 1895 and does over $8 billion in sales annually (Miller & Washington, 2009). The AAFES motto is: "We go where you go" because an AAFES facility can be found almost everywhere the Air Force and Army are located (AAFES, 2014). The majority of AAFES earnings go to the Morale, Welfare, and Recreation (MWR) programs on Army and Air Force installations. MWR programs include recreation centers, golf courses, and libraries (AAFES, 2014). While AAFES supports military personnel, only two per cent of its budget comes from the government. That part of the budget goes to the active duty military personnel assigned to AAFES including a two-star general that serves as the deputy director of the company (Belanger, 2007).

Why did I choose to work for AAFES? My father served in the United States Air Force and I had grown up using AAFES facilities like the Base Exchange, a department store referred to as the BX, or the Shoppette. After my father's retirement, we continued to live near Tinker Air Force Base in Midwest City, Oklahoma. I spent many a summer afternoon at the base pool and my mother was a dedicated user of the base library. My work experience with Dillard's combined with my familiarity with shopping at AAFES stores made a retail manager position with AAFES a natural fit for me. I was hired by AAFES as a college trainee. At that time, college trainees were sent out to various base exchanges (Air Force bases) or post exchanges (Army posts) to learn how the exchange operates by rotating through all the departments in the store. For my training, I was assigned to Nellis Air Force Base in Las Vegas, Nevada. Employment with AAFES has some things in common with being in the military. One of these things is that AAFES arranged to move my household goods. I only had to pack my clothes, and my cat into the car, and I was on my way to Las Vegas from Oklahoma. My household goods arrived a couple weeks later.

My training at Nellis lasted nine months. The first department I learned was the stockroom. I helped check in merchandise as it arrived and assisted with stocking the store shelves with it and placing the merchandise in the stockroom. At Dillard's, I saw the merchandise when it arrived in a box to the lingerie department so this was a new experience for me. After working in the warehouse, I went on to other departments such as customer service, accounting, and the front registers. I also spent time with each of the sales area managers in their departments including sporting goods, electronics, housewares, candy, and tobacco. While my time at Nellis was brief, I gained an appreciation for the effort required to manage a store's operation. I also learned the hard lesson that being nice wasn't enough to ensure a job. The assistant store manager who welcomed me on my first day of work, took me to lunch, and introduced me to people throughout the store—was demoted and reassigned to another exchange just a couple of months after I arrived.

After my training was completed in May 1992, I transferred to Edwards Air Force Base in the Mojave Desert of California. Once again I packed my clothes and cat in the car but thankfully Edwards was only a four-hour drive away from Las Vegas. I was now the sales area manager for electronics, housewares, stationary, health and beauty care, candy, and tobacco. For the first time, I supervised employees with all the associated responsibilities. My department was clustered in two areas of the store, and I managed 15 employees. I hired and trained personnel as necessary. Many base exchange employees are spouses of active duty personnel so turnover is constant. This experience proved invaluable for my time supervising student workers at Texas A & M University. For my area, I oversaw ordering and inventory control within a budget. I interacted with buyers and vendors to take care of the needs of the Air Force personnel stationed at Edwards, and their families. I also handled customer complaints when I was the manager on duty.

I learned the hard way the importance of constant vigilance. Base exchanges frequently have visits from regional or corporate managers. These visits are called inspections. At one inspection, my area received a poor review. The shelves had many holes and the area just did not look as sharp as it could. After the visit, an assistant of one of the managers took the time to meet with me. He advised me that I needed to walk the floor every single day in order to be alert to any potential problems. His advice seems so obvious in retrospect; but I took it to heart and never had a bad visit again.

In 1994, I moved to the Four Seasons building next door to the exchange at Edwards. I was the sales area manager for appliances, home and garden, hardware, toys, and sporting goods. However, we were in a separate building, I actually supervised two managers who in turned supervised the sales associates in the area. During my time at Edwards, my areas averaged $5 million in sales a year. I acquired the important skills of how to manage my department, and its employees.

In 1995, I declined a transfer to Camp Zama in Japan, and I left AAFES and Edwards, and moved back home to Oklahoma. I immediately rejoined AAFES as an hourly paid supervisor at the Class Six store on Tinker Air Force Base. A Class Six store is the base or post liquor store. My store averaged $4 million in sales a year in a store the size of an average convenience store at a gas station. As a supervisor I reconciled the registers at closing, ordered merchandise, stocked the shelves, processed invoices, and trained employees. Of course, I also worked the register. The seasonal fluctuations at the Class Six were comparable to those at Dillard's and Edwards. However, employees at a liquor store have the added stress of customers that are potentially inebriated. We could be held liable if we sold alcohol to someone we suspected was drunk (Rookey, 2011). Fortunately, I rarely encountered this situation, and the base security police were always quick to respond any time we called for assistance. I left AAFES in 2000 to finish my library degree at the University of Oklahoma. My time with AAFES was a good bridge to working in an academic library. While it was still retail and stressful, my work for AAFES gave me the good feeling of serving military families just like mine.

Reference Service

My journey to St Cloud State University includes several retail stops along the way, from a store going out of business, to a liquor store on an Air Force base. A large portion of my reference service is informed by each of my retail work experiences.

I learned many skills along the way that I apply daily. What exactly are the skills required to provide excellent reference service? The Reference and User Services Association (RUSA), a division of the ALA, has developed several guidelines and standards for the provision of reference service. The recently updated *Guidelines for Behavioral Performance of Reference and Information Service Providers* (American Library Association, 2013) has the most alignment with my work in retail. These guidelines include: Visibility/Approachability, Interest, Listening/Inquiring, Searching, and Follow-up. Guidelines like these represent a desire to standardize service to library patrons. Interactions between the patron and service largely determine the customer's perception of the service (Wetzels, Ruyter & Bloemer, 2000). As Saunders (2013) states, "good customer service is the best way for librarians to ensure their continued relevancy in the future" (145). In addition to the five categories listed above I will explain how my retail experiences infuse through to my teaching.

Visibility/approachability

In a retail store, customers need to know who works there, and where they can get service. A library is no different. Self-sufficient customers and library patrons will always exist, but many do require assistance. My Dillard's experience is especially useful here. I was trained to roam around the lingerie department, and make some sort of initial contact with customers. While some of my co-workers were quite aggressive, I just wanted customers to know that I had seen them, and that I was available for assistance if they needed it. If a student comes to the Reference Desk when I'm with another student, I always make eye contact, and nod to acknowledge that the student has been seen.

Approachability means a demeanor that welcomes rather than intimidates. During my time at Edwards Air Force Base I received a wake-up call about the importance of approachability. My supervisor, the store manager, and the manager of all the AAFES facilities on Edwards called me into a meeting, and informed me that my co-workers, and employees at the store regarded me as unfriendly, and standoffish because I did not smile, and speak to them in the aisles and hallways. I have taken this lesson to heart over the years and I make a concerted effort to know everyone that I work with, and to greet them every time I see them. While I may not greet patrons individually, I do attempt to make eye contact with them as I walk through my library.

In order to successfully assist students, reference librarians must approach each interaction with tact and sensitivity. Bra fitters also need those skills in order to properly bra fit a woman. Students feel helpless when they ask a question, and admit they don't know how to find resources in the library. A woman at a fitting feels vulnerable and exposed when she acknowledges she's wearing the wrong size bra.

Interest

According to RUSA, "A successful librarian demonstrates a high degree of objective, nonjudgmental interest in the reference transaction" (2013). I find it much easier to indicate interest with library patrons than with customers. Interactions between customers and sales associates can have an adversarial component. At Dillard's, I learned to master the art of identifying a customer's desire without displaying the pushiness of a car salesman. The reference interview, in some respects, is easier than selling because the exchange lacks the tension of one person trying to sell to another. For the most part, library patrons don't ascribe negative motives to a librarian's questions. As Ross, Nilsen, and Dewdney state, "Clearly one of the most important factors in any interview is the extent to which the interviewer and interviewee share a common purpose" (2002: 2). My work in the Class Six store also taught me to express nonjudgmental interest. Sometimes a customer expressed concern that I thought only an alcoholic would buy a large quantity of liquor. In reality, our store was so busy I did not have the time nor the desire to contemplate a customer's purchase, I merely wanted the transaction to go smoothly and efficiently.

Listening/inquiring

Listening and inquiring are at the heart of every reference and sales transaction. I have to listen carefully and empathetically when a student describes an information need. The librarian has to continue to indicate interest throughout the reference interaction and not just at the beginning. One key to listening well, is to not act surprised or shocked by anything a student says or asks about. My work as a bra fitter definitely prepared me for this. I learned how not to blink or react negatively to anything I heard or saw. Each time I work with a student at the reference desk I try to remember that to ask for help makes a person vulnerable, maybe not quite as a vulnerable as a woman during a bra fitting but it's still a scary proposition to ask for help from someone you don't know. Another similarity between the two groups is that each person requesting help comes with a history that we don't know but that we must respect (Luciani, 2009).

Ross (2003) describes the reference interview as, "a creative, problem-solving process that is collaborative" (p. 38). The best way to solve a mystery is to ask questions. The process is complicated by the fact that the initial question of many library patrons does not accurately describe their actual information need (Dewdney & Michell, 1997). I primarily work with undergraduate students at our Reference Desk, and they are mostly unfamiliar with academic libraries. Like many patrons, they phrase their request in a way they think is most helpful to me. A student may ask for a book when an article would work just as well because books are equated with libraries (Ross, Nilsen & Dewdney, 2002). Interestingly enough, many women have similar misconceptions when they enter a lingerie department. Research reveals that 80 per cent of women do not wear the correct size bra (Shanahan, 2006). When I worked with a customer, I had to ask questions to uncover the issue that drove her to stop in and ask for help. Just like a student may ask for a certain book; a woman might specifically ask for a wire-free bra; when in fact the best professional advice would be: a properly fitted underwire bra—this actually being the woman's best fitting option, albeit not her preferred choice.

Searching

The searching aspect of reference work requires the reference librarian to process the information gathered from listening to the patron and asking questions of the patron, and matching the information need to the available resources. This step is much harder in library work than in bra fitting. The first step in a bra fitting is to measure the woman to determine what size bra she needs. Unfortunately, the result of a reference interview is not quite that precise. Additionally, in my lingerie department I could literally know every piece of merchandise and I could at a glance determine if a bra was available in the needed size. Obviously the large quantity of information resources available to any librarian makes it more complicated to match the information need, with the resource.

One similarity between the two transactions is the need to not overwhelm people with choices. A student doesn't need to know everything about how to use a library. The librarian has to read the cues that the student presents, and determine how much information can be processed. As Ross, Nilsen, and Dewdney describe, "most people would much rather have a small amount of information exactly tailored to their needs" (2002: 26). Oddly enough, I had to do something similar in bra fitting. I usually brought three bras into the dressing room with me. One bra might be a style that I was fairly sure would work for the woman while one might be something less obvious. While my department had a healthy selection of styles and sizes, I didn't want to over-whelm the woman by bringing in 20 bras.

Follow-up

Follow-up is the point in a reference or sales transaction where the librarian, or sales associate issues an invitation to return. While I may send a student off to work on searching the database I just demonstrated at the desk, I also stress that I will provide additional help if needed. During my time at Dillard's, I attended many sales training sessions to learn how to maximize sales. Bra fitting helped me to develop a steady base of customers who would come to the store just to see me. I found the best way to do that was to form a relationship with the customer, and suggest that she ask for me when she returned for additional purchases. The follow-up in reference, and in sales, is useless without the relationship-building that occurs earlier in the transaction.

Teaching

In addition to my reference work, at SCSU I deliver library instruction sessions, and I have also taught a credit-bearing information literacy course multiple times. My expe-rience as a manager, and supervisor for AAFES provides the most support for teaching. As a supervisor, I often coached my employees on new skills, or new procedures. Addi-tionally, I learned to set clear expectations for my employees much like I have to set clear objectives for the students I teach. Finally, I was often called on to deal with customer problems. This experience along with supervising taught me how to project authority; which helps me in the classroom. I'm not authoritarian in the classroom, but the ability to project authority does enable me to gain the students' attention when I need to.

Conclusion

While I draw on my retail experience daily, I won't suggest that every librarian become a bra fitter in order to deliver a superior Reference Desk service. However, I do advocate that librarians imagine a situation in which they are not the expert. Librarians simply know too much about searching and information resources to effectively put themselves in the shoes of a student who needs a peer-reviewed article for the very first time. For some librarians that situation just might be a bra-fitting, or perhaps a visit to the doctor's office. When, in the past, I straightened the panty tables (a Sisyphean task) or rehung bras that had been left in the dressing room—I never dreamed that librarianship was in my future. Although my retail life ended many years ago, I recognize how it shaped me.

References

American Library Association, Reference and User Services Association (2013). *Guidelines for behavioral performance of reference and information service providers.* Available from, http://www.ala.org/rusa/resources/guidelines/guidelinesbehavioral, Accessed 10 August 2014.

Army & Air Force Exchange Service (2014). *About Exchange.* Available from, http://www.shopmyexchange.com/AboutExchange/ Accessed 10 August 2014.

Belanger, M. (22 October 2007). Serving those who serve the U.S. *Convenience Store News, 43* (13), 183–185.

Davis, K. D. (2006). Mind the retail reference gap'. *Library Journal, 131*(9), 66.

Dewdney, P., & Michell, G. (1997). Asking "why" questions in the reference interview: A theoretical justification'. *The Library Quarterly, 67*(1), 50–71.

Gilman, H. (1985). Woolworth expects to post profit rise for its 2nd period, in steady overhaul'. *Wall Street Journal,* (13 August 1985).

Luciani, J. (2009). *The bra book: The fashion formula to finding the perfect bra.* Dallas, TX: Benbella Books.

MarketLine (31 December 2013) *Dillard's, Inc.* (company profile). Available from Business Source Premier database.

Miller, R. K., & Washington, K. (2009). 'Chapter 23: Military post exchanges'. In *Retail Business Market Research Handbook (pp. 141–42).* Loganville, GA: Richard K. Miller & Assoc.

Monget, K., & Eichner, S. (12 May 2008). Dillard outlines lingerie strategy in tough market'. *WWD: Women's Wear Daily, 195*(100), 12.

Nethero, S. (2005). *Bra talk: Myths and facts.* Smyrna, GA: Belle Books.

Rookey, B. (2011). Policies regulating alcohol, U.S. In M. Kleiman & J. Hawdon (Eds.), *Encyclopedia of drug policy* (pp. 645–648). Thousand Oaks, CA: SAGE. Available from, http://dx.doi.org/10.4135/9781412976961.n288, Accessed 10.08.14.

Ross, C. S. (2003). The reference interview: Why it needs to be used in every (well, almost every) reference transaction'. *Reference & User Services Quarterly, 43*, 38–42.

Ross, C. S., Nilsen, K., & Dewdney, P. (2002). *Conducting the reference interview: A how-to-do-it manual for librarians.* New York: Neal-Schuman.

Saunders, L. (2013). Learning from our mistakes: Reflections on customer service and how to improve it at the reference desk. *College & Undergraduate Libraries, 20*(2), 144–155. http://dx.doi.org/10.1080/10691316.2013.789661.

Shanahan, L. (9 October 2006). Bras: Worth having a fi. *Brandweek, 47*(36), 20.

Wetzels, M., de Ruyter, K., & Bloemer, J. (2000). Antecedents and consequences of role stress of retail sales persons'. *Journal of Retailing and Consumer Services, 7*(2), 65–75.

Thinking about meaning: how to be a philosophical librarian

Kevin Michael Klipfel

Meaning and conceptual analysis in Socratic Philosophy

Wise practice and the aims of Philosophy

Philosophers have traditionally sought to understand what the core, or essence, of a concept is, in order to understand its deeper meaning. This is true in the more general sense that philosophy as a discipline thinks systematically about "what it all means" and also, in the more concrete sense that philosophical methodology—*conceptual analysis*—involves a rigorous analysis of the meaning of abstract concepts, such as justice, love, knowledge, free will, and the meaning of life. Socrates, as depicted in Plato's dialogues, is an exemplar of this philosophical approach. For example, in Plato's dialogue, *Meno*, Socrates questions an aristocratic Greek named Meno about the rules by which a person ought to live. A brief examination of the beginning of this dialogue, where the philosophical conversation between Socrates and Meno is first introduced, is instructive for laying out the overall issues in this chapter. For here we see two main components of Socratic philosophy revealed: (1) the unrelenting belief that philosophical reflection has something to do with *practice* (in this case, about how we ought to live our daily lives); and (2) that philosophical analysis can shed light on our practice through *thinking about meaning* (the Socratic method of conceptual analysis).

Many of Plato's dialogues begin with Socrates discussing some ethical concept with an interlocutor after whom the dialogue is named; Plato's (1997) *Meno* is no exception. The dialogue begins when Meno, visiting Athens from Thessaly and aware of Socrates' philosophical reputation, asks Socrates whether Socrates believes that virtue can be taught. Meno, in effect, is asking Socrates whether he thinks young men can taught to be good, or whether the ability to know and act upon what is good is something innate within us.

To Meno's surprise, Socrates—whom Meno considers to be a wise philosopher interested in pursuing questions about how one should live—not only denies knowing whether virtue can be taught; he denies knowing what virtue even *is*. This claim requires clarification since it is prima facie puzzling for Socrates to deny having any knowledge of virtue. For, surely it is reasonable to think that Socrates, simply by existing as a man in the world, has some basic ability to demarcate right actions from wrong ones, and good lives from bad ones. And, indeed, Socrates' denial an understanding of virtue comes at the abstract, conceptual level: he claims not to know

Skills to Make a Librarian. http://dx.doi.org/10.1016/B978-0-08-100063-2.00011-9

what the *nature* of virtue really is (Plato, 1997). What this means, more specifically, is that Socrates seems to operate with the assumption that in order to be wise—to be expert at making good choices about how to live one's life—one must possess a certain kind of *knowledge*. The knowledge one must possess is knowledge of the deep conceptual meanings of ethical terms, according to which one may guide one's conduct. Why think this?

For one, most Western conceptions of morality are based on *rules*. "Don't lie"; "Don't cheat"; "Don't steal"; "Respect your elders"; and so forth, dominate our landscape of moral knowledge. These are the rules, implicitly or explicitly, that guide our conduct. These rules, however, have exceptions. To consider an extreme example, it might be morally permissible to lie if, say, one was protecting a family of German Jews during the Second World War, and the Gestapo was at one's door.[1] Similarly, a college student may feel an internal moral conflict over her desire to pursue a career in writing, versus her family's wishes for her to go to law school, where the moral rules "respect your elders" and "follow your heart" seem to fundamentally conflict. This being the case, if one were to guide one's conduct by the rules one is brought up with in society, one would, in effect, *not* be wise: one would make mistakes in practice; in concrete ethical situations where these rules failed. These mistakes would have practical significance, and would be based on an error in abstract thinking. Socrates was, therefore, after a more universal ethical principle—the "form" of all these rules of conduct—that would give us the proper moral knowledge so that we would be equipped to make wise choices, no matter the life context.

In this sense, Socrates was a philosopher, or a "lover of wisdom", in the deepest sense: philosophical thinking about how one should live was inherently practical. The point was to *become wise*, to think well about the stuff that matters to us, precisely so we can improve our decision-making in our actual lives. This is one reason why Socrates famously attempted to hold his philosophical interlocutors to the principle that they state only what they actually believed (Vlastos; 1991, 1994). Philosophy, for Socrates, was not a debate, and the conversation was not supposed to be theoretical. Rather, its goal was to discover truth: the truth about how the person Socrates was talking to actually lived, and whether the values that person adopted stood up to rational examination. If not, the person ought to revise their beliefs and replace them with better ones, less prone to moral error (Vlastos, 1994; Lear 2009).

It is worth stressing in this context that what we believe impacts what we do. Our ideas and concepts matter. My concept of, for example, what it means to be "man" determines how I conduct myself out in the world: whether I adopt a certain kind of male posturing, whether I am ashamed to cry in front of other people, whether I feel comfortable communicating my real feelings, and leaving myself vulnerable to others, is determined by my beliefs about whether these are appropriately "masculine" ways to behave (cf. Socrates' discussion of "Courage" in his dialogue *Laches*). Since beliefs play a role in determining our actions, and the Socratic Method was about examining individuals' beliefs, Socratic philosophical conversation had the potential to radically change the way people lived. Indeed, the Socratic Method, as actually practiced in Plato's dialogues, had a fundamentally *therapeutic* intent: to help people lead better lives (Lear, 2009). Socrates might have agreed wholeheartedly with

Marx's famous aphorism, that "the philosophers have only interpreted the world, in various ways; the point is to change it" (Marx, 2000: 173). This point is worth bearing in mind when thinking about the more abstract discussions presented here about philosophical inquiry. Our aim is not to think philosophically for its own sake, but to discover how thinking philosophically can improve our practice. Our inquiry is Socratic in this regard.

Thinking about meaning: Socrates and conceptual analysis

Socrates' practical aim was to examine people's ethical beliefs in order to improve the way they live; his method for doing this was what philosophers call "conceptual analysis". Conceptual analysis has long been the central methodology of philosophical inquiry; this form of inquiry is also at the forefront of Plato's *Meno* dialogue (Laurence & Margolis, 2003).[2] When Socrates attempts to elicit a definition of the meaning of virtue from Meno, he is asking one of his famous "What is F?" questions, where Socrates aims to figure out the core meaning of an ethical concept (Vlastos, 1991). He wants a definition that covers all cases of the concept being defined, and only cases of the concept being defined (Vlastos, 1991). This inquiry is important because understanding this core meaning would allow Socrates to have ethical knowledge that *transferred* to other contexts.

For example, when Socrates asks Meno what virtue is, and Meno replies that a man is virtuous when he properly manages his household affairs (*Meno*, 71e), this definition fails, for Socrates, because it merely gives an example of a virtuous action; it tells us (allegedly) what would be virtuous in one case, but not what would be virtuous in many, or even all cases (Vlastos, 1991). This superficial knowledge—knowledge that does not get at the core meaning of our practices—is relevant only in one context; thus, it would only give us the ability to make a wise choice in one context. Instead, we want knowledge that will make us wise, and tell us what to do in many contexts. In short, we want knowledge that is transferrable. And, since it is *knowledge of the core meanings of our practices* that is transferable to other contexts, this is the kind of philosophical understanding Socrates sought: transferrable knowledge of core meanings has practical value; superficial thinking about our practices does not.

Finding meaning in a philosophical education

When I first read Plato's *Meno*, in an Introductory to Ethics class at Houston Community College sometime in the spring of 2003, I had no grasp of philosophy as an academic discipline that attempted to get at the core meaning of things. What I was struck by, more instinctively, was a deep sense of identification with Socrates' quest. I was, let's say, a young man troubled about what he ought to do, and for whom the way most people went about things made little sense. As a young person, it struck me as strange that so few of the people I knew, or grew up with really questioned the values they had been brought up with; they simply went along. As a teenager I loved punk rock, and my suspicion is that the questioning of the rules we are brought up with was a major part of the attraction. Philosophy, it seemed to me, was just punk rock for adults: you got to sit there, and question things, and you got to do this in school, of all places. In philosophy class, a skeptical attitude toward life that had only ever really gotten me in trouble, became my greatest academic asset.

As an adult, I've spent a lot of time thinking about what interested me so much about philosophy, because it was the first time I ever connected with school. Prior to taking my first philosophy course, I experienced school as a boring thing to be endured. It just wasn't *interesting*. Looking back, this is particularly strange to me, because I have always been extremely interested: I always read extensively outside of class about all kinds of things. In fact, my own outside reading is what ultimately led me to sign up for a philosophy class. I'd attempted to read some Kierkegaard and Nietzsche, and ultimately, after realizing this wasn't really the kind of stuff you could understand on your own, I signed up for some classes. And philosophy connected.

For a long time I thought that it was the specific content of philosophy courses that interested me, but this is only partially true. It was not until ten years after first reading about Socrates, in a doctoral course in educational psychology in University of North Carolina at Chapel Hill's School of Education, that I realized exactly what I enjoyed so much about these classes. It wasn't so much that my teachers were Socratic gadfly's questioning the rules of society; in fact, most areas of philosophy had nothing to do with this at all. Rather, it was that my philosophy teachers, virtually without exception, focused on *the core meaning of the material* they were teaching (ostensibly because teaching philosophy *meant* talking about core meanings!). My experience was that their classes weren't about memorizing facts or dates or all those surface things that school had always seemed to be so much about, and that had always bored me half to death. They went deeper. Most teachers I'd previously encountered were like Meno: they'd stayed on the surface. The philosophers were different. The talked about what it all meant. They engaged me.

In my educational psychology class I learned that this is just what good teachers did. Like Socrates, they focused on the core meanings of things. Indeed, in his book *Why Don't Students Like School?*—the University of Virginia cognitive psychologist Daniel Willingham writes that, "a teacher's goal should almost always be to get students to think about meaning" (2009: 61). In order to see why this is important, it is worth getting clearer about the goals of learning. Educational psychologists Richard E. Mayer and Merlin C. Wittrock write that the "primary goal of education is to promote learning" and that "[t]wo classic measures of learning outcomes are retention and transfer" (2006: 289). A student who retains knowledge remembers what was taught; a student with the ability to transfer can use what has been learned; in a variety of new situations where the learning is relevant (Mayer and Wittrock, 2006). With these goals in mind, we can begin to understand the importance of a philosophical approach to teaching—getting students to think about meaning as a primary classroom goal—and its impact on classroom learning, and critical-thinking.

Willingham argues, based on the scientific data, that teachers must carefully choose their lessons so that their teaching makes students focus on the "right" things—the stuff that the teacher wants them to retain, and take away from the lesson.

This is important because, given the way human cognition works, what learners pay attention to—what the lesson actually gets students to think about—is what they will remember (2009). So, for example, a teacher must be careful when using a flashy graphic in an attempt to engage students' attention about some particular piece of subject matter. If what stands out to the student is the graphic, chances are, this is what the student will remember. Similarly, if a teacher's lesson focuses primarily on, say, superficial facts about a painter's life in order to engage them with the material, what the students will remember is that Vincent van Gogh cut off his ear, not the ways in which van Gough was a great artist. The point about student learning, and cognition, and memory that bears emphasis is that "[w]hatever you think about, that's what you remember" (Willingham, 2009: 61).

From this premise, Willingham concludes—much like Socrates encouraging his interlocutors to think about the meaning of their lives—that "[t]he obvious implication for teachers is that they must design lessons that will ensure that students are thinking about the meaning of the material" (p.63). Research indicates that students remember what they pay attention to; so, if we want students to take away from our lessons the core meaning of the material, it follows that this is what our lessons should be about. However, what is so important about focusing on core meanings, from an educational standpoint?

Like Socrates, one major thing educators want their students to do is to *transfer* what they've learned in class to other contexts. The point of learning is not for students to know what to do in *this* situation. Rather, it is for students to take their core under-standings learned in the classroom, and to use them as tools for life. Focusing on core meanings in the classroom prepares students to do this, because core meanings are what students can transfer to similar but unrelated concrete situations in their lives. It prepares students to think critically.

Applications to librarianship: what is the meaning of our practices?

This philosophy talk may be all well and good, but how do we get students to think about meaning in our professional practice as librarians? One obvious context within academic libraries where a philosophical approach will be most directly relevant is in information literacy instruction departments. As such, it will, perhaps, be useful to illustrate these more abstract points with examples drawn directly from this area of our own profession.

At the most general level, it may be useful for instruction librarians to reflect on their professional practice with a: "What is F?"—question of our own: *"What is infor-mation literacy?"* As we've seen, our beliefs about the nature of our practice have a direct influence on how we conduct our practice. In my own experience, I have noticed that our beliefs about what information literacy *is* have a substantial impact on what we *do* in the classroom. Although many instruction librarians may not have a worked out philosophy of what information literacy is, they invariably have a certain *way of looking at things* that impacts their classroom activities. For example, if one believes that the point of librarianship is to show students how to navigate sources, then much of one's time in both the classroom, and at the Reference Desk may be spent showing students the detailed nuances of particular databases. If, however, one looks at librarianship as about teaching students the process of research more broadly, the librarian may focus on conceptual—and, therefore, transferrable—research skills in their sessions.

Consider the simple example of database searching. A librarian who believes that the point of information literacy is to teach students how to use tools may spend a good deal of time during a one-shot information literacy session talking about specific details of many different databases. A philosophical librarian, one who takes as their core aim—to get students to think about the meaning of the material, might instead ask themselves—*"What is the point of teaching students about these databases in the first place? Why am I doing this?"* Reflecting on the deeper meaning of one's practice in this way may help the librarian to realize that the ultimate point of database instruction is not, like Meno, to tell us how to search *this* particular database. Rather, we want to teach students more general principles about how databases work so that they can transfer this understanding to other databases, even if they haven't previously seen this database specifically. As we've seen, this is simply what good teachers (and librarians) do.

A philosophical librarian, then, would think about the core meaning of this particular practice: what is a database? —And teach students the material in such a way that it would give them general principles (à *la* Platonic form) that will help them successfully navigate *many* databases.[3] This helps students learn transferrable skills that will be useful not just for a particular classroom assignment, but in their college careers, and beyond. Many librarians have begun to do this with conceptual, skill-based instructional videos. Two exemplars of this approach are the North Carolina State University Libraries (*http://www.lib.ncsu.edu/tutorials/* [Accessed 10 August 2014]) and EasyBib (*http://content.easybib.com/use-this-video-to-help-teach-the-first-stage-of-inquiry-based-learning/#.UztFsoVrjf0* [Accessed 10 August 2014]). These librarians are thinking philosophically about the *meaning* of the material they are presenting to students. Doing so, has allowed them to move beyond pointing and clicking. This is a principle that can be extended from the online environment to the face-to-face domain of the one-shot, and semester-long information literacy classroom setting.

Asking ourselves about the meaning of any particular practice we engage in as librarians has the potential to radically transform that practice. To take an example from my own experience, I have often considered, more generally, what is it that I would *really* like students to take away from my instruction sessions. Sure, I may have particular learning outcomes for any given information literacy one-shot. However, more deeply, I would like students to come away with a particular answer to the question: *"What is research?"*—with the understanding that research is simply an occasion to further investigate something one would like to know more about. This understanding—that research is just an occasion to look up something you're interested in—has radically transformed the way I approach instruction sessions, and the way I talk to students, and faculty about research. I talk to students about the library as simply a tool for finding quality information about an information problem they care about, rather than something external, imposed on them from without by the academic setting. And I show students practical strategies they can develop for using the library as a way to develop their own curiosity, and authentic interests.

Preliminary research suggests that this approach successfully engages students with research, and information literacy learning at significantly higher rates than instructional approaches that adopt a more "generic", less philosophical approach to library instruction. In 2013 I conducted a study of first-year undergraduates during information literacy instruction sessions at the Robert B. House Undergraduate Library at the University of North Carolina at Chapel Hill. Eight classes of students were randomly assigned into two different groups: (1) an *experimental group* for whom an approach to research as an occasion to look up something that interests you (relative to a class assignment) was modeled by the librarian within the context of searching the library databases; and (2) a *control group* for whom the librarian modeled how to search a more generic topic that did not necessarily fit the librarian's interests. Students were then asked several questions measuring their engagement, and information literacy learning, and asked to rate their responses from 1 (strongly disagree) to 5 (strongly agree) on a Likert scale, administered through Qualtrics (with a p value for significance of $<.05.$).

Students in the experimental group reported to have chosen topics that authentically engaged their interests at significantly higher rates (4.37vs.3.6; p=.000). They also reported increased levels of engagement with their project. For example, when asked whether they cared about their papers independent of the grades they received, students in the experimental group rated their interest at 3.80, as opposed to the control group, at 3.44 (p=.027). Students reported that this increased engagement led to an increase in information literacy learning. For example, students in the control group reported to be able to find information at consistently higher levels (4.08) over students in the control group who received standard database instruction (3.62) (p=.006).

These results are valuable because they provide concrete data that librarians can impact students' engagement with their work, even within the context of a one-shot instruction session. This has an enormous value for campus collaboration, since many faculty may struggle with engaging students in the research process. For this reason, it has been my experience that demonstrating to faculty that an approach to information literacy based on authentic engagement with the research process can help their students become more engaged with their projects, and help students find information more effectively—this being an excellent way to establish the value of information literacy on campus.

My thinking about how to engage students with research was largely drawn from my thinking about the meaning of this practice in a Socratic sense. If the meaning of our practice is to get students to think about research as an occasion to want to learn more about something, then, as the educational literature suggests, this should be the *focus* of our instruction. We want to tailor our session, and our lessons so that students explicitly think about, and are given strategies for approaching research in this way. This will allow them to approach the research process as a way to satisfy their own curiosity throughout their college careers, and also prepare them to be lifelong learners. This example, drawn from my own experience, highlights the fact that our philosophical beliefs about our practice—what research *is*—have a direct bearing on what we *do*. Thinking philosophically about librarianship is no abstract matter; it helps us improve our practice, and impacts how students learn, for the better.

The approach also illustrates a more philosophical way of thinking about student motivation and engagement in the classroom. Instead of asking what *tools* we can use to motivate students in the classroom we can ask ourselves, instead, in response to the question: What will make students want to learn?—*What makes people want to do stuff? What do human beings really want*? There is an extensive history of thinking—from existential philosophy, counseling theory, and the contemporary psychology of motivation—defending the position that supporting human beings' autonomy, and capacity for authentic living is intrinsically motivating. Motivational psychologist Edward Deci sums up this tradition nicely, writing that: "[w]hen autonomous, people are fully willing to do what they are doing, and embrace the activity with a sense of interest, and commitment. Their actions emanate from their true sense of self, so they are being authentic." (Deci & Flaste, 1995: 4). This fact about what it means to be human has serious implications for teaching and learning. Indeed, educational psychologists Assor, Kapan, and Roth (2002) write that:

> the primary task of the teacher is to try to understand their students' authentic interests and goals, and then help students to understand the connection between their personal goals and interests and schoolwork. In addition, teachers may also find or develop tasks that fit their students' interests. When students do not have clear personal interests and goals, teachers may assist them in developing such interests and goals" (2002: 273).

Thus, a philosophical approach to librarianship would involve brainstorming further ways to support students' autonomy, and authenticity in the classroom. This approach would focus on the *meaning* of engagement: it would directly focus on strategies at the core of what motivates human beings in and out of the classroom.

However, let me be even less abstract. When I was a graduate student instructor at the Robert B. House Undergraduate Library at the University of North Carolina at Chapel Hill, we would often get requests from faculty in the first-year writing program to teach students the difference between scholarly *vs.* popular sources. My perception is that there was a sense amongst certain librarians there, myself included, that a library session organized around teaching students this distinction was something we had hoped to move beyond doing. It's not that there was anything actually *wrong* with teaching students this distinction; I just thought that we weren't getting at the deeper meaning of why doing so was actually *important*. Why should anyone actually *care* about this distinction, in any deep way? What was at the core of its *meaning*?

Of course, librarians teaching this distinction were attempting to teach students how to evaluate information quality. This is valuable because many students are required by their professors to use so-called "scholarly" rather than "popular" sources in their papers; therefore, it falls to the librarian (as an expert on research) to inform students about the nature of this distinction. This has led many libraries to provide charts to students outlining the various characteristics of scholarly *vs.* popular sources, so students can delineate between the two. Methods such as the CRAAP (Currency, Relevance, Authority, Accuracy, Purpose) test have become popular ways to teach students information evaluation (http://www.csuchico.edu/lins/handouts/eval_websites.pdf [Accessed 10 August 2014]). So, for example, we teach students to evaluate whether a particular piece of information is credible by checking for bias; to see who published it; whether it has citations; and so forth.

This practice, however, is problematic for the philosophical librarian, for it encourages students to think about superficial indicators of what makes a piece of information credible, instead of what factors are constitutive of something being trustworthy or not *at its core*. These factors fail to get students to think about the deeper meaning of the material, that what makes something worth believing, and what does not, is whether it is reliable, and that reliability is constituted by the type of *evidence* presented (Fallis, 2004). As educators Ed Nuhfer and Victoria Bhavsar write, "the distinctive quality that separates those who do high-level thinking from those who do low-level thinking is effective use of evidence" (*http://tinyurl.com/knry9ue* [Accessed 10 August 2014]). This, then, is the *meaning* of the popular/scholarly distinction and, as such, it is what we want our lesson to get students to think about. This meaning gets lost, however, when the concept of evidence is not given central place (as in general discussions of the C.R.A.A.P. test, or the popular *vs.* scholarly distinction). Thus, in failing to be philosophical in our thinking about evaluating information quality, we have failed to get our students to think about the meaning of what we are teaching. This is just bad practice.

Conclusion

I hope this chapter has made clear that thinking philosophically—focusing on the core meanings of our practices—has enormous potential to influence our everyday practice as librarians. I hope it is also clear that thinking philosophically about librarianship does not require having any philosophical subject expertise *per se*. At bottom, what I learned as a philosophy student, and instructor was to focus on the core meanings of what I was learning or teaching. As an instructor, I believe that my main talent was taking the meaning of some abstract philosophical concept (say, Socrates' famous dictum that "the unexamined life is not worth living") and illustrating its importance through relatable, concrete examples (by, say, showing students Spike Lee's film *The 25th Hour* as a contemporary example of unexamined values leading to an individual's life going badly, or relating examples from my own life). What I could do very well, and which many incoming students could not, was take a basic abstract concept, and transfer it to many concrete life situations. I was able to do this because I had a deep understanding of the meaning of material, and this deeper understanding was what I hoped to transmit to my students.

The philosophical skill of thinking about meaning has been the single most valuable skill I have been able to transfer from my philosophical education, and lecturing career to my practice as an information literacy librarian. I believe that it is one of the single most important skills any instruction librarian can develop as well. Unless the librarian is thinking deeply about the core meaning of the material they are teaching; it is highly unlikely that our students will be thinking about the meaning of the material the librarians are presenting, either. This is not merely a failure in abstract belief, but a limitation in our practice. Our goal as librarians is to be successful practitioners; the surprise, for many librarians, may be that thinking philosophically about what we do can help us get there.

References

Assor, A., Kaplan, H., & Roth, G. (2002). Choice is Good, but Relevance is Excellent: Enhancing and Suppressing Teacher Behaviors Predicting Students' Engagement in Schoolwork" *British Journal of Educational Psychology, 72*, 261–278.

Brecher, D. (2014). Of Databases and Deep Structure. Available from, *Rule Number One: A Library Blog.* http://rulenumberoneblog.com/2014/02/17/of-databases-and-deep-structure/, Accessed 10 August 2014.

Deci, E. L., & Flaste, R. (1995). *Why We Do What We Do: Understanding Self- Motivation.* New York: Penguin.

Fallis, D. (2004). On Verifying the Accuracy of Information: Philosophical Perspectives. *Library Trends, 52*(3), 463–487.

Jackson, F. (2000). *From Metaphysics to Ethics: A Defence of Conceptual Analysis.* New York: Oxford University Press.

Kant, Immanuel (1993). *Grounding for the Metaphysics of Morals: With On a Supposed Right to Lie because of Philanthropic Concerns.* Indianapolis: Hackett Publishing.

Knobe, J., & Nichols, S. (Eds.). (2008). *Experimental Philosophy.* New York: Oxford University Press.

Laurence, S., & Margolis, E. (2003). Concepts and Conceptual Analysis. *Philosophy and Phenomenological Research, LXVII*(2), 253–282.

Lear, J. (2009). The Socratic Method and Psychoanalysis. In S. Ahbel-Rappe & R. Kamtekar (Eds.), *A Companion to Socrates* (pp. 442–462). Hoboken: Blackwell Publishing.

Marx, K. (2000). Theses on Feuerbach. In D. McLellan (Ed.), *Karl Marx: Collected Writings* (second ed. pp. 171–174). New York: Oxford University Press.

Mayer, R. E., & Wittrock, M. C. (2006). Problem Solving. In P. A. Alexander & P. H. Winne (Eds.), *Handbook of Educational Psychology* (pp. 287–303). New York: Routledge.

Plato (1997). Plato: Complete Works. In J. Cooper (Ed.), Indianapolis: Hackett Publishing Co.

Quine, W. V. (2004). Two Dogmas of Empiricism. *Quintessence: Basic Readings from the Philosophy of W.V. Quine.* Cambridge, Mass: Belknap Harvard (pp.31–63).

Vlastos, G. (1991). *Socrates: Ironist and Moral Philosopher.* Ithaca, N.Y: Cornell University Press.

Vlastos, G. (1994). Socratic Studies. In M. Burnyeat (Ed.), New York: Cambridge University Press.

Willingham, D. T. (2009). *Why Don't Students Like School?: A Cognitive Scientist Answers Questions About How the Mind Works and What it Means for the Classroom.* San Francisco: Jossey-Bass.

Endnotes

1. Albeit, see Kant (1993) for a dissenting view.
2. It is important to note that, especially in recent years, conceptual analysis as the dominant philosophical methodology has not gone unchallenged. For example, the Harvard philosopher W.V. Quine famously rejected the "analytic-synthetic" distinction upon which the methodology of conceptual analysis seems to depend (see Quine, 2004); (see Jackson, 2000) for a representative defense. Similarly, the so-called "experimental philosophers" have emerged, in recent years, to challenge *a priori* thinking about meaning in philosophy (although not, it seems to me, thinking about meaning more generally) (see e.g. Knobe and Nichols, 2008). (However, these issues are far beyond the scope of this chapter, and do not bear on its central theses.)
3. For an excellent in-depth discussion of these issues (see Brecher, 2014).

Ladies and gentlemen, welcome aboard!

12

Meredith Lowe Prather

Introduction

For three years I flew the friendly skies as a flight attendant at a regional airline. I began work on my Masters of Library and Information Science while flying for the airline. When I left the airline industry, I went to work as an academic librarian at a local technical college, where I discovered that I could still use many of the skills I had been developing over the previous three years. Effective and successful librarians and flight attendants must provide excellent customer service to a variety of people while still completing set tasks within a limited time period, and dealing with constant change. Skills learned at 20,000 feet translate well into the library setting. I learned that if I can successfully calm fears, subdue anger, and answer questions while in a metal tube flying through the air, I can do it anywhere, including while successfully working with the needy researcher, the demanding attorney, or the mad public library patron. Working as a flight attendant also taught me the importance of time management. There are a lot of tasks that need to be completed within a limited amount of time during a flight. Understanding what was most important and when it really must be done has helped me prioritize tasks, and responsibilities. Airlines and libraries can both be fast-paced environments . . . or mind-numbingly slow. Knowing when to roll with the punches, and to always, always pack a book, my knitting, and a snack—has paid untold dividends. Come fly with me to better librarianship!

During a flight: understanding what was most important, and when it really must be done has greatly helped me prioritize both tasks, and responsibilities on the ground. Airlines and libraries can both be fast-paced environments . . . or mind-numbingly slow. Knowing when to roll with the punches, when to walk away, and to always, always pack a book, my knitting, and a snack has paid untold dividends. Come fly with me to better librarianship!

How may I help you today?

By far the most important skill I learned and honed while flying was how to work with people. Customer service is often talked about, studied, and promoted, but how often do we make a conscious effort to analyze how we interact with our coworkers and customers? A flight attendant's first job is to ensure the safety of her passengers and crew. However, most passengers see her as a supplier of snacks, drinks, and

Skills to Make a Librarian. http://dx.doi.org/10.1016/B978-0-08-100063-2.00012-0

answers to their questions. This is where customer service really is key. It is by far easier to maintain a safe cabin: when everyone is happy, even in trying situations. This meant that I constantly had to perform a role, and reevaluate how I was being perceived. I learned the value of apologies, explanations, confident smiles, and a thick skin.

Apologies are hard but gracefully acknowledging when I had made a mistake, dealing with the repercussions, and moving on, made my life easier. Never was this made plainer to me than one very hot summer day at a small airport in the high desert. My day had started very early and we were on flight four or five. I was simply looking forward to being done for the day soon. The plane was a small one: we only carried 37 passengers, and there was no air-conditioning while we were parked at the gate. The heat and lack of air were stifling.

It was approaching departure time, and all personal electronic devices were required to be turned-off and put away before I could shut the door. A little boy of about seven was sitting with his father in row three. The boy was contentedly playing a game on a handheld gaming system. I began my announcements to prepare the cabin for take-off, directing passengers to stow their bags, and put up their tray tables. I pointedly looked at the little boy when stating that all electronic devices needed to be turned-off, and put away. As anyone who has repeatedly said or read the same thing over and over and over again can tell you, it is very easy to let your mind wander while your mouth continues the rote recitation. I was trying to figure out what the boy's device was called so I could tell him to turn it off. *Gameboy*? *Play Station*? Oh, what was it?! Unfortunately, what I told him was, "Okay son, it's time to put your *Playboy* away now".

Dead silence.

My face flushed as bright as my red uniform polo shirt. Laughter and smiles filled the cabin. Thankfully, the little boy didn't understand what was going on and his father told him to put his *Gameboy* away. I apologized to my passengers, finished my announcement, secured the cabin, and shut the airplane door. Throughout the entire flight, including all the passengers deplaning, I was teased about the *Playboy*. Instead of getting defensive, and confrontational, I just laughed with my passengers, and took the teasing in the good-natured way it was offered. It made for an unforgettable flight, but one I always remember with smiles instead of cringes.

The *Playboy* incident also serves as a good reminder to me to always listen to what I am saying, whether it is at story time, during a presentation to the board of directors, or interacting one-on-one with a patron. The times that I am not paying attention, and consciously thinking about what I am saying are inevitably the ones when I completely mess up . . . or I end up volunteering for a task or giving wrong information to a patron.

Sometimes the situations aren't so fun. Once, I told a passenger he could move to another seat, but then the captain told me he had to stay in his original seat for the plane to take-off safely. This is not an uncommon occurrence on small planes. Knowing I should have checked with the captain first, I had to return to the passenger and tell him to return to his original seat. That did not make for a happy passenger. All I could do was apologize, and try to come up with an alternative to soothe his ruffled feathers, perhaps the ability to move once we had reached cruising altitude or a complimentary glass of wine. It is never easy to admit culpability, but it is the best way to defuse a tense situation, and begin fixing the problem.

For me, this is even harder when I have let down a co-worker or supervisor. This happened to me with a major project at a library. I was tasked with finding, choosing, and implementing a new cataloging system. Unfortunately, a few months into building the new system, it became obvious that it wasn't going to work. It was a disaster. I felt like a complete failure. I summoned my courage, and told my boss that we had to scrap the whole thing, and start again from square one. We did, and I started researching options again. Eventually I did find a new, better program and we implemented that. I felt awful about the failure, and brought it up during my review. Instead of repri-manding me, my boss reminded me that sometimes admitting when you are wrong or have made a mistake shows that you are making the right decision. He didn't consider the project or me a failure because I had been willing to stop the project, and admit I was wrong in choosing the previous software before we invested more time, energy, and money in to the wrong program.

However, sometimes the situation isn't your fault. You've done nothing wrong, yet someone you are working with, co-worker or customer, is creating a problem situation. The flight attendant is the only person a passenger can address on an air-craft when she is annoyed, frustrated, or angry. The Federal Aviation Administra-tion, and its policy writers aren't there to complain to, and explain rules. The airplane is not a good listener, especially when a part is broken, and that is why we aren't moving. The person who stocked the beverage cart isn't there to tell you why he didn't put more beer on board, resulting in you only receiving a single glass instead of the full 22-ounce bottle. However, the flight attendant is, and inev-itably will be confronted.

Apologizing for the situation or the trouble may be appropriate. I cannot tell how often this happens on airplanes (and, I am sure, at public library reference desks). "I'm sorry we will be arriving late, but we want to be sure that we will be arriving safely and our pilots cannot land if they can't see the runway. We will do the best we can to help you with your connection. Here is what you need to do to help your chances of making your connection when we reach the airport". The apology shows that I am listening, I acknowledge the validity of his concern and frustration, and I empathize with his situation. There isn't much I can do but offer what solutions I can. He still might miss his connection and may still be angry, but I did my best to alleviate his concerns.

Being late or canceling a flight due to weather or mechanical issues was one of the three biggest complaint-generating situations I dealt with on board. The other two, the use of personal electronic devices and properly stowing bags, were due to federal regulations. I cannot tell you the number of times that people challenged me or completely ignored my directions to turn-off their cell phones, and other personal electronic devices for take-off and landing, and to not use devices that sent or received a signal during flight.

"But the *Mythbusters* told me I could use my phone during flight. It doesn't really do anything. Besides, the pilots listen to the radio in the cockpit all the time."

"The *Mythbusters* may say so, but federal law disagrees. In fact your cell phone use *can* cause problems with the pilot's headphones and other equipment. The radios the pilots use in the flight deck are built and work differently than your phone. Turn your phone off."

Yes, this conversation actually happened on one of my flights. (In fairness to the *Mythbusters*, several years later I watched the episode when they investigated this issue. They did not say that you could use your phone in flight. They said they couldn't actually test it and that viewers should obey the law.[1]) Instead of apologizing, I explained why the phone needed to be turned-off. Granted, patience isn't easy when you have to deal with the same issues multiple times in a day or are given ridiculous excuses as to why someone is entitled to bend the rules for his own benefit. Explaining to a woman that her purse must be completely under the seat in front of her so that it doesn't become a projectile or a tripping hazard in an emergency gets tiresome. Or, as a librarian explaining to a student or researcher yes, you really do need to cite your sources in an academic paper. The explanation may not always satisfy the passenger, patron, or coworker, but people are often more willing to abide by rules when they are given a logical reason why they should.

When passengers still wouldn't comply, and it was possible and appropriate, I would call in help. If you appear intoxicated before a flight, I'm calling a gate agent to take you off my flight. If you threaten me, I'm calling the police. If you refuse to turn your phone off, I'm letting the captain know, and she/he will tell you to turn it off. If that doesn't work, you'll be removed from the flight. It is important to know your resources, including other people, and to call on them when it is appropriate. I did kick people off my flights for being intoxicated. I rarely hesitated to ask a fellow flight attendant to talk to a difficult passenger. Passengers would often interact differently with different flight attendants, and if that didn't work, the captain always backed us up. Knowing my coworkers would help me was vital in boosting my confidence when dealing with passengers. Even if I didn't get along very well with my fellow crew members or we disagreed about some issues, I knew that when it came to enforcing the rules that make us all safe, I would be supported. Likewise, if they needed that support, I would provide it for them. This was providing good customer service to both my coworkers and my passengers. I still use this policy today even though I no longer deal with safety issues. I know my co-workers will support me when I need it because I strive to treat them with respect, we establish policies, and procedures prior to problems occurring, and I support them when they need help. When a patron asks me if I will scan an entire book for him in violation of copyright laws, I say no, and my boss will back me up because I have proven to him that I make judicious decisions.

One last thought on customer service: providing apologies, and explanations or requesting help doesn't always work. Sometimes passengers just didn't want to comply with what was required, or did so only under stringent protest, or weren't satisfied with the explanations I offered. If I took such interactions personally, it would ruin my flight and my day, so learning to respond with a smile, and develop the ability to not take passengers' meanness, anger, and frustration personally became extremely important. It wasn't easy. I naturally smile a lot, but my skin isn't always that thick. I didn't always succeed, and people or situations rankled me. I couldn't always let them go. It is still a struggle for me some days, but when I manage to remember that it's not personal and tomorrow I get to start over, life becomes much easier.

Through my three years of flying, I gained the confidence that I could handle just about any situation. I learned it is okay to admit when you don't have the answers as long as you are willing to find them out, and to ask others for help, and that an explanation can provide the motivation needed to follow—or prompt compliance with—rules. A smile, personal confidence, and a thick skin are invaluable when working with people. All these skills I learned as a flight attendant, but they remain broadly applicable in my everyday work as a librarian.

You want me to do all that? In 30 minutes?!

There are certain tasks that must be completed during a flight: pre-flight briefings, and cabin walk-throughs, multiple public announcements, at least one beverage service (on most flights), galley inventory, and supply orders filled out, pre-landing briefings and cabin walk-throughs. That is during a normal flight when nothing goes wrong and there are no questions or special requests from passengers. One of our most popular routes that still required a beverage service could be as short as 25 minutes from take-off to landing. After factoring in the time it takes to reach an altitude at which a flight attendant is allowed to leave her seat: that left about 15 to 20 minutes of in-air work time. That is not a lot of time to complete the previously mentioned tasks, including serving beverages to 76 passengers. How were my fellow flight attendants and I successful?

We started by preparing as much as we could prior to the flight. This meant filling out as much of the galley inventory as possible, and prepping the items needed for the beverage service that could still be stowed safely for take-off. After take-off, some of the announcements could be completed while still in my seat. On these flights I would be working with one other flight attendant. We would discuss who would do what during the flight. Some things had to be done at certain times, such as specific announcements, or in a certain order, such as saying the pre-take-off announcement before walking through the cabin to check that bags were stowed, and tray tables up and locked. By working together, we could divide the tasks so as to accomplish them in the most efficient manner possible. During a 25-minute flight, efficiency is the only way to be successful.

Throughout the flight, we would complete our tasks as quickly as possible. This is where practice was extremely helpful. My first few flights were awkward and rushed. By my hundredth flight, I knew the best way to set up the beverage cart in a way that facilitated a speedy service. I had learned the rhythms of the flight, and how to work best within them. The practice made an incredible difference in how well I was able to do my job.

Even with preparing in advance for a flight, delegation of tasks, and practice—there were still days when everything on a flight was just not going to be completed in our allotted time. Some days, we experienced turbulence, and the pilots asked us to stay in our seats longer than usual. Other times, a passenger needed some extra help with some special circumstance. Suddenly, our useful flight time could be reduced from 20 minutes to 10. On those days, prioritizing tasks, and being comfortable not completing tasks when we knew that they were simply not feasible were the only ways to ensure a successful flight. Some tasks are mandated by federal law or company policy, and are required to be completed for the safety of everyone on the flight. Obviously these tasks were of the highest priority, and could not be ignored. On short flights like this, the beverage service was one of the few tasks that we could afford to drop without risking anyone's safety. We might get some annoyed or disappointed passengers, but ensuring a safe cabin was the reason for my job, and the most important aspect of what I did. Establishing my priorities on a legal, company, and personal level made it much easier to ensure that the most vital tasks were completed as well as many or all of the other tasks.

As a librarian, this mentality helps when sorting through my email inbox, and working with multiple research requests. What can be answered quickly, and completed in a few minutes? What is going to take a half-hour, or an hour to complete? What is going to take longer? Is this task something that is urgent? More importantly is it urgent in relation to my professional responsibilities and goals? Just because the requester says it is urgent doesn't mean it really is. I'll ask a few follow-up questions to determine how urgent it really is. It's for a presentation tomorrow, and is for the organization's CEO? Yes, I'll be right on it. The paper is due in a month, and the question answers a minor aspect of the paper? Yeah, I'll get to that soon, but it's not at the top of my list of tasks.

I also try and prepare myself for tasks I know will be coming soon, and delegate when someone else can do the task, or I know I won't have time to complete it in an acceptable timeframe. I enjoy processing and cataloging incoming material. However, I have a lot of other managerial, and research tasks that I must ensure are all completed. This means I tend to assign processing and cataloging to my employee. To help both of us stay focused, I keep two white boards on my office wall where I list out all of our different projects. Under each project are listed the tasks required to complete the project, when they need to be completed, and who is responsible for completing them. All of these are color-coded for quick comprehension. I list any holidays, vacations, conferences, or other events that will be taking staff members out of the office as well. When a task is completed, I strike it out with bright colored ink, and leave it up for a while before erasing the project. It's a good feeling to know that some projects, and tasks are completed. The white boards are an effective, constant visual way to monitor progress, prioritize, and ensure all projects are completed in a timely manner. I also try to pay attention to, and ask about what is happening in other areas of my department and organization. If I know another department has a big event coming up, I can budget my time to be available to assist or have materials on hand that they may need.

Not all flights are short, nor all work-days busy. I distinctly remember working one overnight assignment during which my fellow flight attendant, and I found out that we would have 14 passengers on our two-hour and 45-minute flight later in the day. Thankfully, we had some time before we had to report to the airport, and decided to visit a yarn shop. I bought small needles and fine yarn. During the flight, we spaced our announcements, and the beverage services evenly throughout the time in the air. That still gave us a lot of time without specific tasks to complete other than keeping an eye on the cabin and passengers. I cast on, and re-taught myself to knit. By the end of the flight, I had made significant progress on a scarf. Ever since then, I have been sure to always have a knitting project, a book (audio and/or physical), and a snack tucked in my purse for when the need arises. I have certainly been known to pull out my knitting during a webinar or at a conference. It has often been a great conversation starter, and helped me to meet some wonderful information professionals.

In an office setting, it isn't often appropriate to pull out my knitting, but I don't always have urgent tasks to complete. At these times, it's nice to have a list, or at least be aware of the tasks around the office and library that need to be done, but are easy to start, and stop as needed. Processing and cataloging incoming or backlogged materials, curating bibliographies, and catching up on professional literature are some of the tasks I work on when I don't have anything urgent to complete. They are also good tasks for when I need a change of pace for a little while, or only have a short block of work time before a meeting or the end of the day.

The best way to manage my time is a constantly changing as my circumstances, responsibilities, and energy levels change. I know if I take the time to list out the tasks that I need to complete, and roughly how long they will take, I gain a better understanding of how I need to plan my time to be effective. It allows me to see if, and what needs to be delegated to another person. Sometimes it means acknowledging that something won't be completed in the originally desired timeframe, and adjusting other plans as needed. Being aware of what is going on, and what needs to be done, streamlining tasks as much as possible, delegating when appropriate, and letting go when necessary allow me to be as effective a professional as possible.

What just broke?

One lovely day in a small airport, I greeted my passengers as they boarded for our long flight. My day had been going well. I was flying with pilots I liked, we were running on time, and so far, everything had run smoothly. My passengers were all pleasant, and complied when I asked them to stow their bags, and turn-off their phones. Door shut. I began my next safety announcement. Halfway through, I heard, "ding dong". The pilots were calling from the flight deck. Pilots never call from the flight deck during announcements. Something was up. It turned out that a very important switch, which essentially starts the aircraft's engines, had broken off in my captain's hand. We weren't going anywhere anytime soon. The captain I was flying with that day was a wonderful man who understood both the power of explanations in tough customer service situations, and his influence because of his position. He kindly gave a quick announcement over the intercom explaining to passengers what had happened, and that we would not be taking-off soon. He then finished all of his required tasks in the flight deck, and came out to the cabin to explain in person the situation more clearly and answer any questions he could. The passengers were rebooked on a flight a couple of hours later. It must have been a full moon because even that flight had issues landing due to a deer that wouldn't stop running all over the runway. My crew and I waited for the parts, and a mechanic to fly out, and repair the plane before heading back to base without passengers much, much later that night.

It was not a fun situation for anyone involved. Everyone's day was interrupted, passengers missed connections, and we had our entire work week changed. However, it happened, and there was not anything that anyone on the plane could do to fix it. We all just had to deal with the situation as it was. Thankfully, the passengers on this particular flight were understanding—upset, but not angry or abusive. My crew and I shrugged our shoulders, changed into civilian clothes, borrowed the airport car, and went into town for dinner. We couldn't change the situation, so we adjusted our expectations for the day, and kept positive attitudes. Instead of spending a miserable seven hours at the airport sitting in a broken airplane, we ate a hot meal, and delicious ice cream, and wandered around a small university town.

This is a perfect example of why it is so important to be flexible. It is inevitable that things will go wrong during some work days. The catalog just crashed. Your staff can't process books. The library's website is down. No one can search the catalog for books or access online subscriptions. The printer is down, and all the students have waited until the last minute to print their papers. Handling the situation with grace and flexibility will go a very long way toward making the situation better for all involved. It may even rescue your day. Instead of asking what else can go wrong (believe me, something will)—ask what can we do? The cataloging service is down. Is there other processing that can be done? What about some of those projects you listed out to do when you had some downtime? The website is down. Can you access the catalog from a different route? Are there ways to access the articles needed through other websites? Can you point patrons in the general area of bookshelves where the book they are looking for would be? The printer isn't working. Are students printing to the correct printer? Is there paper? Can you fix the printer? (And how many of us learned early in our careers that much of our time in the library would be spent fixing the printer or the copier?) Is there another printer available?

However, what if the answer is no? What if you have been thrown so many loops that you can't see straight, and a positive attitude is hard to muster? In these times, I have learned I just need to step away.

My last winter as a flight attendant was a particularly brutal one. There was a several week stretch where snow and other weather issues shut down the majority of airports in four States—the four main States we flew out of, and where the majority of our pilots and flight attendants lived, including me. The blizzards hit while I was working a trip in one of the States not affected. Unfortunately, this meant my crew, and our aircraft had to fly flights for crews snowed in. After two weeks of this I was ready to sleep in my own bed, and wash my clothes in a real washing machine. Finally, the snow melted and airports opened. I was headed home. One flight, and a long drive to my house and I would be able to see my bed. Then I got the call saying I was needed to fly one more round trip.

No. I couldn't do it. I didn't have the reserves mentally or physically to safely do my job. I called off the trip. When we landed, I headed to my car knowing I had made the best decision I could make in order to take care of myself, and my passengers. I still didn't make it home for several more days because of snow on the roads, but I was able to rest, and know that no one was depending on me. And I found a washing machine.

Working in a library, I get to go home every night. That doesn't mean I don't get overwhelmed or exhausted or run out of patience. Walking away sometimes is appropriate here as well. I go for a walk around the building. I walk down the street to a café, or to the break room for a snack, and a quick cup of tea. These few minutes away from my desk, and my computer allow me to breathe. I can collect my thoughts, and ponder my current challenges without interruption. It's a chance to refocus, and be prepared to be more productive when I get back to my desk. Really, a snack, and tea make everything better.

As we prepare to land ...

Who would've thought that flight attendants and librarians had so much in common? Both jobs require quality customer service both to our co-workers, and the general public. Sometimes this means that we have to deal with difficult, tense, unsafe, or simply ridiculous situations that we have to navigate to positive outcomes. Keeping a positive attitude while listening to our customers, offering apologies and explanations, and calling for help when needed will help us provide the best customer service possible. Each new successful interaction gives us the experience, and confidence to continue succeeding. Our work days are busy. Being prepared, prioritizing, delegating, and making plans help us to effectively use our time, and resources to complete necessary tasks. Having an understanding of what is happening in the organization, and community around us, allows us to ensure customer satisfaction. Finally, knowing when, and how to adjust plans when things go wrong, and when to take a break— allows us to continue to be productive professionals.

Neither life as a flight attendant, nor life as a librarian is easy. There are days when working with people, the schedule, and the constant change can get the better of us. However, they can also be very rewarding careers if we embrace the challenges presented, and choose to stay positive.

Thank you for traveling with us and have a nice day!

Endnote

1. *MythBusters* (Discovery Channel, 15 March 2006).

Visual literacy meets information literacy: how two academic librarians combined information science, and design in their careers

13

Mary J. Snyder Broussard and Judith Schwartz

Introduction

There is growing discussion of "visual literacy" and a corresponding increase in the use of images and visual media in higher education. The Association of College and Research Libraries (ACRL) (2000) recently felt it was time to address this trend when they published the Visual Literacy Competency Standards for Higher Education in 2011. Additionally, one of the rationales for the need to revise the ACRL Information Literacy Competency Standards is an "explosion of [visual, data, and multimedia modes of scholarship and learning] and the increasingly hybridized, multi-modal nature of learning and scholarship require an expanded conception of information literacy learning and pedagogy beyond the mostly text-based focus of the Standards" (Framework Taskforce, 2014: 3).

Mayer and Goldenstein (2009) demonstrate how the rising use of images in undergraduate teaching and learning is affecting library services. They found that 85% of librarians who responded to their survey reported that they were instructing students on how to find images for school projects, including presentations, papers, posters, exhibits, as well as for fine arts, and theatre inspiration. Many also help faculty to find images for class lectures, class analysis exercises, online instruction, and publication. Finally, a small but significant number of respondents reported helping campus public relations (24%) and development offices (21%) locate images. Nearly half of respondents subscribed to ARTstor, with others reporting subscriptions to other image and map databases.

Not only do academic libraries need visually literate professionals who can assist library users in finding, formatting, creating, and displaying images ethically, but libraries also require attractive and effective visual materials for their website, marketing, instruction, and archives. Because, budgets in academic libraries are usually too restricted to hire professional graphic designers and visual design is often so intertwined with professional philosophies and instructional design that librarians with backgrounds in graphic design are well placed to serve many of the libraries' design needs. This chapter will introduce two academic librarians' previous experiences in graphic design departments and demonstrate how those experiences enhance their role as library professionals.

Skills to Make a Librarian. http://dx.doi.org/10.1016/B978-0-08-100063-2.00013-2

Visual literacy

ACRL defines visual literacy as: "a set of abilities that enables an individual to effectively find, interpret, evaluate, use, and create images and visual media" (Hattwig, D., Burgess, J., Bussert, K. & Medaille, A. 2011). Five of the seven Visual Literacy Competency Standards are directly adapted from ACRL's Information Literacy Competency Standards. The additional standards include an explicit need to interpret and analyze visual media and the importance of being able to create new media. Librarians with graphic design skills are uniquely able to provide library users with advanced assistance in the last two standards, which involve creation and ethical use of images.

Standard 6 of the Visual Literacy Competency Standards states, "The visually literate student designs and creates meaningful images and visual media." Librarians are increasingly collaborating with faculty and various support services on campus to support students as creators of new knowledge. In many (if not most) libraries, reference librarians offer technical help when students ask computer and software questions. Some libraries even offer multimedia labs with design software and access to large-format printers in the library. Regardless of whether or not one's library has such a lab, there is an increasing use of images in academic courses and students are expected to include images in posters, presentation slides, displays, and papers. Librarians are a readily available and highly visible source of help to these students who do not necessarily distinguish such questions from those related to research help. Reference librarians are often helping students print, create and manage PDFs, find images, save and format those images, select the right software for the purpose, and use formatting features in commonly used word-processing programs.

Having a background in graphic design and photo manipulation greatly enables a librarian's ability to help students as image creators. It enables a librarian to assist students with the tools in design programs, use image-related equipment, and take advantage of the lesser-known design tools in more familiar programs such as Power-Point, Publisher, and Word. An advanced understanding of image quality, file size, and the merits of various file types better enables librarians to help users prepare images for the end product. For example, a poster will likely need to be converted to a high-resolution PDF to be sent to a printer to avoid pixilation in large format. In contrast, an image for a website should be set to the final dimensions, and then saved as a low-resolution JPEG, PNG, or GIF file (each of which has its own benefits and drawbacks) in the smallest possible file size in order to load as quickly as possible. Power-Point slides can be compressed for better delivery of online learning or to be loaded into course management systems with file size limits. Librarians with graphic design experience are better equipped to assist with these advanced image creation questions.

Standard 7 of the Visual Literacy Competency Standards addresses the need to understand the "ethical, legal, social, and economic issues surrounding the creation and use of images and visual media." When one has experienced the need to adhere strictly to the copyright laws that govern images in the publishing and marketing world, one develops a different perspective on promoting the ethical, and legal use of images created by others. A solid understanding of copyright and intellectual property is critical in the publishing field. The materials being produced are often widely distributed. The publishing industry takes these very seriously because intellectual property can be worth a lot of money and not respecting the established legal guidelines can leave a publisher or advertising firm subject to expensive lawsuits. Considerable resources are spent documenting who owns the intellectual rights of the materials to be published.

Intellectual property, plagiarism, and copyright are foundations of the ethics of librarians, though their manifestations are different from the publishing world. Librarians are legally bound by the contracts with content vendors, but beyond that they tend to be more concerned with the *ethical* side of this issue, while the marketing and publishing world tends to be more immediately concerned with the *legal* side, and students and faculty are granted a great deal of freedom under Fair Use for educational purposes. Yet sometimes it is useful to have a stronger understanding of the legal side, and that is where a background in publishing is particularly useful. Many librarians do not realize how different (and vastly more complex) copyright laws for images are than for text and how rights for use differ greatly depending on whether the image will be used within the classroom or for campus marketing materials such as theatre posters. A background in image rights research assists a librarian in providing faculty with copyright assistance for publication.

Design needs in academic libraries

Before entering librarianship, neither author was aware of the great need for design in libraries. In library school, Judith learned of the many ways libraries use art and design including branding, wayfinding, signage, renovations, curating revolving art shows, library art installations, and academic publishing in addition to presentations, newsletters, and literary publications. It was not until Mary began her professional career that she found her desire for creative projects was well matched to public services in an academic library. This section will focus on four areas in which the authors have experience with design in academic libraries: marketing, web development, instruction, and archives. While some of these needs can be outsourced to other campus departments or vendors, there are many reasons why some of these design jobs are best done by a librarian.

Marketing and outreach directly affect what potential library users know about and feel towards the library. Academic libraries compete with students' natural tendencies to run to free and easy information that often does not meet the quality standards of their assignments. Libraries have similar missions with faculty, staff, and the broader community. They need to establish their brand as a source of high-quality print, and online resources, attractive spaces for individual and group study, and high levels of customer service. Above all, they must convey themselves as user-centered, and that begins with the marketing material inviting potential users to the physical and virtual library.

Effective marketing relies heavily on visual design as the visual appeal is what initially grabs viewers' attention. Langton and Campbell (2011) write, "The world is visual. We use our eyes to take in much of the content that influences our behavior, tempers our reactions, and informs our decisions. Whether it's on the Web, in a brochure, or live in person, the most effective solutions are the ones that unexpectedly grab our attention". Before viewers even read the library's marketing materials, they are absorbing the non-verbal messages communicated through images, color, and layout. Students (the primary audience of academic library marketing) are bombarded with posters and email messages. When they see a poster from the library, they make instant, unconscious judgments based on visual design about whether reading the text is worth their time and energy. If the answer is no, they will not even read the text. It is therefore important for the library's printed and digital marketing materials to be visually attractive in order to be effective.

Outreach events often bring a particular segment of the wider community into the library with the assumption that some attendees are not regular library users but have the potential to become so. These events also tie into the non-academic mission of the larger institution, which is to provide students with fun and safe extracurricular activities that become an important part of a student's overall college experience. Exactly what such an outreach event entails will vary depending on the particular needs of a library's users and the organizational culture of the larger institution. For example, an outreach event at a university of mostly non-traditional commuter students may be a formal open-house event, while an event at a residential college with mostly traditional students may look a lot like a program one would expect to find at a public library. Regardless of the type of culture, these outreach events often involve visual design to engage participants, as we shall demonstrate later in this chapter.

The academic library's website serves as a front door to the library's online information resources and finding tools, marketing the library's services and collections, and providing various instructional resources. Visual design plays an extremely important role in website development, being nearly indistinguishable from usability, information architecture, and overall effectiveness (Krug, 2006; Nielsen & Loranger, 2006.) Lindgaard, G., et al. (2011) cite numerous studies that tie visual appeal of a website with perceived quality, usefulness, and trustworthiness. Many academic libraries are either required or choose to use the larger institution's web theme, which was most often developed by a group of trained and skilled graphic designers, web coders, and marketing specialists. This requires librarians to negotiate with those administrators responsible for that theme to make sure it meets the unique needs of library users. However, if such negotiations are successful, this facilitates the library in providing their website visitors with a professional, and visually appealing first impression.

Within the institution's web theme, the library should have a visually literate individual to create clear, uncluttered pages, use images to portray effective messages, and create an information structure that allows users to easily find what they are looking for. Newell (2004) studied library website images and found that librarians needed a greater understanding of visual communication principles as they were inadvertently communicating undesirable messages to potential library users. Library website managers should exploit the power of images to portray it as a user-centered organization dedicated to quality.

A recent survey of American library directors shows that a dedication to library instruction is a nearly universal priority of academic libraries (Howard, 2014), and design also plays a role in creating effective instructional materials. In fact, design is so important to instruction that Grassian and Kaplowitz (2009) dedicated an entire chapter to it in their important book titled *Information Literacy Instruction: Theory and Practice*. They write, "Librarians may not be trained in instructional or graphic design, yet often they must create a range of instructional materials and formats to support both in-person and remote learning for many ages and skills" (Grassian and Kaplowitz: 173). Their chapter integrates visual design into suggestions for instructional design, with a breakdown of how visual design should be adapted depending on the medium in which the instruction is delivered. They discuss the need for white space, the importance of color choices on academic performance, how to properly use graphics, and the effect of font choice.

Librarians often rely on class handouts to remind students of the more mechanical or factual information when the students go to do the actual research after the class. Even with few colors or images other than an occasional screenshot, clear organization, layout, use of white space, and font selection make an enormous difference in the educational effectiveness of these class handouts. Similar design principles are required in the creation of online tutorials as well, with the likelihood that more video, audio, and color will be necessary, as well as the ability to select an appropriate technology to create and deliver the tutorial to potential users.

Many academic libraries manage the college or university's archives. These archives house relics and documents of the institution's past to inform current students, administrators, as well as help alumni continue to connect with the institution. Many archives are making their collections more accessible by digitizing them, which is facilitated by having easy access to someone with an advanced knowledge of formatting and ethically managing digital images. Additionally, as one key purpose of an institutional archive is to help various constituents connect with the institution, graphic design skills allow the library to create attractive displays, publications, blogs, and materials for outreach events.

The authors' previous experiences

The two authors of this chapter have each worked in graphic design departments in previous employment positions. Each author will introduce her former life in publishing and marketing and describe how the skills developed in those positions enhance their current careers as academic librarians. In the context of this chapter, Mary and Judith have very complementary experiences. While Mary only spent a year in a graphic design department and the skills she learned were more related to design software than design, the skills developed in that position have enabled many creative projects in her position as an instructional services librarian, though they bear little resemblance to a traditional idea of graphic design. In contrast, Judith is just beginning her career as an academic librarian, but had many years of experience as an art director and graphic designer. Her projects in libraries more closely resemble those of a professional graphic designer. Their combined experiences offer a unique perspective.

Mary J. Snyder Broussard

Shortly after obtaining her bachelor's degree in French and German from Miami University of Ohio, Mary Broussard obtained a job as a copyeditor in a children's craft supply company in the Chicago area. The primary duties of the position included checking accuracy, spelling, and grammar on product packaging, and creating project instructions. Furthermore, she translated all packaging and instructions into French for any products destined for Canada. As the main function of this position revolved around packaging, this position was housed in the graphic design department. Secondary duties included corresponding with relevant magazines to get the company's products featured and posting images and project ideas on the company's website.

While the position was not that of a graphic designer, she was surrounded by graphic designers and expected to learn basic skills in the popular graphic design software Adobe Photoshop (used to manipulate photographs) and Illustrator (used to create line drawings). Photoshop skills were particularly important for the craft project ideas displayed on the company website, as this involved not only creating attractive projects with craft foam, pom poms, and pipe cleaners, but also generating attractive photographs of the project, generating printable templates, and manipulating purchased stock photographs so that the company website showed children playing with new products. Inserting a company's product into stock photography is a common practice for issues of ease and cost. The professional graphic designers that she worked with were busy working on packaging, so she had to quickly learn Photoshop well enough to make the images for the website believable.

During the time that Mary was in this position, she decided to attend library school. She took many experiences and skills from her 14 months in this position, but most tangible of these skills were those directly related to graphic design software, with some basic skills obtained in marketing, and website development. After completing her MLS degree at Indiana University, she began work as an instructional services librarian at Lycoming College, a small private residential institution in central Pennsylvania, where she has been for nearly eight years. At her library, there is a non-librarian employee who serves as production artist for official library marketing, including the popular READ posters of campus professors, and student groups. However, Mary has found that it is often critical for a librarian to directly create some graphics. This eliminates the need to always have to explain one's vision to someone else. There have been many times in Mary's experience that the graphics were too intertwined with technology or instructional design to be given to someone else.

From very early in her position at Lycoming College, Mary took advantage of Banned Books Week to create an outreach event around her love of young adult literature. It began as a display the first year with a poster and an offering of frequently challenged books from the library's collections and quickly developed into a series of trivia games that invite student, staff, and faculty participation. Each of these Banned Books Week events has involved graphics skills, either in the form of advertising or to create the trivia games. In 2009, Mary used Adobe Illustrator to create eleven pictograms representing well-known, frequently challenged book titles (see Figure 13.1). She posted the pictograms around campus and asked students and faculty to submit completed game sheets to be entered into a raffle for a local gift certificate. In 2010, she used Illustrator again to recreate frequently challenged book covers stripped of all text. These were posted around the library and Lycoming community members were invited to submit their title guesses to be entered into a raffle. There was a significant amount of talk about these trivia programs, but only a few students took the time to submit game sheets. Participation increased enormously as the annual trivia games moved to the library's Facebook page with instructions to submit individual guesses for each book title by email. The increase in the participation and visibility of this particular outreach event has meant that each subsequent year Facebook has been used with similar results in attracting large numbers of participants. The trivia games have evolved over the years, but they have always used design software in their creation.

One of Mary's primary duties is to maintain the library's extensive website. At Lycoming College, the library uses the college's website template which was created by professional designers and web developers on staff. The library director and she have worked with the campus web developer to make minor accommodations to the campus template and guidelines to best meet the needs of library users. This allows the library to provide an attractive and sophisticated page that has a consistent feel with other college pages. Within the web theme, Mary uses images to portray the library as a friendly place and promote special events. She also formats logos and images to be inserted into database headers as that customization feature becomes more prevalent among database vendors.

Mary has used graphics software and basic visual design for a number of instructional purposes. She teaches approximately 50 information literacy classes per academic year. Layout, contrast, and hierarchy are important factors she considers when creating handouts for each of these classes. Images such as screenshots are used when they are likely to be helpful, and they often require well-positioned, succinct, and uncluttered labels.

One of Mary's favorite examples of graphics skills transferring to academic librarianship is the game-based learning it has enabled at Lycoming College. In 2013, the Higher Education Horizon Report cited games and gamification as one of the upcoming technology trends that will change education (Johnson et al., 2013). Gamification has the potential to help learners embrace the assigned learning goals and absorb more information because students are enjoying the learning process. Building educational games requires skills in many areas including understanding of basic game mechanics, good pedagogy, relevant technology, and appealing graphics. This is ideally done by a team. However, effective educational games are often built for specific, local learning goals, and therefore often do not have significant resources allocated to them. Mary has worked to make effective, small-scale games where she plays the primary part in all aspects of game development, including the graphic design. She has worked with colleagues to create a number of online, real-world, and hybrid games, each of which involved using design software such as Adobe Illustrator, Photoshop, Dreamweaver, and Flash.

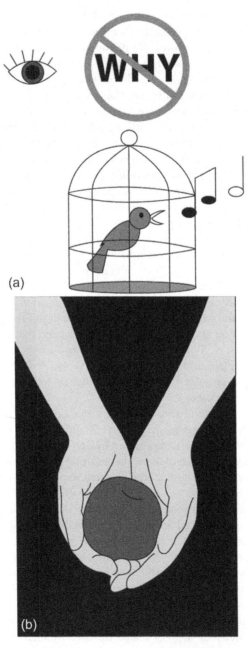

Figure 13.1(a)–(b) Two examples of line drawings created in Adobe Illustrator for the annual Banned Books Week trivia contest. **(a)** A pictogram representing *I Know Why the Caged Bird Sings* by Maya Angelou. **(b)** Representation of the cover of *Twilight* by Stephanie Meyer. Images designed by Mary J. Snyder Broussard.

In an effort to redesign the freshman orientation event to be more engaging for students, it was turned into a treasure hunt game where students completed educational activities to find letters and complete a ransom note that revealed the location of the "missing" unofficial campus mascot (Gregory & Broussard, 2011). One of the learning objectives was for students to simply acknowledge the existence of three locations; the vending machines, the Leisure Reading Collection, and the Academic Resource Center (important, but not administratively part of the library). For these three locations, we borrowed a brilliant low-tech augmented reality game idea from Burke, Kreyche, and Maharas's "Ran Some Ransom" game developed for the 2009 Come Out and Play festival. In "Ran Some Ransom" players lined up transparencies to views in Times Square. The transparencies outlined what existed in reality, with additional circles highlighting letters to be used in the ransom note. To re-create this idea of low-tech augmented reality for the freshman library orientation, Mary imported a digital picture of each of the three library locations into Adobe Illustrator, traced the photograph, and highlighted a letter to be used for the ransom note (see Figure 13.2 below).

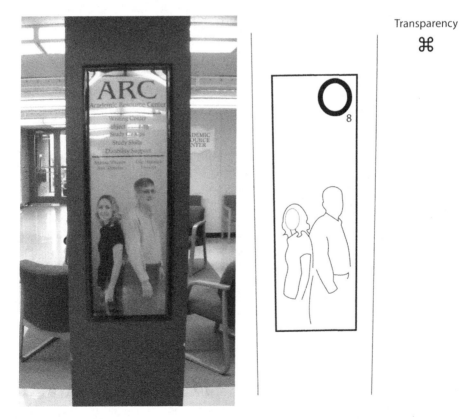

Figure 13.2 A photograph of Lycoming College's Academic Resource Center (ARC) sign next to a transparency outline. When players look through the transparency and line-up the outlines to the poster, the C becomes highlighted as Letter 8 for their ransom note. Photograph and line art designed by Mary J. Snyder Broussard.

Mary created *Goblin Threat*, an online game to teach students how to identify and avoid plagiarism, in 2009 using Adobe Flash (Broussard & Oberlin, 2011). While she had not learned Flash as a copy editor, her knowledge of Adobe Illustrator greatly facilitated the learning curve in drawing figures in Flash. When the graphics and programming were completed, Mary worked with a colleague to write the questions. The resulting project's success has been enormous. Not only was it very well-received on Lycoming's campus, she has received over 70 requests to use or link to the game from other schools, colleges, and universities around the world and has identified over 40 additional institutions that link to the game from their website. Due to this high volume of external traffic to *Goblin Threat*, it is one of the most visited pages on the entire campus website. This is an enormous return on the investment of time to develop the game.

While Mary's time as a copy editor was relatively short, and it would be a far stretch to consider her a *graphic* designer, she is a web designer, an instructional designer, and a game designer. She continues to use Adobe Photoshop, Illustrator, and Dreamweaver on a regular basis in her duties as an academic librarian. Knowledge of this software has enabled her to learn other software such as Adobe Flash and HTML5 to build online games and tutorials. Furthermore, she learned a great deal about the design and editing process, which have further inspired and enabled her creative outreach and instructional projects.

Judith Schwartz

Judith is working on combining her career skills as information professional, and visual-design communicator. Prior to her library career, she worked as an art director and design manager on numerous textbook projects at various design studios for major educational publishers in the K-12, ESL, scholarly and reference, and university press markets. With a BFA from The Cooper Union School of Art and an MA in Advertising and Communication Design from Syracuse University's College of Visual and Performing Arts, Judith has designed book interiors and covers, logos, and marketing materials for clients including McGraw-Hill, St. Martin's Press, Scholastic, Highlights, Harcourt, Pearson, and Oxford University Press.

Her career has included collaboration with editors, authors, designers, illustrators, photographers, photo researchers, and marketing teams to develop marketable book products. Besides designing, doing image manipulation, photo research, and assigning projects to illustrators and photographers, she has years of experience managing projects and staff, as well as working with outside vendors and printers. At various times throughout her career she has been an adjunct professor teaching graphic design-related courses in a classroom setting at Long Island University's Southampton Campus and online at The Art Institute of Pittsburgh, Online Division. Judith is adept with graphics software and uses the Adobe Creative Suite.

Due to the changing climate in the publishing industry, outsourcing, and other factors, she became interested in transitioning to a career in digital archiving. She decided to go to library school and graduated from the Palmer School, Long Island University C.W. Post in the winter of 2012 with an MSLIS and Certificate of Archives and Records Management. While she entered library school leaning towards a digital archives career, she became increasingly interested in academic librarianship. She began interning at Hunter College Library/CUNY as a reference and instruction librarian, and became an adjunct at Hunter upon receiving her degree. She was able to try out many of her new skills and felt very well suited to working on archival projects, teaching, and online and face-to-face research assistance with students.

Judith thought her graphic design career was going to be very separate from her new career direction and was planning on maintaining two separate identities, but to her surprise, it has evolved into one career. She has had interesting short-term positions and internships that have enabled her to utilize many of her prior career skills in her current full-time position as a librarian. In July 2013, Judith was hired as a librarian at Medgar Evers College, City University of New York. Medgar Evers is an urban campus in Brooklyn with an entirely commuter student population. In addition to teaching information literacy one-shot classes and her daily reference desk duties, Judith supervises interlibrary loan. Graphic design quickly became a regular part of her job responsibilities as well.

It was not long after Judith began working at Medgar Evers College that she was asked to design a set of bookmarks to promote the library's services while the library on campus was being renovated (see Figure 13.3). The purpose was to attract students to the library's temporary location and the slogan was "Alive at the Library". The library administration wanted four bookmarks for the departments including "Reference and Information Literacy", "Instructional Media Services", "Circulations and Access Services", and the "Archives", and "Special Collections", Judith's goal was to make the bookmarks fun, colorful, and inviting. She chose a bright color palette for the vertical sidebars so each department would have its own color identity. She sought out images from the library archives that were relevant to the school's mission of civil rights and social justice. She was also able to download royalty-free art that she was able to later manipulate in Adobe Illustrator.

The bookmarks have been distributed at the circulation desk, the reference desk, in instruction classes, and at library exhibits. Additionally, another college office distributes the bookmarks to potential students at area high schools. The initial printing of bookmarks proved to be so successful, they have undergone a second printing. Judith and the library have received many positive comments about the bookmarks from students, faculty, and other campus offices. They were such a promotional success that they evolved into her creating additional projects including a media screen slide to advertise library services on monitor displays around campus and a large tri-fold table display board used as a backdrop at events when promoting the library (see Figure 13.4).

In December of 2013, the Medgar Evers College Library launched a new outreach event called Holiday Extravaganza, which included music, art and photography, break-dancing, and poetry created by the talented library staff. Judith designed the colorful program and performance agenda that would be handed out at the concert and a corresponding media screen slide that would be projected on the monitor displays around campus. As Judith was also showing some of her own photo collage

Figure 13.3 Bookmarks: promote the library's services and direct students to a temporary location. Bookmarks designed by Judith Schwartz.

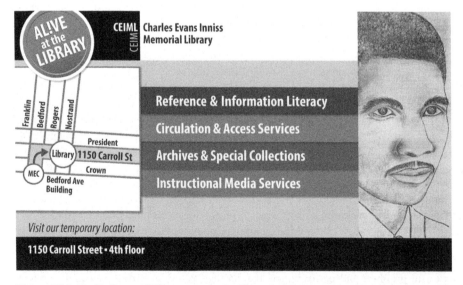

Figure 13.4 Media Screen Slide: promotes the library's services on monitor displays around campus. Slide designed by Judith Schwartz.

Figure 13.5 Event program brochure: *Holiday Extravaganza*. Program designed by Judith Schwartz.

artwork at the event, she decided to carry some of the themes over into the program design (see Figure 13.5). She also photographed the library staff for the program and manipulated images in Photoshop to fit the project specifications. The Holiday Extravaganza event was a major collaborative effort and a great way for the library staff to work as a team. While the turnout for the event was small, it really showed the library staff was "Alive at the Library" in the temporary library space. There was a great deal of enthusiasm generated by the event and this will surely be an annual occurrence for years to come.

Shortly afterwards, the archivist at Medgar Evers College was interested in producing a publication of Library Resources for Black History Month and asked Judith to partic-ipate in the design. The main content of the pamphlet consisted of a bibliography of books that could be found in the library's Special Collections, Caribbean Collection, and eBook Collection. In order to maintain the library brand, Judith designed the pamphlets to com-plement the Archives and Special Collections' bookmark so it looked like it was part of a series (see Figure 13.6). The pamphlets were displayed at the reference and circulation desk and were brought to several outreach events during Black History Month.

Judith's initial interest in archives led to several interesting archival projects. While she was in library school, she volunteered and later became a paid contractor on a pro-ject as an archival photo and film researcher for a documentary related to housing

Figure 13.6 Pamphlet: *Black Diaspora*, a bibliography of select books in the Special Collections, Caribbean Research Library, and Electronic Resources. Pamphlet designed by Judith Schwartz.

rights activism on the lower east side of New York City. Her job responsibilities included locating photos and film footage in online digital photo repositories in addition to research at various historical archives. Excellent data management and organization skills were essential, as she needed to keep track of where images originated, box numbers and folders, online repositories, and image banks. She managed and conducted the tedious photo review meeting process with the other participants. Copyright issues and permissions were also addressed. In addition to the documentary, Judith worked on several digitizing projects at Hunter College's Archives and Special Collections. She scanned and digitized deteriorating scrapbooks of clippings and images that entailed detailed retouching, repairing, and piecing images together in Photoshop, and then created PDF files.

Having established a solid career in the publishing field, Judith is a true graphic designer and artist. Her extensive experience with printers has enabled her to work with the campus print shop and to overcome numerous technical issues that arose in creating a quality product for her library. Her projects and the processes to develop them more closely resemble those of a professional design firm, allowing the library to project a very professional and sophisticated image in their marketing materials.

Abstract skills

The past experiences of the authors have provided each with advanced visual literacy skills. The specific projects described in this chapter show how these skills have benefited their respective libraries. Yet there are many other related skills gained from working in the field of graphic design that adapt well to library work. This section will discuss those skills, and how they can facilitate one's preparation to become an academic librarian and assist users in unique ways.

Organization, in all of its manifestations, is incredibly important in the marketing and publication worlds. Everyone must work together to create an excellent end product that is visually pleasing, easy to read, editorially correct, and delivered on time. This means that designers must be organized, attentive to details, and able to manage their time well. Organization is the foundation of libraries. Resources should be stored in an extremely systematized manner, and finding systems should be built to work within that structure to enable users to efficiently locate relevant resources. Librarians need a solid understanding and appreciation for the organization of library systems in order to meet the mission of the library.

A key part of this organized environment is good time management. It is crucial to create deadlines and keep to the schedule. However, because there are many parties involved in the process, it is important to clearly communicate this schedule with everyone involved. Perhaps one of the more challenging aspects of doing graphic design in the library environment is that academic libraries are less deadline-driven and also most librarians and administrators are not aware of the time the creative process requires. Good communication is particularly important to help them set realistic expectations in regard to a schedule that works for everyone.

As a copy editor in a graphic design department, it was Mary's primary responsibility to pay close attention to details. On the packaging, the image, all words, and product number all needed to correspond to the item contained within. Spelling and grammar also had to be perfect. Many aspects of the packaging needed to be carefully checked during multiple rounds of edits. Sending faulty packaging art to the manufacturers was expensive and time consuming to correct. It needed to be accurate when sent. This attention to detail is important to libraries as well. Catalogers and indexers must be precise in their organization if patrons and reference librarians are to be able to find the items when needed. Marketing materials need to be attractive and editorially correct in order to be effective. Finally, mistakes in computer code may render parts of the library's website or a tutorial unusable.

A final important aspect of organization is good file management. It is important for a department to establish file-naming conventions, organize files so they are findable later, and frequently back-up files. Designers maintain the PSD (Photoshop Document) layered files so they can easily modify them if needed, though these must be converted to other file types such as high-resolution JPEGs or PDFs for printing or low-resolution JPEGs for uploading on a website. As multiple files are created for a single project, some of which may require special fonts, all files should then be properly stored at the conclusion of the project. In a library, organized file management allows for items to be easily found by various members of the staff for editing, reuse, or upgrading to new technology.

In addition to organizational skills, collaboration is also an important skill for designers. Throughout Judith's graphic design career, managing and designing textbooks was an extremely collaborative process. She participated in group concept meetings with authors, editors, and designers, laying out books and deciding what images and text would fall on each page, and assigned photo specs for historical images so that researchers could then acquire the images from stock photography agencies, museums, and archives. She was also a photo researcher on several social studies book projects. Mary worked closely with graphic designers, members of the company's marketing team, magazine editors, and translators. There are so many special skills required in marketing and publication that collaboration and good communication are crucial in working towards a quality end product.

Libraries are also collaborative environments. Librarians in many areas of specialization work together as well as with paraprofessionals and student workers to provide quality collections, and services. Librarians also work with vendors to ensure electronic tools are working properly, and become more useful to the end-user over time. They collaborate with faculty to provide instruction, with patrons to meet their individual information needs, and with various student groups and other organizations on campuses to market their services and generally participate in the mission of the larger institution. Archivists often work with local historians and alumni to collect artifacts that represent the institution's history. These are just a few examples of the many ways librarians work collaboratively to meet the community's needs.

Conclusion

The need for visually literate professionals in academic libraries is twofold. A librarian with advanced knowledge in the area of image ethics and creation can better support students and faculty in an academic environment that is using an increasing number of pictures and photographs. Additionally, libraries have many design needs, particularly in the areas of web development, marketing, instruction, and archives. While many librarians develop a level of proficiency in these areas, having at least one librarian on staff with additional skills and training in design can be quite valuable.

Mary and Judith are creators and designers in addition to librarians. They love the collaborative nature of librarianship that offers the chance to work closely with students, faculty, and staff in other departments. They also love that academic librarianship offers so many creative outlets, which provide a great deal of personal satisfaction. At the same time, academic libraries have an important institutional need for in-house design, and software skills in many areas. This chapter shows a number of examples where their design skills have met a need in their respective libraries, and there were many more examples that could have been included. There is definitely a place for innovative, visually literate librarians who can combine a knowledge and dedication to the philosophies of academic librarianship with various forms of design skills.

References

Association for College and Research Libraries. (2000). *Information Literacy Competency Standards for Higher Education'*. Available from, http://www.ala.org/acrl/standards/informationliteracycompetency, Accessed 10 August 2014.

Broussard, M. J. S., & Oberlin, J. U. (2011). Using Online Games to Fight Plagiarism: A Spoonful of Sugar Helps the Medicine Go Down'. *Indiana Libraries, 30*, 28–39.

Burke, E., Kreyche, C. M., & Maharas, L. (2009). *'Ran Some Ransom', Come Out & Play Festival*. Available from: http://comeoutandplay.org/2009_ransomeransom.php, Accessed 04.04.14.

Framework for Information Literacy for Higher Education Taskforce. (2014). *Framework for Information Literacy for Higher Education, draft'*. Available from: http://acrl.ala.org/ilstandards/wp-content/uploads/2014/02/Framework-for-IL-for-HE-Draft-1-Part-1.pdf, Accessed 31.03.14.

Grassian, E. S., & Kaplowitz, J. R. (2009). *Information Literacy Instruction: Theory and Practice*. New York: Neal-Schuman Publishers.

Gregory, A. S., & Broussard, M. J. S. (31 March 2011). *'Unraveling the "Mystery" of the Library: A "Big Games" Approach to Library Orientation'*, Presentation at ACRL 2011. Philadelphia: PA. Available from: http://www.ala.org/acrl/sites/ala.org.acrl/files/content/conferences/confsandpreconfs/national/2011/papers/unraveling_the_myste.pdf, Accessed 04.04.14.

Hattwig, D., Burgess, J., Bussert, K., & Medaille, A. (2011). *ACRL Visual Literacy Competency Standards for Higher Education'*. Available from: http://www.ala.org/acrl/standards/visualliteracy, Accessed 26.03.14.

Howard, J. (2014). *What Matters to Academic-Library Directors? Information Literacy'*, Chronicle of Higher Education. http://chronicle.com/blogs/wiredcampus/what-matters-to-academic-library-directors-information-literacy/51005?cid=at&utm_source=at&utm_medium=en, Accessed 04.04.14.

Johnson, L., Adams Becker, S., Cummins, M., Estrada, V., Freeman, A., & Ludgate, H. (2013). *NMC Horizon Report: 2013 Higher Education Edition*. Austin, TX: The New Media Consortium.

Krug, S. (2006). *Don't Make Me Think: A common sense approach to Web usability*. Berkley, CA: New Riders.

Langton, D., & Campbell, A. (2011). *Visual Marketing: 99 Proven Ways for Small Businesses to Market with Images and Design*. Hoboken, NJ: Wiley.

Lindgaard, G., Dudek, C., Sen, D., Sumegi, L., & Noonan, P. (2011). An exploration of relations between visual appeal, trustworthiness and perceived usability of homepages'. *ACM Transactions on Computer-Human Interaction, 18*, 1–30.

Mayer, J., & Goldenstein, C. (2009). Academic Libraries Supporting Visual Culture: A Survey of Image Access and Use'. *Art Documentation, 28*, 16–21.

Newell, T. (2004). Representing Library Users and Professionals on Websites: A Visual Grammar Approach for Library Image-Makers and Library Educators'. *Journal of Education for Library and Information Science, 4*, 307–316.

Nielsen, J., & Loranger, H. (2006). *Prioritizing Web Usability*. CA, New Riders: Berkley.

Pedagogy for librarians

14

Megan Hodge

Introduction

While K-12 teachers take numerous classes on teaching methods and educational psychology, and even doctoral students sometimes get a semester on pedagogy before they're thrown into the classroom, most non-school-librarians must learn on the fly, or from colleagues at conferences. What we pick up in the field, though, tends to be things like active learning techniques, pop-culture-sourced research topics with special resonance for our students, and effective assessments that can be executed quickly, all of which are useful and even desirable in the classroom. These may result in engaging lessons, but put us in danger of repeating the same information to students when they return to the library, weeks later, asking for help on their papers because they've forgotten what we covered in class. Without an understanding of pedagogy, and how learning works, we are doomed to teach material without its being learned.

In this chapter, I hope to bridge that gap. I am a relative rarity in the librarian world in that I went through a battery of education classes in college in order to obtain a secondary teaching license, meaning I've had much more training in learning theory than the majority of my librarian peers. This by no means makes me a master teacher—I am a recent library school graduate without many semesters of teaching under my belt—but what I learned in my education classes and my experiences teaching English to middle and high school students informs my practice as an academic librarian. I still have much to learn, and spend a fair amount of time researching instructional design and keeping up with the literature, but I am a much better teacher than I would have been otherwise as a fresh-out-of-library-school instructor. What I bring to the table is a broader understanding of the mechanics of teaching, and how learning works, with an emphasis on linking theory to practice.

I have organized this chapter into three sections: preparing for teaching, things to keep in mind while in front of the room, and improving instruction outside the classroom. While these strategies are hardly comprehensive—all of them could, or do have, entire books written about them—I hope they will be useful on their own, and serve as amuse-bouches for further examination. Many of these strategies are recursive, and feed naturally into and build upon each other. Finally, I have tried to write in a way that will make these recommended strategies painlessly, immediately employable to the practicing instruction librarian, whether that instruction takes the form of a semester-long course or one-shots, as well as provide some recommendations for further reading (with full citations for these recommendations in the References section).

Skills to Make a Librarian. http://dx.doi.org/10.1016/B978-0-08-100063-2.00014-4

Before class: getting ready to teach

Lesson plans: write them

One of the first things future teachers learn in their education classes is the importance of creating and using lesson plans. Ideally, these lesson plans include a list of materials necessary for the class (e.g., handouts), learning objectives (more on which below), and an outline of the class structure: the main topics to be covered, any activities, and notes on anything you'd like to make sure you remember to do or say (special requests from a professor, for example). So essential is lesson planning that it is "often identified in university teacher preparation standards, state teacher certification standards, and more general standards for professional practice" (Norman, 2011: 49).

At its best, lesson planning enables you to focus on crafting classes that are innovative, and meet the learning objectives through the various methods at your disposal: group discussion, demonstration, review, etc. Ideally you tweak something about your instruction each time you teach, whether it's a new example research topic or simply a phrase you heard a colleague use that helps the students click with the material. (If you're teaching the same thing the same way so often that you don't need a lesson plan, you need to mix your instruction up a little! If you're bored, the students will be, too.) Additionally, the presence of learning objectives can ensure that each of the activities, and material blocks that you decide to include in the lesson do, in fact, support the intended learning outcomes. This prevents both content creep, and the addition of activities or subtopics simply to fill the allotted time.

When crafting your lesson plan, keep in mind how *you* like to learn: probably you prefer for your learning to be self-directed, and relevant to your job; you need time to practice and reflect (Gerding & Hough, 2011). How can the content you choose to communicate, and the activities you include ensure that the goal is met? As Mel Silberman notes in *Training the Active Training Way*, beginnings and endings are the most important parts of any story or content because they're what we remember the most (2006). Each class should therefore have as many of those beginnings and endings as possible, which can be done by, for example, chunking material into smaller modules, and using active learning techniques as transitions (Ambrose, et al., 2010: 52).

More prosaically, the lesson plan can be brought with you when you teach to make sure you don't forget anything you meant to say or do, and be used as a vessel for catching your thoughts on how a new activity went either in or just after class. The lesson plan should be thought of as a guide rather than a script, though. Your plan should be flexible enough to adapt for students' unexpected familiarity with your intended material—or, conversely, a lack of understanding of necessary threshold concepts.

Specific aspects of lesson planning are examined in greater detail below.

Additional reading

While geared towards school media specialists, *http://aasl.jesandco.org* [Accessed 10 August 2014] has a collection of lesson plans that are tied into AASL's Standards for the 21st-Century Learner (similar to ACRL's Information Literacy Competency

Standards for Higher Education, but for the K-12 set). In order to be included in this database, lesson plans must meet standards on the inclusion of learning objectives, a list of required materials, etc., and are therefore excellent models even for librarians teaching in higher education.

Articulate learning objectives and base everything—content, activities, assessment—on those objectives

What are learning objectives, and why are they so important? Unlike goals, which are generally teacher-centered, and talk about what *you* will do (e.g. "discuss the Boolean operator OR as a means of increasing the number of search results"), learning objectives are student-centered and indicate what students will be able to do as a result of your class. In the K-12 world, these objectives conventionally start with *"The student will be able to"* or even the acronym TSWBAT, and this is a suitable prefix for learning objectives in higher education as well.

Just as important as that student-centered opening clause is the verb that immediately follows it. Avoid using the catchall "understand" here. Understanding is an amorphous concept; how does one know whether students have understood a concept or not? What if they "understand" 90 per cent of what you said about the Boolean operator OR: Will the class have been successful? What if that "understanding" drops to only 50 per cent two weeks after the class? Additionally, "understand" too often means simple recall.

Learning objective verbs ought to be action verbs, and measurable in some way. Measurability is important: it reveals how successful you were as an instructor, as well as ensures that students walk away from the class with a tangible ability. Benjamin Bloom led a group that produced an inventory of such verbs in the mid-twentieth century that has been a cornerstone of education since its publication. Bloom's Taxonomy classifies learning-related verbs by level of comprehension, specifically by what students will be able to do; exactly what one wants in a learning objective (see Figure 14.1).

Shifting away from what the teacher will do to what the students will learn is a key element in successful lesson planning and teaching because it prompts the instructor to plan the class in a way that meets those objectives, as opposed to simply making sure that each item on a list of concepts has been checked off by the end of class. If the library works closely with a particular department, as mine does, library- or research-related learning objectives may already have been articulated on the course's syllabus. In most cases, though, you will likely have to create your own based on the specific requests of the professor of record.

Each activity, each discussion point, on a lesson plan should support one of that session's learning objectives in some way. An activity-oriented class can therefore be just as ineffective as a lecture-based one: while the students may be more engaged in class, the session ends up consisting of busy work, a way to fill up the time. Including the learning objectives on the lesson plan also helps ensure that there is at least one activity or content chunk which fulfills that objective.

Consider including a learning objective (or phrasing all of your learning objectives in a way) that highlights their usefulness outside the academic environment in "real

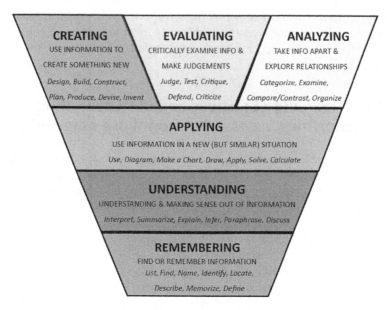

Figure 14.1 Bloom's Taxonomy Inverted Pyramid
Source: Image courtesy of Jessica Pilgreen (2012)

life": for example, "The student will be able to evaluate websites for their reliability based on their author, creation date, and content". Many skills that librarians teach in information literacy classes are ones that will be useful even after the students have graduated, but students are not likely to make such connections themselves. Again, by making yourself as the instructor think about the intended learning outcomes in this way, you ensure that these larger implications are not lost in nitty-gritty explanations of how to, say, use wildcards in ProQuest databases, and the chances are higher that you will make the connections for your students. If students see a benefit to what they're learning beyond a passing grade on whatever research project they're working on, they are more likely to pay attention (Gerding & Hough, 2011).

Additional reading

While aimed at medical school instructors, the University of New Mexico, School of Medicine's *Teaching for Learning Guide* (2003) provides a wealth of information on the effective use of learning objectives (among other useful information such as assessment and reflection). Included are an explanation of the SMART learning objectives system (Specific, Measurable, Attainable, Relevant, Targeted) and advice on how to implement the system, as well as suggested presentational strategies for each of the classifications in Bloom's Taxonomy.

Carnegie-Mellon University's Eberly Center for Teaching Excellence has put together a comprehensive literature review, called *The Educational Value of*

Course-Level Learning Objectives/Outcomes, on the myriad ways that the use of learning objectives is linked to enhanced student learning (n.d.).

Teach less material; move away from what must be "covered"

Out of all the strategies in this chapter, this one will likely be the most difficult to implement and, perhaps, internalize. Teachers at all levels are continually under pressure to cover as much material as possible, to "get through" the textbook. Most instructors have a semester or academic year to get through a curriculum; librarians who teach one-shots have only one class period, unless they're lucky enough to be asked back for additional sessions. Given that we may never have an opportunity to teach these students again (unless they ask a question at the reference desk later), cramming everything students will need into a one-shot can be tempting—indeed, panic-inducing. Alternatively, the session's content may rest entirely outside of our hands; professors sometimes contact us with a very clear idea of what they want us to cover, and are unwilling or unable to spare a second or third class period. The curriculum for our semester-long course may have been created by a committee, and be standardized across all instructors.

Research suggests, however, that learners need to process and interact with information in order for it to be filed away for later retrieval (Ambrose, et al., 2010: 100). This isn't possible if an overview of the library's website, Boolean operators, truncation, and two databases are all on the day's agenda. While each of the library concepts I just listed seem straightforward and easy-to-grasp to us, making a total of four minutes each spent on AND *vs.* OR, and ? *vs.**, seem reasonable and sufficient, chances are that this is not true for your students, even if everyone nods when you ask if they understand. This is called cognitive overload: your brain can only take in so much new information at a time. Think of YouTube video tutorials you've watched or Ikea furniture assembly instructions you've read, or even some conference presentations you've sat through: how much of any of those did you remember afterwards? The implications—that students need to focus on learning one skill at a time in order to reduce their cognitive load—are of particular import to one-shot instructors, who often feel pressured to fit multiple disparate learning objectives into one 50- or 75-minute class.

Try to limit the number of concepts you'll cover to as few as possible. Jane Bozarth, a well-known trainer of trainers, advises spending 50 per cent of your time on the most critical 20 per cent of your content to avoid cognitive overload (2010). This doesn't mean making students repeat "OR = more, AND = less" like a research catechism umpteen times, but allowing enough time to incorporate exercises that lead students to proficiency in the new skill. As much as possible, the rest of your content supports the most important 20 per cent, similar to what is commonly known as the journalism triangle (see Figure 14.2).

Consider which is better: "covering" five concepts, of which students will ultimately retain knowledge of none or one, or demonstrating two concepts, both of which are able to be used again and again outside of class? "Allow[ing] students to focus on

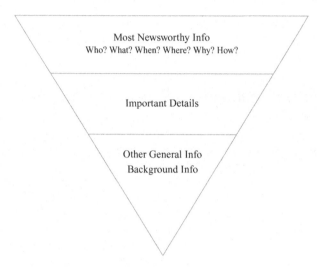

Figure 14.2 Journalism Triangle: Air Force Publishing Office's Newspaper Pyramid
Source: Image courtesy of the Air Force Departmental Publishing Office (n.d.).

one skill at a time [. . .] temporarily reduce[s] their cognitive load and giv[es] them the opportunity to develop fluency before they are required to integrate multiple skills" (Ambrose, et al., 2010: 105). I discuss strategies for doing this in the next section.

Not all of us have the agency to make such changes to what we teach, however. If you are among the ones who don't, show the person or people who do some research on the effects of cognitive overload (Ambrose, et al.'s *How Learning Works* (2010) has a literature review of the topic which would work well) and ask about reducing the number of concepts covered per class. Your request may not be approved, though, and even if you do have autonomy over your class's content, there's still the matter of all those other things the students need to know about. Such situations are when a handout along the lines of Iris Jastram's Subversive Handout comes in handy (see Figure 14.3). Created specifically for classes where the requested list of learning outcomes dwarfs the available time, the Subversive Handout is a handy reminder of the topics covered in class that day, but more importantly also provides a list of all the other usual suspects a librarian can help with. The topics on the Handout may well inspire professors to schedule additional sessions (as Jastram has found to be the case) and will hopefully trigger appointment requests from students as well (2008).

Incorporate exercises where students apply what they've learned to promote deep rather than surface learning

The main benefit of reducing the number of concepts taught per class is gaining additional time to focus on those concepts in order to incorporate exercises and activities into our lesson plans that encourage interaction with the new concepts at the higher levels of Bloom's taxonomy. In other words, you promote the synthesis,

Things to Think About

Here's what I will have covered today (hopefully):
- The difference between catalogs and databases, and why it matters
- Searching MLA International Bibliography
- Finding the full text of articles
    - o   Online
    - o   In the library
- Interlibrary Loan (remember that it can take as little as a few days, or as much as 3 weeks to deliver articles and books to you)
- Sidelong glance at the Arts & Humanities Citation Index

Some things I haven't covered (but you can ask me about at any time)
- Finding books using Bridge and WorldCat
- Finding book reviews
- Finding letters, diaries, images, and other primary sources
- Finding out if journals are peer reviewed or not
- Advanced citation mining
- Effective full text searching (you use different strategies when you're searching through all of the author's words, as we started to learn when searching JSTOR)
- Found an article via Google? How do you know if it's a peer reviewed, scholarly article like those in library databases?
- Locating and using dissertations... and when not to look at them
- And other fun things like using EndNote and del.icio.us to gather and organize your research as you find it.

Getting Help
- My office hours (constantly updated):

    http://people.carleton.edu/~ijastram/schedule.html

Iris Jastram
Librarian for Languages and Literature
ijastram, x7105, or IM me at ijastram (AIM)
http://go.carleton.edu/ijastram

Figure 14.3 An example of a *Subversive Handout*
Source: Image courtesy of Iris Jastram, 2008 (see section on *Teach less material; move away from what must be "covered"*)

evaluation, and creation of knowledge rather than the mere remembering of it to correctly answer the one-minute assessment at the end of class, but no longer than that. One-shot instructors especially are pressed for time, but "what do students remember, much less understand, when there is only *teaching* with no opportunity to really *learn*—to work with, play with, investigate, use—the key ideas and points of connection? Such an approach [teaching] might correctly be labeled, Teach, test, and hope for the best'" (Wiggins & McTighe, 2005: 3). How useful is "knowledge" of truncation where students can correctly define it, but don't think to use it after they've completed the assignment for which they had library instruction?

Phrased another way, as instructors we ought to think about what we'd like students to be able to do with what they learned in our class months or years down the line, both in and outside of academia. The end result we're hoping for, after all, is not the flaw-less truncation of all search terms students use in the future, but the ability to find the best, most relevant sources that fulfill their information needs. This task is arguably much easier for librarians to implement than our discipline-bound peers; so much of what we teach (e.g., the importance of evaluating information for reliability) naturally translates to the world outside academia. Ideally, our classes are really mini-lessons on what it means to think like a librarian, and these questions guide our lesson planning and learning-objective creating: "What are the particular abstract reasoning abilities that students must possess to understand certain concepts central to the discipline? Where are the students likely to have the most difficulty in reading or solving prob-lems in the field?" (Bain, 2004: 51).

The best college teachers, according to Ken Bain's long-term study on the subject, favor teaching methods that amplify their students' "capacity to comprehend, to use evidence to draw conclusions, to raise important questions, and to understand one's thinking. In most disciplines, that means they emphasize comprehension, reasoning, and brilliant insights over memory": in other words, the learning classifications at the higher rather than lower end of Bloom's taxonomy (95). In higher education, we like to think that we prepare our students to be informed, productive citizens as well as well-equipped future employees; it makes sense, therefore, that what we teach should be just as applicable (if not more so) after graduation as before it. "The scholarly work on this issue asks not if students can pass our examinations but whether their education has a sustained, substantial, and positive influence on the way they think, act, and feel" (Bain, 2004: 24).

Students must be able to retrieve that information in order to transfer it to new contexts; incorporating exercises where students must analyze, evaluate, or create their new knowledge (along with proper information organization, discussed in the section on advance organizers, below) can make the difference between a student who remembers information today, and a student who uses that knowledge years from now.

In the classroom

The anticipatory set: preparing students for learning

The anticipatory set should be the very first part of your instruction session: a question or tidbit that piques interest or curiosity in the information to come and, ideally, estab-lishes a rapport between teacher and students. That connection is especially important for librarians who teach one-shots, as they generally have only this one opportunity to convince students that they are worth listening to. One-shot instructors have just one chance to make a positive impression; those who teach over the course of a semester have a much longer window in which to make and modify that initial impression.

Too many instructors launch right into the meat of the lesson without first either making a connection with the students or doing anything that gets them interested in the material. Student expectations are likely to be fairly low; aside from ardent Hermione-types, most students probably view a library instruction session somewhere between a regular class and solving math problems on the excitement spectrum. Note, however, that: "the most basic way to get someone's attention is this: Break a pattern" (Heath & Heath, 2007: 64). There are all sorts of ways in which you can break the expectational pattern of boredom at the library: students will not expect a Top 40 song to be playing when they walk in the classroom, for example. "Teachers [can also] succeed in grabbing students' attention by beginning a lecture with a provocative question or problem that raises issues in ways that students had never thought about before, or by using stimulating case studies or goal-based scenarios" (Bain, 2004: 109–10). Or break the pattern of boring PowerPoint slides with an opening slide of a funny Internet meme that's currently popular.

The first few minutes of class are also key to developing a rapport with the class. Building rapport is important even in one-shots where it's unlikely you'll ever teach the students again. If you make a connection, earn their respect, pique their interest, they are that much more likely to grant you their attention, and suspend any latent cynicism over what you are offering them. I often start my classes by referencing a local or national event that's likely to be at the forefront of the undergraduate's mind: sports championships and extreme weather events are generally pretty safe. For example, in early February I might start class by asking how many students watched the Superbowl, and whether anyone was upset over who won. I could then bring up the statistical whiz Nate Silver, and his predictions for both political elections, and the recent Superbowl, and use that as a segue into the topic of the day: librarians and their professor can predict, like Nate Silver, what grade a research paper will get just by looking at the research question.

If you plan to have the students interact with you or each other at all, "it is also a good practice to set up the expectations of the class right from the start. If they know within the first few minutes of a lesson starting that you will be expecting their active engagement, it will set the tone of the whole lesson, easing them into the rest of the activities you have planned" (Walsh & Inala, 2010: 17). Doing nothing but talk at the students for these first few crucial minutes without any expectation or need for a response lulls them into disconnected passivity. Starting class off with a question that requires participation in the form of a show of hands, or shouted-out responses, on the other hand, alerts students to the fact that the class will not be a straight lecture, and mentally prepares them to participate later on.

The advance organizer: telling them what you're going to tell them

As experts in a particular subject—finding information—we possess a complex network of information about our subject that is continually being added to and refined. When we learn something new about the process of research, we are able to easily fit that new information into our existing schema. Non-experts don't have those schema, however, meaning they don't possess a meaningful way to organize—and therefore remember—the new concepts and ideas they learn in class. Furnishing a preview or outline of what will be covered in class—what is known as an advance organizer—can therefore provide a rudimentary schema into which students can file new information. In essence, you prepare your students' minds for learning. The presentational maxim "tell them what you're going to tell them, tell them, then tell them what you told them" springs from this theory.

"Having a preview of what is to be learned before attempting to use it makes for a much deeper level of organization in which to insert (or attempt to insert) new ideas and concepts. [...] When you know what's coming, you'll get a lot more out of the experience than when you experience it for the first time" (Svinicki, 2013). Providing an advance organizer can be as simple as including the course's learning objectives in the syllabus (in a for-credit course) or writing the day's agenda on the whiteboard prior to the start of class; I also verbally state what I call the class's game plan to make sure students catch this vital information. Additionally, you can make connections explicit between what students already know, and what they will be learning; I discuss this strategy in greater detail in the next section.

There are more sophisticated methods by which one can foster the development of students' organizational models of research. You could furnish an outline or concept map for each class, keeping in mind that the provided language ought to be related to the day's learning objectives, rather than a not-so-helpful list of lesson parts such as "introduction", "lecture", and "recap". Coming to class with a prepared mind is a central tenet behind the flipped classroom movement, which has recently found traction in the library world: "rather than spending class time giving out new information, the students prepare their minds for the applications before class", usually with an assigned reading, video, or other learning object (Svinicki, 2013). Both of these more time-consuming methods of providing an advance organizer can be used in for-credit as well as one-shot classes; the flipped classroom is arguably of greater benefit to the one-shot classroom, as those instructors work within the most limited timeframe. By familiarizing students with the meat of the lesson's content before meeting, the class period itself can be spent refining that knowledge, and providing opportunities for students to interact with it at a more sophisticated level (see *Incorporate exercises* section, above).

Activate students' prior knowledge to scaffold their learning

As knowledge professionals, and especially as we move further and further from being undergraduate or graduate learners ourselves, there develops a disconnect between instructor and student in what we think students already know and can do. As librarians and lovers of learning, many of us have been surrounded by people who are not just smart, but love learning and academia, for a long time. We may also fall prey to stereotypes about our students, such as that all Millennials are tech-savvy, that affect how we decide to teach (Hargittai, 2010: 93). Our expectations of what students already know when they walk in the classroom therefore need to be adjusted to reflect our students' realities, rather than our own.

Many instructors have found that the seemingly specific goals and requirements we have laid out for a particular task cannot be understood by our students; what is happening here? As Ken Bain explains it:

> *We use our existing mental models to shape the sensory inputs we receive. That means that when we talk to students, our thoughts do not travel seamlessly from our brains to theirs. [...] Even if they know nothing about our subjects, they still use an existing mental model of something to build their knowledge of what we tell them, often leading to an understanding that is quite different from what we intend to convey (Bain, 2004: 26–7).*

This conception of students arriving in our classroom with pre-existing knowledge and ideas directly contradicts the traditional notion of students as empty vessels, which just need to be filled up by the knowledge their instructors impart.

When teaching, then, we ought to make connections between the knowledge our students already have to the new material we introduce. We cannot presume that students will make these connections themselves, just as we do not assume that hiring panels will connect the dots between what we (as applicants) see as relevant experience and a list of desired qualifications in a job ad; we make those connections explicit in cover letters. While students likely already have pre-existing knowledge that we would like to draw upon, that knowledge remains inaccessible until we make those connections clear to them.

Students are likely very familiar with Google and other Internet search engines; explicitly comparing and contrasting them with library databases can therefore be helpful. For example, I ask my students to explain to me why they don't type in an entire question into an Internet search box when doing research for their classes (because in the present day, the answers come from sites such as Yahoo! Answers and About.com, which the students know are inappropriate for college work); I then describe how entire questions should not be typed into library databases either (though for different reasons). Similarly, a colleague of mine teaches the use of database facets by explicitly comparing them to the facets on search results screens of shopping websites such as Zappos and Amazon.

Additional reading

Jane Vella's 4-Is instructional model, as outlined in *Taking Learning to Task: Creative Strategies for Teaching Adults*, encourages instructors to connect new material with students' pre-existing knowledge, following it up with an activity that encourages students to interact with the new material, then an activity that gets students to implement their new knowledge (at the upper levels of the ubiquitous Bloom's taxonomy), and end with an activity that integrates the newfound knowledge into their lives. This forms a circle of learning, with the student and his/her life as both the starting and ending point of the learning process (2000). Barbara Fister, a librarian who blogs for Inside Higher Ed, has compiled a useful list of tacit knowledge about libraries and research that librarians are likely to have, and that we may mistakenly assume our students have as well (2013).

Affective learning: how students feel in the classroom is as important as what they're learning there

How students feel in class makes a surprisingly large difference on how receptive, consciously or unconsciously, they are to learning. This is partially due to cognitive load; students have less brainpower to devote to learning if they're thinking about stressors. Research has shown that college-aged students in particular are undergoing social and emotional development that dwarfs their intellectual development (Pascarella & Terenzini, 1991). External stressors are largely out of your control as the instructor, of course, though it's worth remembering that a substantial number of students are affected by library anxiety (Schroeder and Cahoy, 2013: 132). Other affective learning factors, however, are eminently in your power: the relationship between instructor and student, and the overall climate of the class.

Think about how you evaluate information as learned from Rush Limbaugh (if you're a Democrat) or Bill Maher (if you're a Republican). You may take whatever you hear from this pundit at the opposite end of the political spectrum with a grain—or pound—of salt because you believe their political biases lead them to distort the facts. While an extreme example, this is analogous to how students can react if they feel their instructor doesn't have anything of relevance to say, or is intimidating, or off-putting: it is demotivating.

The importance of affective learning is one of the reasons that the anticipatory set is so important: it can help the students relax, and make a connection with you. Developing a rapport with students can begin even before class has started, however, by greeting students as they come in, or making conversation after they've settled in. "This reduces any perceived barrier between [you], and makes for a more informal and receptive class" (Cahoy, p.11). Similarly, the first few sessions of a semester-long class can be used to communicate high expectations: to inform students tacitly and explicitly that your standards are high but that you believe they are capable of reaching the bar you've set. "Expecting students to perform well becomes a self-fulfilling prophecy, having direct impact upon student learning" (Woodard & Hinchliffe, 2010: 324).

"Frequent student-faculty contact in and out of classes is the most important factor in student motivation and involvement" (Woodard & Hinchliffe, 2010: 321). This is great news for librarians who teach for-credit classes; you have a semester of opportunities to develop and nurture connections with students. One-shot instructors needn't feel disconsolate, however; I have found from personal experience that my students respond better—in terms of greater participation with each other, willingness to answer questions, openness to untraditional activities, and reduced classroom management issues—if I am my natural self when teaching, rather than a personality-less librarian automaton. Providing positive feedback in class—when warranted—can further develop a rapport as well. And both one-shot and for-credit library instructors can make themselves known to students by setting up regular office hours in their liaison departments.

Connecting with students is also a crucial part of classroom management, even for one-shot instructors. Students are less likely to engage in inappropriate behaviors—texting, intentionally taking a nap—with instructors they like and respect. You'll still encounter the occasional insolent or argumentative student, however. The old maxim "kill them with kindness" is useful here; it is a surprisingly successful strategy, though likely to be more effective when used in a semester-long class. Additional classroom management techniques are discussed in the next section.

Additional reading

While everyone has a sense of humor, few of us are likely capable of successfully taking the stage at a stand-up comedy club. Eamon Tewell on The Desk Set (2014), and Joshua Vossler in *Humor and Information Literacy* both explain how your personality can constructively inform your instructional practice, and provide strategies for effectively using comedy as an affective learning technique (2011).

Classroom management

One might think that classroom management wouldn't be a concern when teaching in higher education. However, what teacher hasn't witnessed chatting, or texting in class, or tardy students who continually arrive five minutes late—missing 10 per cent of the day's material, and distracting all of their classmates, as they shuffle up to the remaining seat at the front of the classroom?

The proverb "an ounce of prevention is worth a pound of cure" is especially true in education; creating a positive atmosphere in the classroom with clear expectations goes a long way towards forestalling potential disruptions. "Praise is one of the most powerful, and certainly one of the most underutilized, tools in any teacher's repertoire" (Eyster & Martin, 2010: 16): it can neutralize negative forces in your class, reinforce excellence, and prevent the hardworking but quiet student from remaining invisible and unacknowledged. See the section on the importance of affective learning, above. Additionally, try to unchain yourself from the instructor's podium as much as possible. Walking around the classroom is a good way to ensure attention even from students at the far reaches of the classroom, and pre-empt disruptive behaviors before they occur.

While instructors may be tempted to ignore the occasional muttered aside because they don't want to make a big deal of something trivial, I urge you to take a stand. "Everyone in the class will quickly sense what you will tolerate and what you will not. Turn a blind eye [. . .] and they will understand that you are giving up part of your rightful authority and that they are the ones who get to set the social guidelines in the room"; advice that is as true for one-shot instructors as it is for those who have the luxury of teaching semester-long courses (p.60). Unfortunately, the instructors of record often check out at the back of the room when they bring their classes to the library for instruction—that is, if they haven't dropped their students off, and left them for you. This doesn't necessarily mean that you need to call out every giggling student; proximity can be a surprisingly effective classroom management technique. Simply moving closer to the inattentive student is often enough to quell the undesirable behavior.

If you are fortunate enough to teach a semester-long information literacy class, you have an additional set of issues to deal with, tardiness likely foremost among them. This is more likely to be an issue in college than K-12 education, as class attendance is usually not mandatory. You could lock the door precisely one (or two or five) minute after class starts, but this is a bit harsh. Less draconian is giving a short quiz as soon as class starts, with no make-ups allowed. This alternative to giving a grade for prompt attendance—arguably not appropriate in college—encourages not only punctuality, but close reading of the assigned homework text as well.

Additional reading

While geared towards the K-12 teacher, Eyster and Martin's *Successful Classroom Management* is a treasure trove of classroom management strategies, especially the preventative kind. Additional topics covered include ways to guarantee lesson plan variety, and why a passion for the subject should not be underestimated, both of which have implications in ensuring the attentiveness and good conduct of your class.

After class: completing the instruction loop

Reflective practice

What you do as an instructor after class can matter as much as the time you spent preparing or actually teaching. If you use an activity or analogy that unexpectedly bombs, do you do more than cross it off your repertoire? What about when your class is an unsurprising success? Taking the time to reflect on your class—what worked, what didn't, anything else that comes to mind—helps you work through the more important implications of that information: *why.*

Was the class immediately after the lunch hour, making students sluggish (and therefore, perhaps, in need of something to get them up and moving about)? Did you chat with the students while they waited for class to start, thereby forming a rapport that helped carry the lesson in the form of increased participation? Some of these factors will be outside your control, but it's still worth reviewing them in case any of them could be mitigated through planning. Additionally, reflection helps prevent you from subconsciously overlooking (and rectifying) instructional shortcomings you may have.

Ideally, this reflection will take place as soon after the class has ended as possible, especially if multiple sessions are taught in a short period of time. Small but important details are more likely to be lost the longer the delay between teaching and reflecting. Regardless of whether you teach one-shots or for-credit classes, the chances are high that you will teach the same content in some shape or form again. Unless you somehow take note of what you'd like to do differently or emphasize next time, you are likely to either forget those changes, or fall back on "the spiel", especially when stressors such as too little time to prepare during the instructional busy season are factored in. Depending on how much you tend to shift into autopilot when teaching, this can even happen between different sessions of the same class on the same day; making a note on the lesson plan to allot only 2.5 minutes for a discussion, instead of 3, can mean the difference between a more focused classroom and one that keeps descending into off-topic chatter.

Blogging can be an especially effective medium for the reflective process. In addition to all of the above benefits, blogging has the added advantage of providing a mechanism for feedback from other librarians and instructors without asking for it outright (e.g., on Twitter or Facebook). The commiserating replies will assuage your disappointment, the congratulatory ones heighten your feeling of success, and you're likely to get some good tips as well.

Finally, "incorporating metacognitive elements [. . .] can also prevent the boredom that can result from teaching the same concepts over and over" (Booth, 2011). Reviewing what you said and did after class, when the heat of the moment has passed, can remind you of having read or heard about a similar technique elsewhere, or prompt you to research solutions to small problems that presented themselves in class.

Additional reading

Char Booth has several extremely helpful chapters on the importance and benefits of reflective instruction, including easy-to-follow methods by which it can be made a regular part of one's instructional practice, in her book *Reflective Teaching, Effective Learning* (ALA, 2011).

Provide prompt, formative feedback

"Feedback is the teacher's way of communicating with students, and it is key to helping the student learn" (Woodard & Hinchliffe, 2010: 324); as such, it is the most vital tool in an instructor's arsenal. Feedback ensures that students comprehend and are capable of using the information you are responsible for teaching. Feedback on formative assessments—that is, assessments conducted during the learning process rather than afterwards—is therefore the most useful kind of teacher-student communication: as it enables you to correct missteps on the journey that (if left unchecked) may lead the student to entirely the wrong destination.

If you teach semester-long courses, there will be many opportunities to check student progress and provide feedback, both formally and informally. If you find yourself in this fortunate position, it is important to return graded—and commented-upon—assignments as quickly as possible to students. The grades students receive for homework and more substantial assignments are how they gauge how they're doing in the class; as library research is a foundation class, few students will have mastery over the material. Ambrose, et al., 2010 call this stage of learning unconscious incompetence, when students "have not yet developed skill in a particular domain, nor do they have sufficient knowledge to recognize what they need to learn" (p.96). Students may think they understand a concept when in reality they only partially understand or have a flawed understanding. Providing meaningful feedback on assignments in a timely fashion ensures that these misunderstandings are corrected before learned behaviors and foundational concepts must be unlearned. However, do not neglect to provide written commentary in the interests of providing a timely grade: "although grades and scores provide some information on the *degree to which* students' performance has met the criteria, they do not explain *which aspects* did or did not meet the criteria and *how*" (emphasis Ambrose, et al., 2010: 140).

However, many of us do not have the luxury of meeting with students a dozen or so times over the course of a semester; fortunately, formative feedback can still be provided in the one-shot classroom. Especially in the instance of one-shot instruction, it is important to have "more tasks of shorter length or smaller scope [to] provide the frequency of feedback that allows students to refine their understanding" (Ambrose, et al., 2010: 150). It is thus preferable to assess understanding after each new concept is introduced, and students have had an opportunity to wrestle with that concept discretely, rather than conducting a more general assessment at the end of class.

Keep in mind that feedback does not necessarily need to come from you, or even be given individually; students can, with appropriate guidance (e.g., rubrics) provide feedback for their peers, and feedback is still useful when given for group rather than individual work. For example, after I've introduced the concept of truncation and we've discussed it for a while, I often ask the class to truncate a couple of words by selecting one of four multiple-choice options on PollEverywhere. This enables me to see how well this concept of truncation has been understood, and for me to explain why the other answer options are incorrect to the class as a whole, rather than individually. Another activity I use, borrowed from my supervisor, is to divide the class into small groups, and to ask each group to put a set of cards with call numbers on them in order. The teams then stand up (this exercise is also helpful for reinvigorating a sleepy class) and I call out the order the call numbers should be in, one card at a time, with teams sitting down once one of their cards is shown to be out of sequence. With each progression—if a team has had to sit down—I explain why the cards should be in this particular order, and again am able to provide feedback collectively rather than individually. Group feedback can, therefore, be as useful as individual feedback, in addition to having the benefits of speed and student anonymity (sparing students potential embarrassment in the case of a wrong answer).

Articulate your teaching philosophy

Technically, teaching philosophy statements could appear in the preparing-for-class division of the chapter; education students generally prepare them in their final semesters in preparation for their job search, as schools (and often institutions of higher education as well) ask for them as part of the application process, and they are, therefore, created before the students begin teaching. Education majors have had the advantage of several years of cumulative study of learning theory, instructional strategies, and educational psychology before they get to this point, however, and these subjects are all necessary to inform a robust teaching philosophy. I have placed this section in the after-class division of the chapter to mimic the education major's practice of placing it in the penultimate stages of study, as the reader has, at this point, had a rudimentary orientation on these topics.

So, what *is* a teaching philosophy? It is a narrative—between a couple paragraphs and a couple pages long—that articulates how you feel the teaching and learning process works, in addition to describing and justifying the way in which you teach. There is a multitude of best practices in the canon of educational research, but no one-size-fits-all scientific method for flawless instruction: it is a highly personal practice. Explaining, to yourself and potential employers, how the theories you've learned and your experiences have shaped your methods can, therefore, help you reflect upon, and refine your teaching. While most commonly used as part of the educational job application process, the teaching philosophy, therefore, has a formative purpose as well, and thus is useful for librarians who teach.

As the creation of learning objectives and their inclusion on a lesson plan help ensure that the content and activities you choose support those learning objectives, so the construction and refinement of a teaching philosophy helps ensure that you teach both mindfully and intentionally. Especially during busy times, it can be difficult—both preparing for class and actually teaching—to break out of instructional autopilot. Revisiting your teaching philosophy and revising it as necessary can keep it fresh in your mind, and serve as a reminder that asks: "Is this how I want to teach?"

Where to start? Think about what you love most about teaching, the greatest student needs you see in the classroom, and what inspired you to become a librarian in the first place. For example, Iris Jastram, an instruction librarian I've mentioned earlier in this chapter, calls her blog Pegasus Librarian; the About Me page of her blog explains why the mythological creature is the namesake for her blog, and why it is her instructional inspiration: in a nutshell, because her "favorite symbolic concept places Pegasus at the point where innovation, creativity, wisdom, deliberation, and a healthy sense of humor intersect. That's the place [she]'d like teachers, learners, and librarians to inhabit" (2006). As she demonstrates, the inspiration for your teaching philosophy can lie outside of librarianship, and even academia.

Additional reading

A number of graduate schools have created guides for their students on the writing of teaching philosophies; these often include leading questions to help jog your memory. Among these are Cornell (2011) and Washington University in St Louis (2013). The University of Minnesota has created a highly regarded tutorial that walks you through the statement-creation process step-by-step (2010).

It can be helpful to see how other librarians have envisioned their teaching philosophies, especially since librarians are so rarely asked to create them. There is a collection of librarian teaching philosophies on the 21st Century Teacher-Librarians Ning that could give you an idea of how you might approach creating your own; an Internet search for "librarian teaching philosophy" yields some additional examples (University of Colorado at Denver, 2014).

Finally, the Chronicle of Higher Education has posted an article online on how to write a teaching philosophy that goes beyond a discussion of fundamentals (such as being student-centered) to reflect your own unique voice and experiences (Lang, 2010).

Conclusion

The concepts and strategies discussed in this chapter are just the tip of the educational psychology and learning theory iceberg. There are entire bodies of research devoted to aspects of learning theory that I have not even touched on: learning styles, learning development stages. While no crash course can replace a systematic study, hopefully the principles discussed herein will still be of immediate practical use, and serve as a stepping stone for further research. I hope that you will view teaching as "an endeavor that benefits from careful observation and close analysis, from revision and refinement, and from dialogues with colleagues and the critiques of peers, [...] never completely satisfied with what [you have] already achieved" (Bain, 2004: 20–1). One of the things we learn as librarians and educators is that the best teachers are themselves constantly learning; this is just as valid for technique as it is for content.

Bibliography

Air Force Departmental Publishing Office (n.d.). US Air Force, Shawn Air Force Base, 20th FW Editorial *Policy & Submission Guidelines* Graphic: Journalism Triangle). Available from: *http://commons.wikimedia.org/wiki/File:Inverted_pyramid.jpg*, Accessed 10 August 2014.

Ambrose, et al. (2010). *How learning works.* Available from: San Francisco, CA: Jossey-Bass. *http://c4ed.lib.kmutt.ac.th/sites/default/files/HowLearningWorks-Ambrose.pdf*, Accessed 17 August 2014.

Bain, K. (2004). *What the best college teachers do.* Cambridge, MA: Harvard University Press.

Booth, C. (2011). *Reflective teaching, effective learning (ALA).*

Bozarth, J. (8 June 2010). *Nuts and bolts: Find your 20%.* Available from, *Learning Solutions Magazine.* http://www.learningsolutionsmag.com/articles/472/nuts-and-bolts-find-your-20, Accessed 10 August 2014.

Cahoy, E. S. (2013). The quarterly interview: Ellysa Stern Cahoy. *LOEX Quarterly, 40*(1), 11–12. Available from, http://commons.emich.edu/loexquarterly/vol40/iss1/5.

Cornell University Graduate School (2011). *Teaching philosophy statement.* Available from, http://www.gradschool.cornell.edu/career-development/put-your-qualifications-writing/teaching-philosophy-statement, Accessed 10 August 2014.

Eberly Center for Teaching Excellence, Carnegie Mellon University. (n.d.). 'The educational value of course-level learning objectives/outcomes'. Available from, *http://www.cmu.edu/teaching/resources/Teaching/CourseDesign/Objectives/CourseLearningObjectives Value.pdf,* Accessed 10 August 2014]

Eyster, R., & Martin, C. (2010). *Successful classroom management: Real-world, time-tested techniques for the most important skill set every teacher needs.* Napierville, IL: Sourcebooks.

Fister, B. (25 June 2013). *Tacit knowledge and the student researcher.* Available from, http://www.insidehighered.com/blogs/library-babel-fish/tacit-knowledge-and-student-researcher, Accessed 10 August 2014.

Gerding, S. and Hough, B. (presenters); Griffiths, K. (facilitator) (9 February 2011) 'Delivering tech workshops', *TechSoup.org.* Webinar available from: *www.techsoup.org,* Accessed 10 August 2014.

Hargittai, E. (February 2010). Digital na(t)ives? Variation in Internet skills and uses among members of the "Net Generation" *Sociological Inquiry, 80*(1), 92–113. http://dx.doi.org/10.1111/j.1475-682X.2009.00317.x.

Heath, C., & Heath, D. (2007). *Made to stick: Why some ideas survive and others die.* Random House: New York.

Jastram, I. (29 March 2006). *Why Pegasus?* Available from, http://pegasuslibrarian.com/2006/03/why-pegasus.html, Accessed 10 August 2014.

Jastram, I. (16 January 2008). *Subversive handouts: One librarian's secret weapon.* Available from, http://pegasuslibrarian.com/2008/01/subversive-handouts-one-librarians-secret-weapon.html.

Lang, J. M. (29 August 2010). *4 steps to a memorable teaching philosophy.* Available from, https://chronicle.com/article/4-Steps-to-a-Memorable/124199/ Accessed 10 August 2014.

Norman, P. J. (2011). Planning for what kind of teaching? Supporting cooperating teachers as teachers of planning. *Teacher Education Quarterly, 38*(3), 49–68.

Pascarella, E. T., & Terenzini, P. T. (1991). *How college affects students: Findings and insights from twenty years of research.* San Francisco, CA: Jossey-Bass.

Pilgreen, J. (6 July 2012). *Simplified Bloom's taxonomy visual (Graphic of Bloom's taxonomy).* Available from, http://www.meandmylaptop.com/2/post/2012/07/simplified-blooms-taxonomy-visual.html, Accessed 10 August 2014.

Schroeder, R., & Cahoy, E. S. (April 2010). Valuing information literacy: Affective learning and the ACRL standards. *Portal: Libraries and the Academy, 10*(2).

Silberman, M. (2006). *Training the active training way.* San Francisco, CA: Pfeiffer.

Svinicki, M. (September 2013). Flipped classrooms – old or new? *National Teaching and Learning Forum, 22*(5).

Tewell, E. (25 February 2014). *Using comedy to inform library instruction.* Available from, http://thedeskset.org/using-comedy-to-inform-library-instruction/ Accessed 10 August 2014.

University of Colorado at Denver, School of Education & Human Development (2014). *Philosophy statement.* Available from, http://21centurylibrarian.ning.com/group/

sl5530foundationsofschoollibrarianshipspring2010/forum/topics/philosophy-statement?
xg_source=activity, Accessed 10 August 2014.

University of Minnesota Center for Teaching and Learning (8 September 2010). *Writing your teaching philosophy.* Available fromhttp://www1.umn.edu/ohr/teachlearn/tutorials/philosophy/[Accessed 10 August 2014].

University of New Mexico School of Medicine (2003). *Teaching for learning: Learning for health: Quick reference guides for planning, implementing, and assessing learning experiences.* Available from, http://som.unm.edu/omed/_docs-dev/go_far_handbook_eng.pdf, Accessed 10 August 2014.

Vella, J. (2000). *Taking learning to task: Creative strategies for teaching adults.* San Francisco, CA: Jossey-Bass.

Vossler, J. (2011). *Humor and information literacy: Practical techniques for library instruction.* Santa Barbara, CA: Libraries Unlimited.

Walsh, A., & Inala, P. (2010). *Active learning techniques for librarians: Practical examples.* Oxford, UK: Chandos Publishing.

Washington University in St. Louis, The Teaching Center (2013) *Writing a teaching philosophy statement.* Available from: *http://teachingcenter.wustl.edu/About/ProgramsforGraduateStudentsandPostdocs/resources/Pages/Writing-a-Teaching-Philosophy-Statement.aspx*, Accessed 10 August 2014.

Wiggins, G., & McTighe, J. (2005). Understanding by design *(expanded second edn).* Alexandria, VA: Association for Supervision & Curriculum Development.

Woodard, B. S., & Hinchliffe, L. J. (2010). Teaching the teachers: Developing a teaching improvement program for academic librarians. In Scott Walter & Karen Williams (Eds.), *The Expert Library: Staffing, Sustaining, and Advancing the Academic Library in the 21st Century.* Chicago: Association of College and Research Libraries.

Index

Note: Page numbers followed by *f* indicate figures and *t* indicate tables.

Made in the USA
Coppell, TX
09 February 2022

73187485R00115

The library and information profession builds skills and expertise that cover a wide spectrum. These skills are often desirable in other fields and industries. Likewise, the skills built before entering the library and information professions benefit those professionals. *Skills to make a Librarian* looks at both sides of this equation through a collection of essays by current and former librarians and information professionals who make use of this wide range of cross disciplinary skills. Chapters have been contributed from authors working at various academic libraries, and focus on different skills and experiences, including critical thinking, marketing and information science.

Dawn Lowe-Wincentsen is the Wilsonville Campus librarian for the Oregon Institute of Technology. She graduated with her MLIS from Louisiana State University in 2003, though she has been involved in libraries since 1996. Dawn has been editor for the Learning Exchange, newsletter of the Learning roundtable of the American Library Association since 2008. She has co-authored A Leadership Primer for New Librarians: Tools for Helping Today's Early Career Librarians to Become Tomorrow's Library Leaders (Chandos) and co-edited Mid-Career Library and Information Professionals: A leadership primer (Woodhead Publishing) as well as written various chapters and articles about librarianship.

Key Points

- explores which skills developed outside of librarianship benefit other practices and careers
- presents a look at how the skills of librarianship fit into life outside libraries
- authors open up about personal experiences while keeping it professional
- chapters written by authors at various points in their careers

CP

CHANDOS
PUBLISHING

ELSEVIER

An imprint of Elsevier • store.elsevier.com

ISBN 978-0-08-100063-2

9 780081 000632